TRAT·TO·RIA (trät-ə-ˈrē-ə)
(IT RHYMES WITH PIZZERIA)
A SMALL FAMILY RESTAURANT
SERVING SIMPLE
ITALIAN FARE

PATRICIA WELLS'

TRATTORIA

· ·

Simple and Robust Fare

Inspired by the

Small Family Restaurants

of Italy

· ·

WILLIAM MORROW
75 YEARS OF PUBLISHING
An Imprint of HarperCollinsPublishers

First published in hardcover by William Morrow in 1993.

First William Morrow paperback edition published 2001.

Cover art by Richard Beards

The Library of Congress has catalogued the hardcover edition as follows:

Wells, Patricia.
  Patricia Wells' trattoria / Patricia Wells.
      p.   cm.
    ISBN 0-688-10532-7
1. Cookery, Italian.   I. Title.
TX723.W45   1993   93-16679
641.5945—dc21   CIP

ISBN 0-06-093652-5 (pbk.)

09 10 11 12 QW 15 14 13 12 11 10 9

The memory of my maternal grandfather, Felix Ricci, who as a young man left his farm in Ateleta in the Abruzzi region of Italy for a new life in America. Arriving at Ellis Island in 1910, he worked his way across the country, building railroads and saving money to purchase a plot of land. Here he is, in 1934, on his dairy farm in Comstock, Wisconsin.

My mother, Vera Catherine Ricci Kleiber, and my sister, Judith Frances Kleiber Jones, with gratitude for their support all along the way. Here they are, in 1945, the year before they added my name to the Ricci family tree.

■ ■ ■

Acknowledgments

W hat are you working on?" is the question posed almost daily by friends, colleagues, readers, acquaintances. During the past several years, of course, the response was *Trattoria!* and, almost universally, that single word managed to inspire eager smiles of recognition and anticipation. For we instantly identify "trattoria" with a simple, generous, full-flavored style of food that is so appealing today.

This book is a testament to the many people—friends and strangers, colleagues and family—who joined me physically and spiritually along the trattoria trail, as I collected the recipes, anecdotes, quotes, tips, and suggestions contained here.

Years ago, when I was a fledgling food journalist, a variety of cooking instructors shared great insights into the Italian way of cooking and of life. Most important among them were Marcella and Victor Hazan—both extraordinary ambassadors of Italian cooking. I will always be grateful to them for their rare spirit of sharing and openness. I also want to thank Giuliano Buglialli for his friendship and the discerning classes he has offered in New York and in Florence.

Many editors have consistently offered support to this and other writing projects, and I specifically want to thank John Vinocur, Pamela Fiori, David Breul, Donna Warner, Ila Stanger, Barbara Peck, Carole Lalli, Mary Simons, and Malachy Duffy for their past, present, and future encouragement.

As I have traveled within Italy, dozens of cooks, chefs, and restaurateurs have kindly allowed me into their kitchens and have shared recipes, tips, and techniques. I particularly want to acknowledge some of them here, including all of the staff at La Frateria di Padre Eligio in Cetona; Ugo and Gigi Salis at Trattoria da Graziella in Fiesole; Maria and Vittorio Becarria and Bruno Galaverna of Osteria Barbabuc in Novello; Angelo Maionchi of Del Cambio in Turin; Carlo Citerrio at Locanda dell'Amorosa in Sinalunga; Elio, Francesco, and Ninetta Mariani at Checchino dal 1887 in Rome; Diana and

Cesare Benelli of Al Covo in Venice; and in Florence, Piero Giannacci at Quattro Stagioni, Francesco Masiero at Il Cammillo, and Fabio and Benedetta Picchi at Cibrèo; and in Milan, Roberto Fontana at Trattoria Casa Fontana and Ezia Calatti at Antica Trattoria della Pesa.

Thank you to Bianca Vetrino in Turin, Enrico and Patricia Jacchia in Rome, Maria Manetti Farrow in Florence, Johanne Killeen and George Germon in Providence, Maggie and Al Shapiro in Normandy, Judith Symonds in Paris, and Rita and Yale Kramer in New York, all friends who made my days in Italy that much more special. Thank you Carlo Scipione Ferrero and Giovanna Bologna for helping with research on the history of the trattoria, and Maria Sanminiatelli for assistance in organizing many of my excursions. I am also grateful to Calvin Trillin for first sending me to Da Giulio in Lucca, where my curiosity about their recipe for "smashed" chicken—pollo al mattone—inspired this book.

Thank you Judy Jones for the care and attention you gave to each of my recipes, and to Steven Rothfeld for your friendship, your shared devotion to the details of life, and, of course, your masterly photos. I am also grateful to Alexandra Guarnaschelli for her expert assistance in the kitchen during our photography sessions. At home, I thank Laura Washburn for her fidelity and last-minute assistance in editing the final manuscript. And thank you Kyle Cathie, for believing in me.

At William Morrow, I am grateful to Barbara M. Bachman.

For almost fifteen years, Susan and Robert Lescher have acted as my literary agents, advisers, and friends, and I thank them for their continued support in helping shape and direct my career.

But my deepest gratitude is saved for my editor and dear friend, Maria Guarnaschelli, who gave one thousand percent to this project. Her insight, encouragement, and vision are unparalleled, not to mention her terrific sense of humor and ability to transform long, intense work sessions into memorable good times.

As ever, this book and I owe everything to Walter Newton Wells, my dear husband and partner in this wonderful life.

Contents

■ ■ ■

Take Me to a Trattoria

Homey, unpretentious, honest, and homemade, that's the heart and soul of Italian trattoria cooking. Robust food—served without frills or fuss—makes up the body and the substance of small family restaurant fare all over Italy.

Several years ago, I began my quest for the quintessential trattoria, along quiet roads framed by rolling vineyards in the Piedmont, by the blue waters of the Ligurian resort of Santa Margherita, down stone alleyways in Siena, through the doors of bustling vineyard eateries in Tuscany, into the back rooms of loud, lively trattorias in Rome, and inside a quirky family spot on the edge of Milan, where they serve more than twenty different versions of risotto. In brief, a joyous land of bright lights, loud voices, full flavors.

Italian food needs no introduction, and even those who neither speak nor read Italian are probably on a first-name basis with many of the dishes found on a typical trattoria menu. Is there anyone who needs a translation of spaghetti, scampi, risotto, or tagliatelle?

But that's only the beginning, and a rather limited one at that. Authentic trattoria cooking—as found in small and large establishments from one end of the country to the other—is as rich, diverse, and pleasurable as any cuisine in the world.

The Italians are masters at roasting, at frying, at composing dishes of pasta, rice, meats, and poultry and salads of infinite variety and surprise. And no culture better understands simplicity and the magic of culinary understatement: Only the Italians can manage to slice a few tomatoes, drizzle them with olive oil, sprinkle them with sea salt and basil, and convince you to make a meal of it.

Along the trattoria trail I've been enraptured by the perfection of a crusty-roasted lamb in Rome, mesmerized by the feather-light delicacy of fried artichokes in Florence, and, in the Tuscan countryside, been brought to my knees by the subtleties of a dish no less noble than spaghetti in tomato sauce.

Whether it's found in the heart of the city or along a dirt road in the country, a trattoria is a essentially a small, informal, family-run restaurant, with home cooking and a homey atmosphere. And because trattorias are generally family ventures, no one is exactly like another.

The word *trattoria*—first appearing in print in 1859—probably comes from the French word *traiteur,* or caterer. But others suggest the word stems from the term *littarae tractoriae,* letters that in Latin times were carried by royalty as they traveled, and were given to messengers as a means of obtaining food and board on their journeys.

Many trattorias—including many featured here—have been in the same family for generations. And though they may have originally served as makeshift gathering spots for card playing and an afternoon sip of wine, they're now full-fledged restaurants, with a true family presence and a commitment to tradition. Other establishments take on a more modern posture, where the owners are young couples who work in tandem, around the clock, updating and re-creating the regional dishes of their childhoods.

When it comes to design and decoration, there is a definite trattoria "look." In the city, in particular, you're almost certain to find glass-paneled doors covered with simple and elegant embroidered white linen curtains; the chairs are almost always bentwood, the china thick and white, the tableware of ordinary stainless steel. If you order the house wine in "caraffa," you're likely to drink it out of small squat juice glasses. Order a bottle of wine from the list, and you'll be upgraded to simple stemmed wine glasses.

Traditionally, the walls are decorated with paintings, drawings, or even frescoes, offered by artists in exchange for food, wine, and atmosphere. Likewise, many establishments are adorned with all manner of thick glazed pottery or with majolica, resting on shelves or covering the walls. While today, little ashtrays, bowls, or plates bearing the name of the establishment may be offered to customers as pleasant souvenirs, they were once sold or swapped for different commodities, mostly wine and pork products.

Often, the kitchens open directly into the dining room, so diners can see the happenings in the kitchen, and the cooks can keep an eye on diners. You may or may not share tables with other diners, and in most cases, you may order one course at a time, adding courses until you say *basta,* or "enough." (For this reason, portions are rarely gargantuan: It is not uncommon to order soup as a first course, pasta as a second course, and meat, fish, or poultry as a main course. But there is nothing to stop one from ordering two pastas in succession, as I've seen Italian businessmen do on many an occasion.)

In the countryside, a trattoria may be little more than a small kitchen and a few outdoor tables, generally canopied by a flourishing grape arbor. Many vineyards boast their own trattoria, where the house wines can be shown off to best advantage.

While regional specialties abound, Italians are highly mobile within their own country, so it's not uncommon to find a Sardinian restaurant in Rome, a Tuscan trattoria in Milan, or a Piemontese eatery in Florence.

Seasonality is the key to all good cooking, and the roster of month-by-month trattoria specialties is no exception. In late August in Tuscany, restaurants offer the prized ovoli mushroom, and come fall you can't pass through the Piedmont without encountering the fragrant white truffle. And if it's December, you're sure to find puntarelle (a sort of wild chicory) on every trattoria menu in Rome.

Wine is hardly an afterthought in trattoria dining, though one's unlikely to find a sommelier in such down-home establishments. The budget-minded (meaning a healthy percentage of the diners) will order the house red or white by the carafe, often (but not always) a wise choice.

Likewise, desserts do not take a place of honor in the trattoria repertoire: Fruit tarts may be purchased from a pastry shop in the neighborhood, or prepackaged ice creams may be served. And always there are bowls of fresh fruit, ranging from slices of plump ripe pineapple to bowls of succulent, rosy-fleshed blood oranges.

While this book represents a decade's worth of expeditions throughout Italy in search of the authentic flavors of this rich land, it is also an attempt to offer—in the one hundred and fifty or so recipes gathered here—a faithful portrait of the colors, aromas, and tastes of Italian cooking today. Intentionally, I have mixed both traditional and modern fare, in hopes that your kitchen might also serve as a model of that rich and generous table.

Patricia Wells
1993

A Trip to
Antipasto Heaven

■

Nothing makes most diners happier than a generous selection of salads, vegetables, and spreads, little bits and bites of this and that. While the litany of dishes may appear intimidating, each can be prepared in advance. Offer, as well, a generous choice of wines, such as a white Vernaccia de San Gimignano from Tuscany, a red Barbera from the Piedmont.

Anchovies Marinated in Lemon Juice, Oil, and Thyme

Grilled Zucchini with Fresh Thyme

Sardinian Parchment Bread

Marinated Baby Artichokes Preserved in Oil

Salt-Cured Black Olives

Seared and Roasted Tomatoes

Individual Eggplant Parmesans

Red Bean and Onion Salad

Silky Sautéed Red Peppers

Aunt Flora's Olive Salad

Lemon-and-Oregano-Seasoned Tuna Mousse

White Bean Salad with Fresh Sage and Thyme

Black Olive Spread

Goat Cheese and Garlic Spread

ANTIPASTI, STARTERS, AND SALADS

Goat Cheese and Garlic Spread

Crema Formaggio all'Olio

"There are two Italies—one composed of the green earth and trans-parent sea, and the mighty ruins of ancient time, and aerial moun-tains, and the warm and radiant atmosphere which is interfused through all things. The other consists of the Italians of the present day, their works and ways. The one is the most sublime and lovely contem-plation that can be conceived by the imagination of man; the other is the most degraded, disgusting, and odious. What do you think? Young women of rank actually eat—you will never guess what—garlick!"

PERCY BYSSHE SHELLEY, LETTER TO LEIGH HUNT,
22 DECEMBER 1818

One spring evening in the Piedmont, more than a dozen of us gathered around a long table at the Osteria Barbabuc, in the hamlet of Novello, for a multi-course feast enlivened with plenty of the local Dolcetto d'Alba and Barbaresco. Little ramekins of this pure white cheese were waiting for us when we were seated, and we quickly devoured this garlic-rich, appetite-stimulating spread. The osteria's cook, Bruno Galaverna, prepares the cheese spread with the local robiola cheese, which is made with either cow's milk, goat's milk, or sheep's milk. When robiola is fresh—no more than three days old—it has a soft, delicate, almost buttery taste. In the Piedmont, one finds many variations of this cheese; sometimes herbs, lemon juice, and freshly ground black pepper are added. I prefer the simplicity of this version, nothing but good fresh cheese, a touch of oil, and a hit of garlic. Be certain to use fresh garlic—stale garlic will make for a bitter spread. Robiola can be found in some specialty shops, but top-quality domestic goat cheese is a worthy substitute.

8 ounces (250 g) robiola or mild fresh goat cheese

2 teaspoons extra-virgin olive oil

2 plump fresh garlic cloves, degermed and minced

In the bowl of a food processor, combine all the ingredients and blend until smooth and silky. Spoon into a ramekin and smooth out with a spatula. Serve immediately, as an appetizer or as part of a cheese course, with breadsticks or slices of toasted Italian bread. (The cheese can be stored, covered and refrigerated, for up to 3 days.)

■ Yield: 1 cup (250 ml) ■
cheese spread

WINE SUGGESTION: We sampled this with the dry, red, and graceful Dolcetto d'Alba, and you might, too.

VARIATION: On a visit to the trattoria Cibrèo in Florence, I sampled a thyme and olive oil version of this spread: To prepare it, simply combine the robiola or goat cheese, oil, and 2 teaspoons fresh thyme leaves, omitting the garlic. Blend in the food processor until smooth and fluffy, and serve as a dip or spread for fresh toast, for an appetizer.

The Germ Question

Take a clove of garlic, halve it lengthwise, and examine it. Garlic that is exquisitely fresh, plump, and moist will have a pale, barely visible green sprout running through the center. As garlic gets older that sprout grows, turns darker green, and gives the garlic a more intense flavor. The germ can also add a touch of bitterness to foods when garlic is added in its raw state. As a matter of course, I always remove the germ when garlic will be used raw, leave it in when garlic will be cooked.

■ ■ ■

Silky Sautéed Red Peppers

Peperoni in Aceto

With an agreeable flavor balance of both sweet and acid, these smooth, shiny, sautéed red peppers make a welcome first course, can star as part of a antipasto buffet, or are superb as a side dish to a summer meal of cold meats or poultry. The recipe comes from George Germon, chef and owner of Providence, Rhode Island's fine Italian restaurant, Al Forno. He prepared the peppers one day in my kitchen, and kindly allowed me to include them here. Rather than sautéeing the peppers in oil—the more traditional method—he cooked them in vinegar, tossing in a bit of oil at the end. I have also successfully prepared the peppers with balsamic vinegar, making for a sweeter, but no less appealing, dish.

6 red bell peppers (about 2 pounds; 1 kg)

½ cup (125 ml) plus 3 tablespoons best-quality red wine vinegar or balsamic vinegar

1 teaspoon sea salt, or to taste

¼ cup (60 ml) extra-virgin olive oil

1. Wash the peppers, quarter them lengthwise, and remove and discard the seeds and membranes. Place in a very large skillet and toss with the ½ cup (125 ml) vinegar and the salt. Cover and cook over low heat until soft and tender, about 25 minutes. Toss from time to time, adjusting the heat so the peppers cook slowly. By the end of the cooking time, most of the liquid will have evaporated. Do not increase the heat to speed up cooking, or the peppers will scorch and toughen.

2. Once the peppers have softened, transfer them to a large platter. Return the skillet to the heat, increase the heat to medium, and deglaze with the final 3 tablespoons vinegar, using a metal spatula to completely remove any flavorful bits that may have stuck to the pan. Add the oil, and heat just until warmed through, less than 1 minute. Pour the liquid over the peppers, toss, and taste for seasoning. Cool for at least 30 minutes before serving at room temperature: As they cool, the peppers will continue to soften and to absorb the oil and vinegar, giving them a complex, subtle flavor.

■　Yield: 6 to 8 servings　■
as an appetizer

. . .

Oven-Roasted Peppers

Peperoni al Forno

Whenever I have a batch of these delicious red and green roasted peppers ready at hand, I feel secure, as though my larder were somehow complete. These peppers can wear many hats: as a quick lunch with a slice of grilled bread; as a sauce tossed with warm pasta; as a member of a lovely antipasto table. I've sampled these at trattorias all over Italy. Sometimes they're roasted and served as is with just a touch of oil and salt, and sometimes they have a nice, vinegary tang. Take your choice. Be sure to watch the peppers as they bake: The goal here is peppers that are soft and fully cooked, with most of the skin still attached. If they scorch, or bake at too high a temperature, the skins fall away and the peppers become unpleasantly dry or rubbery, and sometimes bitter. Should you also find yellow or orange peppers in the market, try all four varieties for a festival of color. Or, if you're partial to red peppers, stick with a single hue. Even those who profess a dislike for peppers will be surprised by the sweetness of this dish.

4 red bell peppers (about 1½ pounds, 750 g)

4 green bell peppers (about 1½ pounds, 750 g)

¼ cup (60 ml) extra-virgin olive oil

Fine sea salt to taste

1 tablespoon best-quality red wine vinegar (optional)

1. Preheat the oven to 350°F (175°C; gas mark 4/5).

2. Wash the peppers, quarter them, and remove and discard the seeds and membranes. Place in a covered baking dish large enough to hold them comfortably. Toss with the oil and season lightly with salt.

3. Cover and place in the center of the oven. Bake for 1 to 1½ hours, turning the peppers from time to time so they do not scorch. Remove from the oven and, if desired, toss with the vinegar. Taste for seasoning. Serve warm or at room temperature.

Yield: 8 to 10 servings
as an appetizer

Lemon-and-Oregano-Seasoned Tuna Mousse

Mousse di Tonno

S pread it on toast, place it atop a bed of crisp, dressed greens, or serve it alongside a salad of green beans or steamed beets. This rich and vibrantly flavored tuna appetizer is a standby from Florence's up-to-date trattoria Cibrèo, a place where creativity and imagination are thoroughly uninhibited. This is a great dish to know about when the cupboard is ostensibly bare: Open the pantry, then the refrigerator, and, wow, you've a great snack, a quick lunch, a simple appetizer.

One 6½-ounce (190-g) can imported tuna packed in olive oil (do not drain; see Note)

4 tablespoons (2 ounces; 60 g) unsalted butter, softened

Grated zest (yellow peel) of 1 lemon

2 tablespoons freshly squeezed lemon juice

2 tablespoons extra-virgin olive oil

½ teaspoon dried leaf oregano

1 plump fresh garlic clove, degermed and minced

With a fork, flake the tuna in the can. Transfer, oil and all, to the bowl of a food processor. Add the remaining ingredients and process until smooth and creamy. Taste for seasoning. Transfer to a medium-size bowl and serve at room temperature. (The mousse can be stored, covered and refrigerated, for up to 3 days.)

▪ Yield: 1 cup (250 ml) mousse ▪

NOTE: If tuna packed in olive oil is unavailable, use top-quality white tuna packed in water. Drain the tuna, discard the water, and add an additional tablespoon of extra-virgin olive oil when preparing the mousse.

Caponata

"Plato, when he visited Sicily, was so much struck with the luxury of the Agrigentum, both in their houses and their tables, that a saying of his is still recorded; that they built as if they were never to die, and eat as if they had not an hour to live."

PATRICK BRYDONE, A TOUR THROUGH SICILY AND MALTA, *1773*

C aponata—a smooth, jam-like mixture of eggplant, red peppers, onions, and celery, punctuated by a touch of sugar and vinegar and accented by green olives and capers—is one of my favorite trattoria dishes. I love to make it and adore eating it, especially when the market is filled with glistening purple eggplant. A close cousin of the French ratatouille, caponata is generally chunkier, accented with the crunch and flavor of celery, and laced with the saltiness supplied by the olives and capers. I've sampled many versions of this Sicilian dish throughout Italy, and even tasted one version—north of Venice—that included huge chunks of potatoes. You've succeeded at caponata if each vegetable manages to maintain its own integrity and texture. The vegetables should remain slightly firm, almost crunchy, and should in no way turn to mush. This is achieved by carefully cooking the vegetables separately, then folding them together near the end. Note also, it's important to season this dish lightly as you cook, so in the end, no additional seasoning is necessary. The added step of blanching the olives makes the dish more sophisticated, for unblanched olives can add an aggressive edge. Caponata can be served warm or at room temperature, as part of an antipasto assortment, or as an accompaniment to roast meats or poultry.

(continued)

2 medium onions

2 red bell peppers

1 cup (250 ml) extra-virgin olive oil

Fine sea salt to taste

One 16-ounce (480-g) can imported Italian plum tomatoes in juice or one 16-ounce (480-g) can crushed tomatoes in purée

Several parsley stems, celery leaves, and sprigs of thyme, tied in a bundle with cotton twine

4 plump fresh garlic cloves, thinly sliced

8 ribs celery hearts with leaves, diced

2 teaspoons fresh thyme leaves

1 firm medium eggplant (about 1 pound; 500 g), cubed (do not peel)

2 tablespoons sugar

½ cup (125 ml) best-quality red wine vinegar

1 cup (5 ounces; 150 g) drained pitted green olives

¼ cup (60 ml) drained capers, rinsed

1. Peel the onions, trim the ends, and cut in half lengthwise. Place each half, cut side down, on a cutting board, and cut crosswise into very thin slices. Set aside. Cut the peppers into thin vertical strips, then halve each strip crosswise. Set aside.

2. In a deep 12-inch (30-cm) skillet, combine the onions, ¼ cup (60 ml) of the oil, and a pinch of salt, and stir to coat the onions with oil. Cook over low heat until soft and translucent, about 5 minutes. Add the peppers and a pinch of salt. Cover and continue cooking for about 5 minutes more. If using whole canned tomatoes, place a food mill over the skillet and purée the tomatoes directly into it. Crushed tomatoes can be added directly from the can. Continue cooking for another 5 minutes. Add the herb bundle and garlic and taste for seasoning. Cover and simmer gently for about 20 minutes, stirring from time to time. Do not overcook: The vegetables should be cooked through but still firm, not mushy. Remove and discard the herb bundle. Remove from the heat and set aside.

3. Meanwhile, in another 12-inch (30-cm) skillet, heat ¼ cup (60 ml) of the oil over moderate heat. Add the celery and cook until it is lightly colored and beginning to turn soft and translucent, 7 to 10 minutes. Transfer to a bowl, and season lightly with salt. Add the thyme, and set aside.

4. In the skillet in which the celery was cooked, heat the remaining oil over moderate heat. When hot, add the eggplant and cook until lightly colored, about 5 minutes. (The eggplant will soak up the oil immediately, but allow it to cook without added oil, and keep the pan moving to avoid scorching.) The eggplant should remain firm.

5. Transfer the eggplant and the celery to the tomato mixture. Taste for seasoning. Cover and simmer gently over low heat until the mixture takes on a soft, jam-like consistency, about 20 minutes.

6. Meanwhile, in a small bowl, combine the sugar and vinegar, and stir to dissolve. Set aside.

7. In a medium saucepan, bring 1 quart (1 l) of water to a boil over high heat. Add the olives and blanch for 2 minutes. Drain and rinse under cold running water. Taste an olive: If it is still very salty, repeat the blanching.

8. Add the sugar-vinegar mixture, the blanched olives, and the capers to the vegetable mixture, and simmer over low heat for 1 to 2 minutes to allow the flavors to blend. Taste for seasoning. Transfer to a large serving bowl to cool. Serve warm or at room temperature, but not chilled.

Yield: 8 to 12 servings
as an appetizer

■ ■ ■

Seasoned Raw Beef

Insalata di Carne Cruda

Carne cruda, or lightly seasoned chopped, raw beef, is Italy's answer to the French steak tartare. This recipe is a specialty of the Piedmont. I've come to prefer this pure, unadulterated version, and particularly love it as the first course of a leisurely Sunday lunch. Use the finest olive oil you can afford, and serve this with plenty of crusty homemade bread. And select the leanest beef available, mixing in the seasoning as lightly as possible so the meat is not packed. Some people prefer seasoning the beef ahead of time and refrigerating it for about an hour before serving so the beef absorbs the seasoning. I prefer to serve it right away, making for a fresh, vibrant flavor.

1 pound (500 g) lean top-round beef or trimmed filet mignon or very lean trimmed sirloin, well chilled, and finely chopped

½ cup (125 ml) celery leaves, snipped with a scissors

½ cup (125 ml) fresh flat-leaf parsley leaves, snipped with a scissors

½ cup (125 ml) extra-virgin olive oil

1 tablespoon freshly squeezed lemon juice

Fine sea salt and freshly ground black pepper to taste

1 lemon, thinly sliced, for garnish

1. In a bowl, combine the beef, half the celery and half the parsley, the oil, and the lemon juice. Toss gently with a fork. Season to taste with salt and pepper.

2. Mound the beef on four chilled salad plates, showering with the remaining parsley and celery leaves. Garnish with slices of lemon.

■ Yield: 4 servings ■

WINE SUGGESTION: Bring out a good red from the Piedmont, a Dolcetto or Nebbiolo.

Seared and Roasted Tomatoes

Pomodori al Forno

Few dishes are simpler or more welcoming than a giant platter of fragrant seared and roasted tomatoes. These often take a place of importance in a huge antipasto feast, for they're easy to make and just as easy to love. I've prepared these with both round and oval tomatoes, served warm or at room temperature, with equal success. Just be sure to use a large well-seasoned pan (I use an old, very thin black tin frying pan) that will allow the tomatoes to sear over rather high heat before you roast them in the oven. When served warm, they are a great accompaniment to chicken, meat, or fish.

¼ cup (60 ml) extra-virgin olive oil

8 firm medium-size tomatoes, cored and halved crosswise

Fine sea salt to taste

2 teaspoons fresh thyme leaves

1. Preheat the oven to 400°F (200°C; gas mark 6/7).

2. In a very large skillet, heat the oil over moderately high heat. When hot, place as many tomatoes as will easily fit in the pan, cut side down. Sear, without moving the tomatoes, until they are dark and almost caramelized, 5 to 6 minutes. Transfer the tomatoes, cooked side up, to a baking dish just large enough to hold the tomatoes comfortably. Continue until all the tomatoes are seared. Pour the cooking juices in the skillet over the tomatoes. Season lightly with salt and the thyme.

3. Place the baking dish in the center of the oven and bake, uncovered, until the tomatoes are browned and sizzling, about 30 minutes (or about 15 minutes for oval Roma tomatoes). Serve immediately, or at room temperature.

■ Yield: 8 servings ■

Individual Eggplant Parmesans

Parmigiani di Melanzane

I like to think of these delicious individual eggplant "parmesans" as crustless pizzas. I sampled them one August evening at a trattoria on Lake Garda, where the waterside eatery offered some twenty-five or thirty different items from the self-service antipasto table. They make a quick main dish for a light meal, or a luncheon dish served with a green salad. Although trattorias often serve these at room temperature, I think they lose much of their charm. So, for best results, serve hot from the oven. And although this is a simple dish, it requires careful timing and no distractions!

1 firm medium eggplant (about 1 pound; 500 g) (do not peel)

3 to 4 tablespoons extra-virgin olive oil

Fine sea salt to taste

Fresh flat-leaf parsley leaves, fresh thyme leaves, fresh basil leaves, and/or dried leaf oregano to taste (optional)

½ cup (125 ml) Tomato Sauce (page 256)

4 ounces (125 g) fresh whole-milk mozzarella, thinly sliced

¼ cup (1 ounce; 30 g) freshly grated Italian Parmigiano-Reggiano cheese

Dried leaf oregano, for garnish

1. Preheat the oven broiler.

2. Cover a broiling pan with aluminum foil, for easier cleanup. Slice the eggplant crosswise into ½-inch (1-cm) slices. Place the slices on the broiling pan, lightly brush the top of each slice with oil, and season with salt.

3. Place the broiling pan about 5 inches (12.5 cm) from the heat. Broil until the slices are thoroughly and evenly browned, about 5 minutes. Remove the broiling pan from the oven and turn each slice of eggplant. Lightly brush the uncooked sides with oil. Season with salt, and the herbs, if using. Return to the oven and broil until brown, about 3 minutes.

4. Remove the broiling pan from the oven and top each slice with a spoonful of tomato sauce, a thin slice of mozzarella, and a light sprinkling of Parmesan and of oregano. Return to the oven and broil until the sauce is hot and the cheese is bubbly, about 2 minutes more. The eggplant should be soft when pierced. Serve immediately.

■ Yield: 4 to 6 servings ■
as an appetizer

Oregano: Fresh versus Dried

Oregano—known as *origano* in Italian—is perhaps the only herb that is better dried than fresh, for dried leaf oregano has a sweeter, more pungent, more distinctive flavor. It is, in fact, the only dried herb allowed in my spice drawer, and dried oregano finds its way into tuna mousse, salads, and tomato sauces, it's sprinkled on pizzas, and it marries well with both green and black olives. When shopping for the dried herb, be sure to distinguish between ground oregano (which can taste like dirt) and the preferred leaf oregano. Replenish stocks of dried oregano every six months.

Oregano is closely related to marjoram, which has a more delicate, flowery flavor. Wild marjoram—a tall perennial herb—is also sometimes called oregano. To profit from its sweet and pungent flavor, always add oregano near the end of cooking.

■ ■ ■

Grilled Zucchini with Fresh Thyme

Zucchini alla Griglia

Once you've secured firm, small zucchini and have good olive oil and sea salt on hand, there's little more for you to do than heat up the broiler or grill. The pure, sweet, golden freshness of young zucchini should star here, so just brush—don't douse—with oil and seasonings. I like to serve this as part of an antipasto buffet or as a side dish to meats, fish, or poultry. While instructions are given here for broiling in the oven, the zucchini can also be grilled, following the same basic procedure. Just be certain to slice the zucchini very thin, so that it cooks quickly and evenly, and carefully stem the fresh thyme leaves.

5 fresh firm small zucchini (about 1¾ pounds; 875 g), cut into thin lengthwise slices

About 3 tablespoons extra-virgin olive oil

Sea salt to taste

1 tablespoon fresh thyme leaves

1. Preheat the oven broiler.

2. Cover a broiling pan with aluminum foil, for easier cleanup. Place the zucchini slices side by side on the foil-covered broiling pan. Lightly brush with oil, and season with salt.

3. Place the broiling pan about 5 inches (12.5 cm) from the heat. Broil until the slices are golden brown, 2 to 3 minutes. Remove the broiling pan from the oven and, using tongs, turn each slice of zucchini. Lightly brush the uncooked sides with oil. Season with salt. Return to the oven and broil until golden brown, 2 to 3 minutes.

4. Remove the zucchini from the oven and transfer to a shallow dish, layering in overlapping slices. Drizzle lightly with oil and sprinkle with the thyme leaves. Serve warm or at room temperature. The zucchini is best consumed the same day. Refrigeration will alter the vegetable's fresh, delicate flavor, so store at room temperature.

■ Yield: 4 servings ■

Tips for Better Broiling

Broiled—or "grilled"—vegetables are greatly in vogue, but, alas, all too often we are served vegetables that are burnt on the outside and raw on the inside, or were cooked so far in advance they loose all their fresh appeal. Proper oven broiling is simple: Just think of it as baking at intense heat. For best results, vegetables should be cooked quickly at high heat so they do not dry out. Be careful not to broil too close to the heat, or the vegetables will simply burn, not cook.

HERE ARE SOME TIPS:

■ Preheat the broiler for a good fifteen minutes, to ensure a very high and even temperature.

■ Slice the vegetables thin, to expose a maximum of surface area.

■ Broil about 5 inches (12.5 cm) from the heat, so the vegetables cook quickly, but thoroughly, and do not burn.

Marinated Baby Artichokes Preserved in Oil

Carciofi sott'Olio

I consider my cupboard bare if I don't have at least one jar of these delicious pickled artichokes on hand. I love them as a snack, as an accompaniment to warm or cold meats or poultry, as a quick topping for pizzas or pasta, or layered in a bowl as part of a large antipasto buffet. I've experimented with many versions of this simple-to-prepare condiment, and find I prefer a very weak pickling solution prepared with white wine vinegar. The light solution and the quick cooking makes for a pickle that's not overly acidic. The hot artichokes are then covered with extra-virgin olive oil, and they take on a special, rich flavor.

In the United States, "baby" artichokes are simply small but fully mature secondary-growth globe artichokes from the "green globe" variety. An average full-sized artichoke weighs in at about two pounds (1 kg). The baby globe artichokes are simply volunteers that appear after the main crop has been picked. The tiny artichokes are sweet and more tender than the larger version, and since the feathery choke is so small and delicate, the heart and choke are both completely edible. In Europe, however, tiny violet-tinged artichokes (in Italy, a favorite variety is "Violetto"—usually weighing about three ounces [90 g] each) are varieties unto themselves, prized for eating raw or for pickling like this.

2 cups (500 ml) Champagne vinegar

2 cups (500 ml) water

2 teaspoons fine sea salt

8 bay leaves, preferably fresh

2½ pounds (1.25 kg) small artichokes (about 25) (see Mail Order Sources, page 325)

1½ cups (375 ml) extra-virgin olive oil, or as needed

4 plump fresh garlic cloves, degermed

2 tablespoons fresh flat-leaf parsley leaves, snipped with a scissors

1. In a large stainless steel saucepan, combine the vinegar, water, salt, and 4 of the bay leaves.

2. Prepare the artichokes: Rinse the artichokes under cold running water. Using a stainless steel knife to minimize discoloration, trim the stem of an artichoke to about ½ inch (1 cm) from the base. Carefully trim off and discard the stem's fibrous exterior. Bend back the tough outer green leaves one at a time, letting them snap off naturally at the base. Continue snapping off the leaves until only the central cone of yellow leaves with pale green tips remains. Lightly trim the top of the cone of leaves to just below the green tips. Trim any dark green areas from the stem. Depending upon its size, leave whole or halve or quarter the artichoke lengthwise, and transfer immediately to the vinegar mixture to prevent discoloration. Continue until all the artichokes are trimmed.

3. Bring the liquid and artichokes to a simmer over medium-high heat. Simmer, reducing the heat if necessary, until the artichokes are tender but still offer a bit of resistance when pierced with a knife, 7 to 10 minutes. (Cooking time will vary according to the size of the artichokes.) Drain the artichokes, discarding the vinegar mixture and bay leaves.

4. While the artichokes are still warm, marinate them: If the artichokes will be consumed the same day, arrange them in a single layer in a shallow dish and partially cover with oil. To preserve them, arrange in layers in a sterilized 1-quart (1-l) canning jar, or several smaller sterilized jars: Layer the artichokes, garlic, parsley, and the remaining 4 bay leaves, finishing with a layer of artichokes. Completely cover the artichokes with oil. Set aside, uncovered, until the artichokes are completely cool. If necessary, add additional oil to come to the top. Cover securely. Refrigerate, covered, for up to 2 months, making sure that the artichokes are always covered in oil. The artichokes preserved in this manner can be consumed as soon as they are cool, but will have greater depth of flavor if allowed to marinate for at least 24 hours.

■   Yield: 1   quart   (1   liter)   ■

Anchovies Marinated in Lemon Juice, Olive Oil, and Thyme

Acciughe al Limone

Tiny bites that precede a meal—such as those included in the huge selection of varied antipasti found at many trattorias—are often among the most satisfying. They open the palate and refresh the spirit and the body. One of my favorites is a healthy serving of fresh anchovies that have simply been filleted and marinated ever so quickly in a touch of lemon juice, then anointed with extra-virgin olive oil and a touch of seasoning. Although most of us don't come across fresh anchovies on a regular basis, should you stumble upon them (or beg them off a fisherman or fishmonger), go for it!

1 pound (500 g) fresh anchovies (about 24)

3 tablespoons freshly squeezed lemon juice

2 tablespoons extra-virgin olive oil

Fine sea salt to taste

4 bay leaves, preferably fresh

2 teaspoons fresh thyme leaves

1 shallot, finely minced

1. Lightly rinse (don't wash or soak) the anchovies. Individually head and gut the fish by holding each anchovy firmly just beneath the head and gently pull off the head and attached entrails. Discard the head and entrails. Run your thumb down the center of the fish, and it will easily spread open. Remove and discard the central bone. Carefully pull the anchovy apart into 2 fillets. Lightly run your fingers along each fillet to remove any pieces of bone or entrails. Pat dry, and place the fillets, skin side up, side by side on a platter. Drizzle with the lemon juice, cover with plastic wrap, and refrigerate for 10 minutes.

2. Remove the fish from the refrigerator. Drain off and discard the lemon juice. Drizzle another platter with the olive oil, sprinkle lightly with salt, and cover with the bay leaves. Arrange the anchovy fillets side by side on the platter. Sprinkle with the thyme and minced shallot. Season very lightly with salt. Cover with plastic wrap and refrigerate for 10 minutes. Serve as an appetizer, with freshly grilled toast.

■ Yield: 4 servings ■
as an appetizer

• • ■

Fresh Artichoke Omelet

Tortino di Carciofi

Green and golden, this dish reminds me of springtime and daffodils. Although a tortino is generally a vegetable pie without the pastry, this Florentine specialty is more a cross between an omelet and scrambled eggs. I love artichokes so much that on one trip to Florence I sampled this dish two days in a row: once at the charming little trattoria Sostanza, the next day at the tiny family eatery Il Francescano, near Santa Croce. In this version, the baby artichokes are sliced very thin, then quickly sautéed in olive oil. The eggs are then cooked much like an omelet, but the omelet is not folded: Rather, the cooked artichokes are placed in the center of the cooked eggs, which are gently folded over toward the center. You'd never think of eggs and artichokes as a marriage made in heaven, but they are!

1 lemon

4 baby artichokes (see Mail Order Sources, page 325)

2 tablespoons extra-virgin olive oil

Fine sea salt and freshly ground black pepper to taste

8 extra-fresh large eggs, at room temperature

4 tablespoons (2 ounces; 60 g) unsalted butter, at room temperature

1. Prepare the artichokes: Halve the lemon, squeeze the juice, and place the halved lemon and juice in a bowl filled with cold water. Rinse the artichokes under cold running water. Using a stainless steel knife to minimize discoloration, trim the stem of an artichoke to about ½ inch (1 cm) from the base. Carefully trim off and discard the stem's fibrous exterior. Bend back the tough outer green leaves one at a time, letting them snap off naturally at the base. Continue snapping off the leaves until only the central cone of yellow leaves with pale green tips remains. Lightly trim the top of the cone of leaves to just below the green tips. Trim any dark green areas from the stem. Slice the artichoke lengthwise into very thin slices and transfer immediately to the lemon juice mixture to prevent their discoloring. Continue until all artichokes are trimmed and sliced.

2. Drain the artichokes and pat them dry. In a seasoned or nonstick 10-inch (25-cm) skillet, heat the oil over moderate heat. When the oil is hot but not smoking, add the artichokes and sauté until lightly browned, 3 to 4 minutes. Drain in a sieve set over a small bowl, and season to taste with salt and pepper. Set aside.

3. Prepare the omelet: Break the eggs into a bowl. Cut 2 tablespoons of the butter into small cubes, and add to the eggs. Season with salt and pepper. (Do not beat the eggs at this point.)

4. Warm the seasoned or nonstick pan for several seconds over high heat. Add the remaining 2 tablespoons butter. While the butter melts, beat the eggs lightly with a fork. Tilt the pan to coat the bottom with melted butter. When the butter begins to foam, but before it begins to brown, pour in the beaten eggs. Stir the egg mixture by gently passing a fork through the eggs several times to expose as much of the mixture as possible to the heat of the pan. (Be careful not to scrape the tines of the fork over the bottom of the pan, or the surface will scratch, making the omelet stick.)

5. When the underside of the omelet begins to set, use the fork to lift the edges of the omelet. At the same time, tilt the pan so that any uncooked egg from the top will run under the cooked egg and set. Continue lifting and tilting the pan until all of the egg has set. When the edges of the omelet are firm, but the top is still moist, quickly spoon the artichokes into the center. Fold the edges over about 1 inch (3 cm) all around, slightly enveloping the artichokes. Slip the omelet, right side up, onto a warmed round platter, and season generously with salt and pepper. Slice and transfer to warmed dinner plates.

Yield: 4 servings as a first course,
2 servings as a main course

Tips for a Fluffy, Moist Omelet

■ Begin with fresh eggs at room temperature.

■ Beat the eggs lightly, and be careful not to overbeat. The yolks and whites should be beaten just to combine them without forming air bubbles that might make the omelet dry out.

■ Heat the pan thoroughly before adding the eggs.

■ Cook any bulky ingredients beforehand—such as the artichokes here—and add them to the omelet at the last minute.

■ Use a well-seasoned (or nonstick) pan that is wide enough to allow the eggs to cook quickly. An omelet that is cooked too slowly will tend to dry out.

. . .

Raw Vegetables Dipped in Olive Oil

Pinzimonio

Pinzimonio—a mix of raw vegetables that are dipped in olive oil seasoned with a touch of salt and perhaps fresh black pepper—is an ideal summertime dish, a communal affair that gets everyone eating with their hands, sitting elbow to elbow at long, festive tables. Or, on the more serious side, pinzimonio is the ideal way to "test" the flavors of extra-virgin olive oils. When oils are sampled in their pure state, with just a hint of salt, you can truly judge the flavors, and select a favorite. So, next time you have four or five oils together, make a visit to your greengrocer, invite over a group of friends, and chomp away! The following is simply a suggestion of the vegetables you might include. Arrange them attractively in a large bowl of ice water, to keep them cool. I like to supply each diner with a several small bowls, so they can season their oils (or not) to taste. Also make sure everyone has a good sharp paring knife, for slicing and for trimming the artichokes.

Tender ribs celery with leaves, washed

Baby artichokes

Cherry tomatoes

Fresh baby fava beans in their pods

Fennel bulbs, quartered lengthwise

Red and green bell peppers, quartered lengthwise

Carrots, peeled and quartered lengthwise

Fresh baby onions or scallions

Small cucumbers, quartered lengthwise

Extra-virgin olive oil (several brands if desired)

Fine sea salt and freshly ground black pepper to taste

Fresh country bread

• • •

Spinach-Parmesan Frittata

Frittata Fredda alla Rustica

I once spent a week in Florence, visiting a different café each morning for breakfast and the morning paper. Since I don't have much of a sweet tooth, I'd opt for an assortment of tiny sandwiches, or panini, ideal Italian finger food. Often, the filling was made up of varied frittate—highly seasoned cooked egg and herb mixtures—perfect for waking up morning tastebuds.

A frittata is a close relative of the omelet, but it is served flat, not rolled, more like a Spanish tortilla, and at room temperature. A frittata is cooked very slowly over low heat, then placed under the broiler until firm. This version is the most classic, and one of my favorites. Try to use the smallest, freshest spinach leaves you can find. When sliced into thin wedges, or used as a sandwich filling, this frittata—always cooled to room temperature before eating—makes perfect snack, luncheon, or picnic fare.

6 large eggs, at room temperature

Fine sea salt and freshly ground black pepper to taste

Freshly grated nutmeg to taste

4 cups (3 ounces; 90 g) loosely packed fresh spinach leaves, rinsed, dried, and finely chopped

1 cup (4 ounces; 125 g) freshly grated Italian Parmigiano-Reggiano cheese

1 tablespoon extra-virgin olive oil

1. Preheat the oven broiler.

2. Crack the eggs into a large bowl and beat lightly with a fork. Add the salt and pepper, nutmeg, spinach, and half the cheese, and beat lightly to combine the ingredients.

3. In a 9-inch (23-cm) ovenproof omelet pan or skillet, heat the oil over moderate heat, swirling the pan to coat the bottom and sides evenly. When the oil is hot but not smoking, add the frittata mixture. Reduce the heat to low and cook slowly, stirring the top two-thirds of the mixture (leaving the bottom part to set, so it doesn't stick) until the eggs have formed small curds and the frittata is brown on the bottom and almost firm in the center, about 4 minutes. The top should still be very soft. With a spatula, lightly loosen the frittata from the edges of the pan, to prevent sticking later on. Sprinkle with the remaining cheese.

4. Transfer the pan to the broiler, placing it about 5 inches (12.5 cm) from the heat, so that the frittata cooks without burning. Broil until the frittata browns lightly on top and becomes puffy and firm, about 2 minutes. (Watch carefully: A minute can make the difference between a golden-brown frittata and one that's overcooked.) Remove the frittata from the broiler and let cool in the pan for 2 minutes. Place a large flat plate over the top of the pan and invert the frittata onto it. Let the frittata cool to room temperature.

5. To serve, cut into wedges and serve with a salad or as a sandwich filling.

■ Y i e l d : 4 t o 6 s e r v i n g s ■

• • •

Individual Gorgonzola Soufflés

Tortino Gorgonzola

These rich and memorable individual Gorgonzola soufflés were served as part of a multi-course feast one spring Saturday evening at the Osteria Barbabuc, in the hamlet of Novello in the Piedmont. With my first taste of the warming soufflé, all I could think of was presenting this to guests at home, with a sparkling green arugula salad alongside. That's the way I love to serve this soufflé, for it's a perfect, elegant, and satisfying luncheon dish. If all the ingredients are measured out and ready beforehand, it takes little last-minute preparation. The recipe was shared with me by the osteria's chef, Bruno Galaverna. A tortino is traditionally a simple, rustic vegetable pie, prepared without pastry. Although the quantities of cream and flour here take this beyond the realm of a classic soufflé, the little tortinos puff up beautifully, as if defying tradition.

Butter for preparing the ramekins

2 cups (500 ml) heavy cream

¼ teaspoon fine sea salt

Freshly ground black pepper to taste

¾ cup (100 g) unbleached all-purpose flour

5 large eggs, separated

5 ounces (150 g) imported Gorgonzola cheese, at room temperature, crumbled

1. Preheat the oven to 425°F (220°C; gas mark 8).

2. Thoroughly butter the bottoms and sides of eight ½-cup (125-ml) ramekins.

3. In a large saucepan, combine the cream, salt, and pepper, and scald over moderately high heat, bringing the mixture just to the boiling point. Reduce the heat to low, and add the flour all at once, whisking constantly to prevent lumps from forming. The sauce

will thicken almost immediately. Remove from the heat, and stir in the egg yolks one by one. Then add the Gorgonzola, and stir until the cheese melts into the cream mixture. Set aside.

4. In the bowl of an electric mixer fitted with a whisk, beat the egg whites until stiff but not dry. Whisk one-third of the egg whites into the soufflé mixture and combine thoroughly. (Do not be concerned about deflating the egg whites at this point.) With a large rubber spatula, gently fold in the remaining whites. Do this slowly and patiently. Do not overmix, but be sure that the mixture is well blended and almost no streaks of white remain.

5. Spoon the mixture into the prepared ramekins, filling them three-quarters full, and smoothing out the tops with a spatula. Place the ramekins on a heavy-duty baking sheet and place in the center of the oven. Bake until the soufflés are well risen and the tops are browned, about 15 minutes. Carefully remove from the oven and place each ramekin on a small salad plate. Serve immediately.

■ Yield: 8 servings ■

WINE SUGGESTION: With this soufflé, I love a nice Barbera d'Alba or a Dolcetto d'Alba, both from the Piedmont.

For Easier Separating, and Better Whipped Whites

Eggs are easier to separate when they are cold, but whites whip better at room temperature. So when preparing dishes such as this one, separate the eggs immediately after removing them from the refrigerator, then allow them to come to room temperature before you begin cooking.

Herb-Infused Savory Custards

Tartra all'Antica

Creamy, fragrant, and infused with the scents and flavors of fresh rosemary and bay leaf, this elegant and unusual first course is, as chef Angelo Maionchi of Turin's Del Cambio says, "like pasta." That is, it's an appealing backdrop for all sorts of sauces, which can be paraded out to celebrate each season in turn. While a cheese sauce is classic, the chef also serves a cream and asparagus sauce in the spring, and a mushroom and tomato sauce (page 257) in the fall. Any sauce you love for pasta would go well as an accompaniment to this shimmering, molded starter. I love it best with a tomato-based sauce, for I enjoy the play of textures and flavors, as the soft, rich, and refined custard is contrasted with the mildly acidic sauce. Eating this dish is, in fact, a little like having dessert as a first course! I always prepare this in advance, earlier in the day, so there is little last-minute work.

Butter for preparing the ramekins

1½ cups (375 ml) whole milk

2½ cups (625 ml) heavy cream

3 tablespoons minced fresh rosemary leaves, measured after mincing

4 bay leaves, preferably fresh

4 large eggs

2 large egg yolks

¼ cup (1 ounce; 30 g) freshly grated Italian Parmigiano-Reggiano cheese

¼ teaspoon freshly grated nutmeg

¼ teaspoon fine sea salt

Freshly ground black pepper to taste

2 cups (500 ml) warm Tomato-Mushroom Sauce (page 257)

1. Preheat the oven to 350°F (175°C; gas mark 4/5). Butter six 1-cup (250-ml) ramekins.

2. Prepare a large kettle of boiling water for the water bath; set aside.

3. Cut 3 slits in a piece of waxed paper, and use it to line a roasting pan large enough to hold the ramekins. Place the ramekins in the pan, on top of the paper, and set aside. (The paper will prevent the water added to the pan from boiling and splashing up on the custards.)

4. In a medium-size saucepan, combine the milk and cream, and scald over high heat, bringing the mixture just to the boiling point. Remove from the heat, add the rosemary and bay leaves, cover, and set aside to infuse for 10 minutes. Strain the liquid through a fine-mesh sieve into a large bowl. Discard the herbs. Set aside to cool.

5. In a small bowl, blend the eggs and egg yolks lightly with a fork, but do not let the mixture become foamy or frothy, or the custard will be filled with bubbles.

6. When the milk mixture has cooled, add the eggs and stir to blend. Stir in the cheese, nutmeg, salt, and pepper. Taste for seasoning.

7. Divide the custard evenly among the prepared ramekins. Add enough hot water to the roasting pan to reach to about half the depth of the ramekins. Place in the center of the oven and bake until the custards are just set at the edges but still trembling in the center, 50 to 55 minutes.

8. Remove from the oven and carefully remove the ramekins from the water. (The custards can be baked earlier in the day and reheated in a warm water bath for about 10 minutes before serving.) To serve, invert the molds onto warmed salad plates, spooning the warm sauce attractively around the molds.

■ Yield: 6 servings ■

WINE SUGGESTION: A smooth, balanced red is right here, such as a Dolcetto d'Alba from the Piedmont.

∎ ∎ ∎

Swiss Chard and Parmesan Torte

Torta di Biete

his savory snack is a favorite Mediterranean specialty. Vegetable pies such as this one—prepared with a quick and wholesome olive oil pastry—can be found at pastry and snack shops in many parts of Italy. There are versions flecked with pine nuts and raisins as well, but I prefer the simplicity of this torte. I often prepare it early in the day and serve it with a glass of white wine as an appetizer before dinner. If you have a garden, raise Swiss chard, for it grows like wild and has a sturdy, sensible personality in the kitchen. Short of chard, fresh spinach is a totally worthy substitute.

PASTRY

- *1 cup (135 g) unbleached all-purpose flour*
- *¼ teaspoon fine sea salt*
- *¼ cup (60 ml) water*
- *¼ cup (60 ml) extra-virgin olive oil*

FILLING

- *1 pound (500 g) Swiss chard leaves (or substitute fresh spinach leaves)*
- *Fine sea salt and freshly ground black pepper to taste*
- *3 large eggs*
- *1 cup (4 ounces; 125 g) freshly grated Italian Parmigiano-Reggiano cheese*

1. Preheat the oven to 375°F (190°C; gas mark 5).

2. Prepare the pastry: In a medium-size bowl, combine the flour and salt. Stir in the water, then the oil, mixing until thoroughly blended. Knead briefly. The dough will be

very moist, much like a cookie dough. Press the dough into the bottom of 10½-inch (27-cm) tart tin with a removable bottom. (You do not need to cover the sides of the tin.)

3. Prepare the filling: Wash and dry the green leafy portions of the chard or spinach, trimming and discarding the center stems. Tear the leaves and chop, in several batches, in a food processor.

4. Place the chard in a large shallow frying pan and season with salt and pepper. Wilt the chard or spinach over low heat, and cook until most of the liquid has evaporated, 2 to 3 minutes. Remove from the heat.

5. Combine the eggs and cheese in a medium-size bowl and stir to blend. Stir in the chard or spinach, mix well, and taste for seasoning. Spoon the mixture into the prepared tart tin.

6. Place in the center of the oven and bake until the filling is lightly browned and firm to the touch, about 45 minutes. Remove to a baking rack to cool. Serve at room temperature, cutting into thin wedges. (Do not refrigerate, or the filling will become tough.)

■ Yield: 8 to 12 servings ■

WINE SUGGESTION: I love a bubbly white with this, such as a Prosecco *frizzante*, or a dry white such as a Soave or Orvieto Secco.

Celery Salad with Anchovy Dressing

Insalata di Puntarelle

One Saturday morning I was wandering through the Campo dei Fiori food market in Rome and noticed that each salad merchant displayed little buckets of water filled with what appeared to be "celery flowers." I asked one vendor, who explained that it was called puntarelle, a local form of wild chicory that is traditionally trimmed into flowers. I sampled the salad the next day at Trattoria Piperno, and wasn't at all surprised to find that puntarelle taste remarkably like celery. The salad can be found in most Roman trattorias, where it is regularly served with this garlic-rich anchovy dressing. Since puntarelle are not easily found outside of Italy, I've taken the liberty of substituting celery, a full-flavored, readily available vegetable we shamefully take for granted. This salad must be served immediately after it is tossed: If left to linger, the dressing wilts the celery and turns it soggy. Note that even though the dressing is prepared in the food processor, the garlic should be minced by hand.

1 head of celery (about 1½ pounds; 790 g), ribs separated, rinsed, and trimmed into 3-inch (8-cm) lengths

ANCHOVY DRESSING

6 tablespoons extra-virgin olive oil

Two 2-ounce (60-g) cans flat anchovy fillets in olive oil

3 plump fresh garlic cloves (or to taste), degermed and minced

Freshly ground black pepper to taste

1. Prepare the celery: Prepare a large bowl of ice water. With a small, sharp knife, cut a celery flower from each piece of celery: Make several lengthwise cuts about one-third the length of each rib, so that the end of each piece fans out into a flower. Place them in the ice water and refrigerate. They will fan out as they chill. (The celery fans are best prepared several hours in advance.)

2. Prepare the dressing: In the bowl of a food processor or a blender, combine the oil, the anchovies and their oil, and the minced garlic, and process or blend into a fairly smooth dressing. Transfer to a small bowl and set aside.

3. At serving time, carefully drain and dry the celery with a clean towel. Place in a large salad bowl. Toss with just enough dressing to lightly coat the celery. Serve immediately, for once tossed, the celery quickly loses crispness and zest. Serve as a salad, with knife and fork, and pass the pepper mill.

■ Yield: 6 to 8 servings ■

Aunt Flora's Olive Salad

Insalata di Olive

A s a child I always loved the family gatherings at which my mother's sister, Flora DeAngelo, would prepare her multi-course Italian feasts. This crunchy, fiery, green olive salad was a favored dish in her repertoire. The salad can be served as part of an antipasto platter, or offer it as an accompaniment to cheese, sausages, and crusty bread. I also like it as a spicy condiment for a simple meal, such as Chicken Cooked Under Bricks (page 218), served with Sautéed Spinach (page 62) and Roasted Rosemary Potatoes (page 54). This is an instance in which I depart from my general disdain for dried herbs: Dried leaf oregano does have a special flavor, one that is perfectly natural here.

1 cup (5 ounces; 150 g) drained pimento-stuffed green olives, cut into 4 crosswise slices

3 ribs tender celery hearts with leaves, diced

1 teaspoon best-quality red wine vinegar

1 tablespoon extra-virgin olive oil

4 plump fresh garlic cloves, degermed and minced

¼ teaspoon dried leaf oregano

¼ teaspoon crushed red peppers (hot red pepper flakes), or to taste

In a small bowl, combine all the ingredients and toss to blend. Cover and refrigerate for at least 2 hours and up to 2 days, tossing occasionally. Serve at room temperature, as a condiment.

■ Y i e l d : 6 t o 8 s e r v i n g s ■

■ ■ ■

Green Olive, Tuna, Celery, and Red Pepper Salad

Insalata di Olive Verde, Tonno, Sedano, e Peperoni

Whenever I prepare a large antipasto buffet, this spunky, colorful, zesty condiment is always on the table. I've seen this dish served at many trattorias, in varied versions. Some cooks add cooked white beans, a pleasant touch that makes for a filling and hearty condiment. I like to serve this with a platter of sliced red tomatoes and good crusty country bread, as a luncheon dish.

1 cup (5 ounces; 150 g) drained pimento-stuffed green olives, halved crosswise

4 to 5 ribs celery hearts with leaves, thinly sliced

1 6½-ounce (190-g) can imported tuna in olive oil (do not drain; see Note)

1 red bell pepper, minced

3 tablespoons extra-virgin olive oil

1 teaspoon best-quality red wine vinegar

Fine sea salt to taste

With a fork, flake the tuna in the can and transfer, oil and all, into a small bowl. Add all the remaining ingredients, and toss to blend. Taste for seasoning. Serve immediately, or cover and refrigerate for up to 8 hours. Serve at room temperature.

■ Yield: 6 to 8 servings ■

NOTE: If tuna packed in olive oil is unavailable, use top-quality white tuna packed in water. Drain the tuna, discarding the water, and add an additional tablespoon of extra-virgin olive oil when preparing the salad.

■ ■ ■

Fresh Fava Bean and Pecorino Salad

Baccelli al Pecorino

As you step inside Cibrèo in Florence—one of my favorite restaurants in all of Italy—your eyes instantly fall on the welcoming sideboard laden with varied appetizers and desserts. The assortment might well include a giant white porcelain bowl of garden-fresh fava beans marinating with cubes of pecorino cheese, oil, lemon juice, and a touch of herbs. While most of us may not be very familiar with these deliciously nutty little beans, they make a vibrant palate-teaser—more like a snack or appetizer than a whole course. When you prepare this at home, don't make the mistake of serving large portions of this filling starter—just a bite or two will do. For this recipe, scour your farmers' markets, and use the smallest and youngest fava beans or broad beans you can find: Once they mature, the skin covering the beans becomes coarse and tough and must be removed before eating. I like the tinge of bitterness in the raw, uncooked beans: It's a great contrast to the almost-sweet young pecorino. If the only sheep's milk cheese you can find is the hard grating variety, use any good-quality soft fresh goat's milk cheese that can easily be cut into cubes.

2 pounds (1 kg) fresh unshelled fava beans or broad beans (about 2 cups [500 ml] shelled beans)

3 tablespoons extra-virgin olive oil

1 tablespoon freshly squeezed lemon juice

1 teaspoon dried leaf oregano

3 tablespoons fresh flat-leaf parsley leaves, snipped with a scissors

⅛ teaspoon crushed red peppers (hot red pepper flakes), or to taste

8 ounces (250 g) soft sheep's milk cheese (pecorino) or goat's milk cheese, cut in cubes the size of a fava bean

Fine sea salt and freshly ground black pepper to taste

1. Shell the beans. You should have about 2 cups (500 ml) of beans. Taste one; if the beans are tender and not too bitter, they can be served raw, without removing the skin that covers each bean. If they are tough, blanch the beans in boiling salted water for 30 seconds, then slip off the outer skin, revealing two smaller beans. (This is a very tedious operation, but worth the effort.)

2. In a medium-size bowl, combine the beans and all the remaining ingredients, and toss to blend. Taste for seasoning. Serve immediately, in small portions, as a snack, an appetizer, or as part of a series of antipasto.

■ Yield: 8 to 12 servings ■

NOTE: Should there be any leftovers, sauté the beans and cheese with a touch of oil in a small skillet: They are fragrant and equally delicious as a warm appetizer.

Knowing Beans About Beans

Fresh fava beans—long and round, with velvety pods—are one of the world's great gastronomic treasures. Tender, only faintly bitter, and a brilliant spring green, fava beans—known as *fave* in Italian—are so nourishing they are called the meat of the poor. Fava beans, also known as broad beans, are similar to but not the same as kidney-shaped lima beans, which can become quite tough. When very young and fresh, lima beans—sometimes called wax or butter beans—may be eaten raw. They can be found in farmers' markets, in the pod, or in some supermarkets, already shelled.

Red Bean and Onion Salad

Insalata di Borlotti

T his is a favorite antipasto and one that can easily be made in advance. Red-and-white-speckled borlotti, or cranberry (Roman) beans, have a delightfully earthy flavor and always make me feel very healthy and wholesome. I sampled this dish one Sunday evening at a little trattoria on Lake Garda, in the Veneto. Before serving, always retaste the beans, adding additional oil, vinegar, and seasoning as desired. A handful of minced flat-leaf parsley leaves tossed in at the last minute adds a fine touch of color and flavor.

2½ cups (1 pound; 500 g) dried cranberry (borlotti) beans

1 small onion, halved

1 medium carrot, peeled

3 bay leaves, preferably fresh

4 plump fresh garlic cloves, crushed

1 large rib celery

Generous sprig of fresh sage

6 tablespoons extra-virgin olive oil, or to taste

2 small red onions (about 8 ounces; 250 g), minced

¼ cup (60 ml) best-quality red wine vinegar, or to taste

Fine sea salt and freshly ground black pepper to taste

Minced fresh flat-leaf parsley leaves (optional)

1. Rinse the beans, picking them over to remove any pebbles. Place the beans in a large bowl, add boiling water to cover, and set aside for 1 hour. Drain the beans, discarding the water.

2. Place the onion, carrot, bay leaves, garlic, celery, sage, and 2 tablespoons of the oil in a large covered saucepan and add cold water to cover by 1 inch (2.5 cm). Bring just to a simmer over moderate heat, and cook for 15 minutes. Add the drained beans and return to a simmer. Cover and continue cooking just until tender, about 30 minutes to 1 hour more. Check the beans from time to time: They should be slightly firm but not mushy when fully cooked. If necessary, add additional water to keep the beans from drying out. (Cooking time will vary depending upon the freshness of the beans; fresh beans cook more quickly than old ones.)

3. Meanwhile, in a small bowl, toss the minced onions with 2 tablespoons of the oil. (The oil will serve to soften the harshness of the raw onions.) Set aside.

4. Once the beans are cooked, drain them, discarding the herbs and vegetables. Transfer the beans to a large bowl. While still warm, toss with the minced onions and the remaining 2 tablespoons of oil, the vinegar, and the salt and pepper. Taste for seasoning. (The proportions of vinegar and oil given here are only a suggestion: You may prefer more or less.) The beans may be served warm, but are generally served at room temperature, as part of an antipasto table or salad buffet, as a luncheon side dish, or as a simple condiment. The beans remain fresh-flavored for 2 to 3 days, refrigerated.

■ Y i e l d : 8 t o 1 0 s e r v i n g s ■

Bean Lore

The ancient Romans used beans for balloting, both in the courts and in elections. Black beans signified opposition or guilt, white stood for agreement or innocence.

White Bean Salad with Fresh Sage and Thyme

Fagioli all'Olio

T his fragrant marriage of white beans and oil, enriched with a few herbs and seasonings, is one of Italy's purest treats. Tuscan trattorias offer these beans year-round, serving them warm as a first course, or at room temperature as part of an antipasto buffet. Sage and thyme add a special depth of flavor.

2½ cups (1 pound; 500 g) dried small white beans (navy, cannellini, or toscanelli)

1 small onion, halved

1 medium carrot, peeled

3 bay leaves, preferably fresh

4 plump fresh garlic cloves, crushed

1 large rib celery

1 generous sprig each of fresh sage and thyme

About ½ cup (125 ml) extra-virgin olive oil, to taste

Sea salt and freshly ground black pepper

3 tablespoons fresh thyme leaves, for garnish

1. Rinse the beans, picking them over to remove any pebbles. Place the beans in a large bowl, add boiling water to cover, and set aside for 1 hour. Drain the beans, discarding the water.

2. Place the drained beans in a large covered saucepan and add cold water to cover by 1 inch (2.5 cm). Add the onion, carrot, bay leaves, garlic, celery, sage and thyme sprigs, and 2 tablespoons of the oil. Bring just to a simmer over moderate heat, and simmer for 30 minutes. Season with salt and simmer just until tender, about 30 minutes more. Check the beans from time to time: They should be slightly firm but not mushy when fully cooked. If necessary, add additional water to keep the beans from drying out. (Cooking time will vary depending upon the freshness of the beans; fresh beans cook more quickly than old ones.)

3. Once the beans are cooked, drain them, discarding the herbs and vegetables. Transfer the beans to a large bowl. While still warm, toss with the thyme leaves, season with salt and pepper, and add the remaining 6 tablespoons (95 ml) olive oil. The beans may be served warm, but are generally served at room temperature, as part of an antipasto table or salad buffet. The beans remain fresh-flavored for 2 to 3 days, refrigerated.

■ Y i e l d : 8 t o 1 0 s e r v i n g s ■

Tomato and Bread Salad

Panzanella

This is one of those rustic, peasant-style salads that makes you want to pack up a wicker picnic basket and take off for a sunny hill with a beautiful view, a group of friends, and a jug of red wine. Panzanella is a traditional Tuscan salad found in many variations at trattorias throughout the region. No doubt, tomato and bread salad was created out of a need to do *something* with that leftover country bread, whether whole wheat or sourdough. I first sampled panzanella at Il Latini, a boisterous and popular Florentine trattoria where the waiter patiently explained their method of making the salad. The traditional recipe always includes chunks of slightly dried out bread and cubed ripe tomatoes, along with cucumbers, onion, celery, vinegar, and oil. Some cooks trim the crusts from the bread (I don't) and others peel the tomatoes (I don't). The bread can be cubed with a knife or simply ripped into chunks with your hands. I've seen versions with and without garlic, and some enjoy the flavors of green olives or tuna. This is the version I like best, with a pungent hit from both the garlic and the green olives. While some recipes suggest soaking the bread in water first to soften it, I don't unless I am using rock-hard cubes of bread. Soaking makes the bread get soppier faster, and I like to keep the crunch going as long as possible. I prefer to let the natural vegetable juices, vinegar, and oil do the job. Serve this as a luncheon main dish, along with sausages and cheese, and, of course, a simple but fruity red wine.

4 cups (about 8 ounces; 250 g) slightly dried out country bread cubed or torn into pieces

About 1½ pounds (750 g) ripe tomatoes, cored and coarsely chopped

1 red onion, thinly sliced

½ hothouse cucumber, peeled and cut into small cubes

2 ribs celery hearts, cut into small cubes

½ cup loosely packed fresh basil leaves

3 plump fresh garlic cloves, degermed and minced (optional)

1 cup (5 ounces; 150 g) drained pitted green olives, halved crosswise (optional)

1 to 2 tablespoons best-quality red wine vinegar

Fine sea salt to taste

3 to 4 tablespoons extra-virgin olive oil

Freshly ground black pepper to taste

1. Place the bread in a large bowl. Add the tomatoes, onion, cucumber, celery, and basil, and toss gently to blend. If using, add the garlic and green olives. Sprinkle with the vinegar and salt, and toss gently to blend. Spoon the oil over the salad, sprinkle with freshly ground black pepper, and toss once more. Set aside for 30 minutes to allow the bread to absorb the dressing and the flavors to blend.

2. To serve, use a slotted spoon to transfer portions to large dinner plates.

■ Yield: 6 to 8 servings ■

Arugula, Pine Nut, and Parmesan Salad

Insalata di Rughetta, Pignoli, e Parmi

Peppery, vibrant arugula—also known as rughetta or rucola, in Italian—is a remarkable salad green. Its energy can perk up tired palates and spirits like nothing else I know. Here the fresh green is combined with lightly toasted pine nuts and fresh shavings of Parmesan cheese. It's a variation on a dish I sampled at the traditional Florentine trattoria Il Cammillo. There they serve a first course of layered pine nuts, chopped arugula, and shaved Parmesan. I was frustrated by the "tightness" of the dish when I sampled it, and have taken the liberty of turning the combination into a full-fledged salad. Toss it very lightly with a mixture of top-quality vinegar and oil. I serve this often at dinner parties, to welcome raves.

½ cup (2 ounces; 60 g) pine nuts

3 ounces (90 g) stemmed arugula leaves, washed and dried

One 2-ounce (60-g) chunk of Italian Parmigiano-Reggiano cheese

Fine sea salt to taste

About 1 tablespoon best-quality red wine vinegar

Freshly ground black pepper to taste

About 2 tablespoons extra-virgin olive oil

1. Preheat the oven to 350°F (175°C; gas mark 4/5).

2. Spread the nuts loosely on a baking sheet. Toast until lightly browned, about 10 minutes. Check every few minutes to avoid burning the nuts. Remove from the oven, and turn out onto a large plate to cool. (The nuts can be toasted several hours in advance.)

3. In a large shallow salad bowl, combine the arugula and toasted pine nuts. Using a vegetable peeler, shave the Parmesan cheese into long thick strips directly into the bowl. (If the chunk of cheese becomes too small to peel, grate the remaining cheese and add to the bowl.) Season the salad with fine sea salt and toss gently to blend.

4. Drizzle 1 tablespoon vinegar over the salad, season with pepper, and toss to blend. Add just enough oil to very lightly coat the arugula, and toss to blend. Serve immediately, arranging on large serving plates.

■   Y i e l d :   4   s e r v i n g s   ■

• • •

Walnut and Pecorino Salad

Insalata di Noci e Pecorino

On my last visit to Florence's Cibrèo, a giant white bowl of marinated walnuts and pecorino (sheep's milk cheese) was sitting on a sideboard, welcoming hungry guests as they took their places for the multi-course feast to follow. This simple preparation has since become a family favorite; I serve it sometimes as a before-dinner snack, or, more often, alongside a salad of baby spinach leaves tossed only with fine sea salt and extra-virgin olive oil. The combination is a great substitute for a full cheese course, and yet the wholesome crunch of the toasted walnuts and the soft saltiness of the cheese on the palate make for a fabulous course all its own. The varied ingredients can be measured out in advance, but toss the salad at the last moment, for a fresher, more distinct flavor. If you cannot find top-quality sheep's milk cheese, substitute a good domestic or imported goat's milk cheese.

2 cups (8 ounces; 250 g) freshly cracked walnut halves, toasted and cooled

3 tablespoons extra-virgin olive oil

1 tablespoon freshly squeezed lemon juice

1 teaspoon dried leaf oregano

3 tablespoons fresh flat-leaf parsley leaves, snipped with a scissors

8 ounces (250 g) soft sheep's milk cheese (pecorino) or goat's milk cheese, cubed

Fine sea salt and freshly ground black pepper to taste

In a medium-size bowl, combine all the ingredients and toss to blend. Season to taste. Serve immediately, in portions, as an appetizer or as part of a series of appetizers.

▪ Y i e l d : 4 t o 6 s e r v i n g s ▪

VEGETABLES

Asparagus with Butter and Parmesan

Asparagi alla Parmigiana

This is one of the finest and most flavorful ways I know of preparing asparagus. First the slim and tender green stalks are cooked in boiling salted water, and immediately plunged into ice water to stop the cooking and to keep the delicious spears firm and green. They are then sautéed in a blend of butter and olive oil, and sprinkled with a touch of Parmigiano-Reggiano cheese just before serving. This is a perfect simple first course, which can be followed by a more complicated main course, such as Braised Oxtail with Tomatoes, Onions, and Celery (page 251) or Beef Braised in Barolo Wine (page 247). I sampled this dish one sunny Sunday afternoon in May, at the Trattoria del Castello in Grinzane Cavour in the Piedmont, when everyone had been impatiently awaiting the season's first asparagus, and the true arrival of spring.

Coarse sea salt to taste

1 pound (500 g) small green asparagus stalks, trimmed

2 tablespoons (1 ounce; 30 g) unsalted butter

1 tablespoon extra-virgin olive oil

½ cup (2 ounces; 60 g) freshly grated Italian Parmigiano-Reggiano cheese

1. Prepare a large bowl of ice water and set aside. Bring a large pot of water to a boil, and add 1 tablespoon salt for each quart (liter) of water. Add the asparagus and cook until crisp-tender, about 8 minutes. Remove the asparagus with a slotted spoon and immediately plunge it into the ice water, to cool it down as quickly as possible. (Do not let the asparagus sit in the cold water too long, or it will lose its crispness and fresh flavor.) As soon as the asparagus is cool, drain, and transfer to a thick towel to dry. (The asparagus can be cooked up to 2 hours in advance.)

2. When ready to serve, combine the butter and oil in a large skillet over moderately high heat. When hot, add the asparagus, stir to coat with the fat, and sauté just until warmed through, 2 to 3 minutes. Transfer the asparagus to 4 warmed dinner plates, sprinkle with the cheese, and serve immediately.

■ Y i e l d :   4   s e r v i n g s ■

WINE SUGGESTION: Asparagus is a difficult flavor for wine: A safe choice would be a good Chardonnay.

Panfried Potatoes with Black Olives

Patate alle Olive

I first sampled this simple dish at a small restaurant in Santa Margherita, along the Ligurian coast near Genoa. I love the play of textures, colors, and flavors in this dish: the softness of the olives contrasted with the crunch of the potatoes; the black against white; and the saltiness of the olives paired with the delicately flavored potatoes. I particularly like this as a side dish to fish or poultry.

1½ pounds (750 g) small red potatoes

3 tablespoons extra-virgin olive oil

½ cup (125 ml) brine-cured black olives, such as Italian Ligurian or French Niçoise olives, drained, pitted, and halved (see page 282)

Fine sea salt and freshly ground black pepper to taste

1. Peel the potatoes and cut them lengthwise into quarters. Rinse in several changes of water and dry thoroughly with a thick, absorbent towel.

2. In a very large heavy skillet, heat the oil over moderately high heat until hot but not smoking. Add the potatoes in a single layer. Reduce the heat to moderate and brown the potatoes thoroughly on one side before turning. Cook the potatoes until they are browned on all sides and tender when pierced with a fork, 15 to 20 minutes total. Add the olives to the pan and cook until warmed through, tossing from time to time, about 1 minute more. Transfer to a warmed serving bowl. Season to taste with salt and pepper, toss, and serve immediately.

■ Yield: 4 servings ■

Tips for Crispy Panfried Potatoes

■ Be sure the potatoes are well rinsed and completely dried before frying them.

■ Do not salt the potatoes until the end of the cooking time. Salting beforehand will encourage them to give up their liquid, making them limp.

■ Do not use a nonstick pan: The potatoes will not brown properly.

■ Heat the oil first, then add the potatoes to the pan.

■ Resist the urge to turn the potatoes too often. Allow them to brown on one side before turning.

■ Season with salt and pepper immediately after removing the potatoes from the frying pan.

Roasted Rosemary Potatoes

Patate al Forno

The Romans are great at serving meats roasted in a good hot oven, and these attractive, delicious, mouth-watering potatoes are a fine accompaniment. I serve them with just about everything, but love them best with roasted chicken or pork. This is the ideal recipe for someone who insists he doesn't know how to cook, for the preparation takes little skill and little time. I've sampled these using various varieties of both roasting and boiling potatoes with equally good results. The key here is to use small, firm potatoes. The smaller the potatoes are cut, the more quickly they'll cook. Sometimes as a variation, I cut the potatoes crosswise into thin slices for maximum crispiness. These are also delicious served with a dab of Garlic Mayonnaise (page 275).

1½ pounds (750 g) small, firm potatoes
1 tablespoon minced fresh rosemary leaves
3 tablespoons extra-virgin olive oil
Fine sea salt and freshly ground black pepper to taste

1. Preheat the oven to 450°F (230°C; gas mark 9).

2. Peel and quarter the potatoes. Rinse them well and pat thoroughly dry with a thick towel. (To achieve the desired crispy skin when baking, the potatoes must be completely dry.)

3. On a baking sheet, combine the fully dried potatoes, rosemary, and oil, and, with your fingers, toss until the potatoes are well coated and the rosemary is well distributed. Spread the potatoes out in a single layer.

4. Place the baking sheet in the oven, and roast until the potatoes are golden brown and tender when tested with a fork, 20 to 25 minutes. Shake the baking sheet from time to time to redistribute the potatoes. When cooked, season with salt and pepper. Serve immediately.

■ Yield: 4 to 6 servings ■

Deep-Fried Zucchini and Zucchini Blossoms

Fritto di Zucca e Fiori di Zucca

Italians are masters at frying and have proven that fried foods need not be fatty, heavy, soggy, or indigestible. Properly fried foods are fragrant, golden, and taste of themselves, for the frying process fixes the flavor of the ingredient. My favorite fried food is the delicate, sunshine-yellow zucchini blossom, which often can be found at farmer's markets in season. If you have a garden, pick the blossoms early in the morning, when they are still tightly closed. While traveling about Italy, I've seen these blossoms served on their own, in tandem with slices of zucchini, or alongside sliced raw baby artichokes. The batter used for frying varies from chef to chef. My favorite version comes from Cesare Benilli at Al Covo in Venice. Beer batter produces a crunchy crust with a slightly—and pleasantly—bitter tang.

BEER BATTER

¼ cup (60 ml) water

¼ cup (60 ml) beer, at room temperature

½ cup (70 g) superfine flour, such as Wondra

3 large egg whites

About 2 quarts (2 l) peanut or safflower oil, for deep-frying

16 very fresh zucchini blossoms

About 1 pound (500 g) large fresh zucchini, scrubbed and sliced diagonally into ¼-inch (½-cm) slices (or substitute 1 pound [500 g] fresh baby artichokes, trimmed and quartered)

Fine sea salt to taste

1. Prepare the batter: In a medium-size bowl, whisk together the water and beer. Slowly whisk in the flour, whisking until smooth. The batter will be fairly thick. Set aside for 1 hour, to allow the flour to absorb the liquid.

2. Preheat the oven to 200°F (100°C; gas mark 1) to keep the first batches of fried ingredients warm, as you prepare the others.

3. Pour the oil into a wide 6-quart (6-l) saucepan, or use a deep-fat fryer. The oil should be at least 2 inches (5 cm) deep. Place a deep-fry thermometer in the oil and heat the oil to 375°F (190°C).

4. In the bowl of an electric mixer fitted with a whisk, beat the egg whites until stiff but not dry. Whisk the batter one more time, and, with a spatula, thoroughly fold the egg whites into the batter.

5. With your fingers, dip the ingredients to be fried, a few at a time, into the batter, rolling them to coat evenly with batter. Shake off the excess batter, letting it drip back into the bowl. Carefully lower the blossoms or vegetables, a few at a time, into the hot oil. Fry until the blossoms or vegetables are golden on all sides, turning once, for a total cooking time of about 2 minutes. With a wire skimmer, lift from the oil, drain, and transfer to paper towels. Immediately season with sea salt. Place the first batch in the oven—with the door slightly ajar—to keep warm. Continue frying until all of the ingredients are cooked, allowing the oil to return to 375°F (190°C) before adding each new batch. Serve immediately.

■ Yield: 4 servings ■

WINE SUGGESTION: Sample these with a light white Sauvignon Blanc, perhaps one from Italy's northeast corner, Friuli-Venezia-Giulia.

Tips for Successful Deep-Frying

■ Make sure all the ingredients are dry (moist ingredients will splatter).

■ Use fresh oil and plenty of it. Since vegetable oil is fairly inexpensive, I use fresh oil each time I fry. I prefer peanut oil, but safflower or corn oil can also be used. Olive oil is a luxury, and I prefer to save it for other cooking and for salads.

■ Make sure there is at least 2 inches (5 cm) of oil in the pan, and use a pan large enough to contain any splattering. (I use a large, wide enameled steel pan.)

■ Use proper heat and even heat. Invest in a deep-fry thermometer, and leave it in the pan while you cook.

■ Don't crowd the pan. When you add ingredients to hot fat, the temperature is instantly reduced. Always allow the oil to return to the proper temperature before frying another batch.

■ When frying in batter, use superfine flour: It won't cake up and it results in a more delicate batter.

■ Unless otherwise noted, when frying in batter, dip ingredients in the batter at the very last minute, to prevent sogginess.

■ Preheat the oven to keep the first batches of cooked food warm while you continue frying.

■ Drain the ingredients immediately after frying, placing on absorbent paper towels or clean cloth towels. Season with fine sea salt immediately after draining.

■ Serve fried foods hot.

Eggplant Parmesan

Parmigiana di Melanzane

One finds versions of this rich, earthy, and familiar vegetable dish everywhere in Italy. Like so many popular dishes, eggplant Parmesan has been banalized, and cooks often don't take the time to do it right. There are a few keys to a perfect version: Carefully deep-fry the eggplant in oil (if done properly, it won't absorb any more oil than you would use in grilling or baking the slices). Use a good homemade tomato sauce and the freshest mozzarella and Parmesan you can find. And do not prepare it in advance: part of the earthy charm of the dish is its very freshness. If top quality tomatoes cannot be found, substitute 2 cups (500 ml) tomato sauce made from canned tomatoes (page 256). No matter how you make it, you'll be amazed at the fresh look of this dish as it comes from the oven, with a touch of green basil, the golden tones of the lightly browned cheese, and the red tomatoes peeking through—yummm.

(continued)

TOMATO SAUCE

¼ *cup (60 ml) extra-virgin olive oil*

1 *small red or yellow onion, minced*

2 *plump fresh garlic cloves, minced*

Fine sea salt to taste

8 *to 10 (about 2 pounds; 1 kg) small ripe tomatoes, peeled, cored, seeded, and chopped*

2 *firm medium eggplant (about 2 pounds; 1 kg)*

2 *quarts (2 l) peanut or sunflower oil, for deep-frying*

Fine sea salt to taste

1 *pound (500 g) fresh whole-milk mozzarella, thinly sliced*

1 *cup (4 ounces; 125 g) freshly grated Italian Parmigiano-Reggiano cheese*

½ *cup (125 ml) loosely packed fresh basil leaves, snipped with a scissors*

1. Preheat the oven to 400°F (200°C; gas mark 6/7).

2. Prepare the tomato sauce: In a large skillet, heat the oil, onion, garlic, and salt over moderate heat and cook just until the onion is soft and translucent, 3 to 4 minutes. Add the tomatoes, stir to blend, and simmer gently, uncovered, until the sauce begins to thicken, about 15 minutes. Set aside.

3. Rinse and trim the eggplant and cut lengthwise into very thin slices. (Do not peel the eggplant and do not salt it. See box.)

4. Pour the oil into a heavy 3-quart (3-l) saucepan, or use a deep-fat fryer. Heat the oil to 360°F (180°C). Fry the eggplant in batches (2 or 3 slices at a time), until deep golden, 3 to 4 minutes per batch. With a flat wire mesh skimmer, transfer the eggplant slices to paper towels to drain. Season immediately with salt.

5. Spoon several tablespoons of the tomato sauce into a rectangular gratin dish measuring about 9 by 13 inches (23 × 33 cm). Place one-third of the fried eggplant side by side over the sauce. Spoon a thin layer of sauce over the eggplant. Cover with slices of mozzarella, using about half the cheese. Continue with another layer of eggplant, a layer of tomato sauce, and about half the Parmigiano-Reggiano cheese. Continue with the remaining eggplant, tomato sauce, mozzarella, and the final half of the Parmigiano-Reggiano cheese. Sprinkle with the fresh basil.

6. Place the gratin dish in the center of the oven and bake until the cheese is melted and the dish is fragrant and bubbling, about 40 minutes. Remove from the oven and serve warm or at room temperature, but not cold. (Since this dish tends to release a fair amount of liquid, it is best to serve with a slotted spoon.) The dish can be served the next day, but refrigeration tends to change the texture, so it is best to store at room temperature.

■ Yield: 6 to 8 servings ■

Please Don't Salt or Peel the Eggplant

I do not agree with the common practice of salting eggplant as a method of removing bitterness from the vegetable. Truly fresh, firm eggplant is never bitter, so does not require advance salting to extract unwanted flavors. Likewise, the skin of the eggplant imparts a rich, deep flavor, so please do not peel it.

Sautéed Spinach with Garlic, Lemon, and Oil

Spinaci Saltati

Verdant green spinach that's been blanched and rinsed with cold water to drain, then tossed in a pan with oil and the scent of garlic, is one of my favorite vegetables. I serve it alongside roast meats or eat it all on its own. And I love it as I had it served to me at the Osteria del Cinghiale Bianco in Florence, mounded on toast that had been rubbed with garlic, for a classic fettunta, the Florentine version of the antipasto more commonly known as bruschetta.

3 tablespoons coarse sea salt

2 pounds (1 kg) fresh spinach, washed and stemmed, and dried

4 plump fresh garlic cloves, halved

2 tablespoons extra-virgin olive oil

Fine sea salt and freshly ground black pepper to taste

2 tablespoons freshly squeezed lemon juice

1. In a large pot, bring 6 quarts (6 l) of water to a rolling boil over high heat. Add the salt, then add the spinach, stirring to evenly wilt the spinach. Cook just until wilted through, 2 to 3 minutes. Drain the spinach, and rinse thoroughly with cold water to stop the cooking and set the bright green color. Drain again.

2. With a stainless steel knife, coarsely chop the spinach. Place in a fine-mesh sieve set over a bowl and set aside to drain once more, pressing as much liquid as possible from the spinach.

3. In a large skillet, combine the garlic and oil, and cook over moderate heat just until the garlic turns golden, but does not brown, 2 to 3 minutes. Remove and discard the garlic. Add the chopped spinach and cook, tossing gently with the tines of a fork, until warmed through, 2 to 3 minutes. Season with salt and pepper and the lemon juice, and serve immediately.

■ Yield: 4 to 6 servings ■

ITALIAN ADAGE:

"Salt the salad quite a lot,
then generous oil put in the pot,
and vinegar, but just a jot."

Sautéed Baby Artichokes

Carciofi Saltati

If you have a favorite, top-quality extra-virgin olive oil, bring it out for this dish. Nothing makes my palate happier than to bite into these fresh-flavored little artichokes, bathed with the perfume of a great olive oil. The artichokes can be served as a vegetable course or alongside roast pork or chicken. They're also delicious the next day, tossed into an omelet or a salad.

3 tablespoons freshly squeezed lemon juice

1 quart (1 l) water

Sea salt to taste

10 baby artichokes (about 1 pound; 500 g)
(see Mail Order Sources, page 325)

3 tablespoons extra-virgin olive oil

Freshly ground black pepper to taste

1. In a large stainless steel saucepan, combine the lemon juice, water, and ½ teaspoon salt. Set aside.

2. Prepare the artichokes: Rinse the artichokes under cold running water. Using a stainless steel knife to minimize discoloration, trim the stem of an artichoke to about ½ inch (1 cm) from the base. Carefully trim off and discard the stem's fibrous exterior. Bend back the tough outer green leaves one at a time, letting them snap off naturally at the base. Continue snapping off the leaves until only the central cone of yellow leaves with pale green tips remains. Lightly trim the top of the cone of leaves to just below the green tips. Trim any dark green areas from the stem. Depending upon its size, halve or quarter the artichoke, and transfer immediately to the acidulated water to prevent discoloration. Continue until all the artichokes are trimmed.

3. Bring the liquid and artichokes to a simmer over medium-high heat. Simmer, reducing the heat if necessary, until the artichokes are just tender but still offer a bit of resistance when pierced with a knife, 3 to 4 minutes. (Cooking time will vary according to the size of the artichokes.) Thoroughly drain the artichokes, discarding the cooking liquid. (The artichokes may be cooked up to 3 hours in advance. Just be sure to drain them. If they are allowed to cool in the cooking liquid, they will turn mushy.)

4. In a large skillet, heat the olive oil over moderately high heat until hot but not smoking. Add the drained artichokes and sauté just until crisp and evenly browned, 3 to 4 minutes. Season with salt and pepper and serve immediately. The artichokes are also good leftover, served at room temperature.

■ Yield: 4 to 6 servings ■

On Artichokes

In Italy, no soil goes idle. One delight of driving through the Italian countryside is the host of vegetable gardens found tucked into the most unforeseen spots. Gardens are crammed along the side of the road, inserted next to the railroad line, tucked at the edge of a parking lot, stuffed between a ravine and the road's shoulder. Almost always, giant, thistle-like flowering artichokes—*carciofi* in Italian—form the garden's centerpiece.

Artichokes are prized for their rich, sweet, almost grassy flavor, and serve to stimulate salivation, which is why they often appear at the beginning of a meal.

When purchasing artichokes, look for those with flat, tightly closed leaves and bright-green coloring. They should be heavy for their size. (Lightness is a sign they have dried out, and are certain to be tough.) Artichokes thrive on moisture: If they will not be used immediately, lightly trim the stems, wrap in dampened paper towels, and refrigerate.

Braised Artichokes with Garlic and Parsley

Carciofi alla Romana

A marvelously fragrant, vibrant, multipurpose dish. I first sampled this version of the popular Roman-style artichokes at La Frateria di Padre Eligio in Cetona, in Tuscany. I spent a thoroughly educational morning with Chef Walter Tripodi in the restaurant/monastery kitchen, following him about as he prepared the day's luncheon. This was one of that day's dishes, an appealing blend of artichokes, parsley, mint, garlic, and a touch of hot pepper, all braised in white wine and extra-virgin olive oil. Serve the artichokes warm as a first course, or toss them with strands of thick pasta—linguine is great—as a main course. Although Chef Tripodi used tiny, violet-hued choke-less artichokes, I adapted the recipe for the more common globe artichokes.

4 globe artichokes

1 lemon

1 cup (250 ml) loosely packed fresh flat-leaf parsley leaves

1 cup (250 ml) loosely packed fresh mint leaves

8 plump fresh garlic cloves, halved

½ teaspoon crushed red peppers (hot red pepper flakes), or to taste

Fine sea salt to taste

½ cup (125 ml) extra-virgin olive oil

2 cups (500 ml) dry white wine, such as a Chardonnay or Pinot Grigio

1. Prepare the artichokes: Prepare a large bowl of cold water. Halve the lemon, squeeze the juice, and add the juice, plus the lemon halves, to the water. Rinse the artichokes under cold running water. Using a stainless steel knife to minimize discoloration, trim the stem of an artichoke to about 1½ inches (4 cm) from the base. Carefully trim off and discard the stem's fibrous exterior. Bend back the tough outer green leaves one at a time, and snap them off at the base. Continue snapping off the leaves until only the central cone of yellow leaves with pale green tips remains. Lightly trim the top of the cone of leaves to just below the green tips. Trim any dark green areas from the base. Halve the artichoke lengthwise. With a small spoon, scrape out, and discard, the hairy choke. Cut each trimmed artichoke half lengthwise into 8 even wedges. Place the wedges in the acidulated water to prevent discoloration. Repeat with the remaining 3 artichokes. Set aside.

2. Prepare the cooking liquid: With a large chef's knife, finely chop together the parsley, mint, garlic, crushed red peppers, and salt. Transfer to a 1-quart (1-l) nonreactive heavy saucepan, such as a stainless steel or enameled steel pan. Add the oil and wine. Thoroughly drain the artichoke slices and add to the saucepan. Cover and bring just to a simmer over moderate heat. Reduce the heat to low and simmer very gently until the artichokes are soft and offer no resistance when pierced with a knife, about 45 minutes. (They should still be swimming in liquid.)

3. To serve warm as a first course or vegetable side dish: Transfer to warmed shallow soup bowls, spooning the sauce over the artichokes. Pass plenty of crusty bread, for sopping up the delicious sauce.

To serve with pasta: Toss the artichokes with cooked and drained dried linguine, using all the liquid as the sauce. The pasta does not require cheese.

■ Yield: 4 to 6 servings ■

WINE SUGGESTION: Serve the same simple white wine used in cooking the artichokes, preferably a Chardonnay or Pinot Grigio.

ON THE BANKS

OF THE ARNO

■

After a diet of Florentine beans and grilled or roasted meats and poultry, Florence always manages to offer up some fine fare from the sea. Here's a Florentine fish menu, to enjoy with a glass or two of Pinot Grigio or Sauvignon Blanc.

SPICY TOMATO-MUSSEL SOUP
SEA BASS WITH POTATOES AND TOMATOES IN PARCHMENT
LEMON-RICE TEA CAKES

SOUPS

Tuscan Five-Bean Soup

Minestrone alla Toscana

"A first-rate soup is more creative than a second-rate painting."

ABRAHAM MASLOW

Throughout the streets of Florence, one finds an abundance of food and specialty shops, some of them devoted solely to the legume family—dried beans, peas, and lentils—a testament to the Florentine's love for one of nature's healthiest gifts. Many shops even sell customized bean soup "kits," tiny sacks that contain a colorful mix of tiny dried legumes, sometimes with a few grains added for good measure. The mixtures vary, but inevitably include cranberry (borlotti) beans, navy (cannellini) beans, red and green lentils, split peas, and black-eyed peas. You could add tiny adjuki beans, small kidney beans, baby lima beans, barley, or brown lentils to the mix. Just be sure to keep the beans small, and of rather uniform size, so they cook fairly evenly, and estimate about 1 pound (500 g) of beans for every 3 quarts (3 l) of water. I've purchased packages with as many as ten different beans, peas, and grains. This recipe is simply a blueprint: Combine the best beans you can find in your market, and don't be concerned if you have an abundance of dried ingredients remaining. Simply put together your own personalized bean soup kits for your pantry, or create gift packages, with the recipe included, for your friends. If you use fairly fresh beans, and keep them small, you can have dinner on the table in just one hour. The end result is what I think of as a "light" bean soup, one with a complexity of flavors and textures, a dish that's delightfully filling, but not overwhelmingly so. Be sure to serve it with plenty of crusty homemade bread. Wine is not generally served with soups such as this.

½ cup (3 ounces; 90 g) dried cranberry (borlotti) beans

½ cup (3 ounces; 90 g) dried red lentils

½ cup (3 ounces; 90 g) dried green lentils

½ cup (3 ounces; 90 g) dried green split peas

½ cup (3 ounces; 90 g) dried small white (navy) beans (cannellini or toscanelli)

½ cup (3 ounces; 90 g) pearl barley

3 tablespoons extra-virgin olive oil

1 medium onion, diced

1 medium carrot, diced

1 rib celery, thinly sliced

2 plump fresh garlic cloves, minced

Several sprigs of fresh thyme, bay leaves, fresh sage leaves, and celery leaves, tied in a bundle with cotton twine

3 quarts (3 l) water

Sea salt to taste

Extra-virgin olive oil, for the table

Freshly ground black pepper to taste

1. In a colander, combine the legumes and pearl barley. Rinse thoroughly under cold running water. Drain and set aside.

2. In a 6-quart (6-l) heavy-bottomed stockpot, combine the olive oil, onion, carrot, celery, garlic, and herb bundle, and stir to coat with the oil. Cook over moderate heat until the vegetables are fragrant and soft, about 5 minutes. Add the legumes and pearl barley, stir to coat with oil, and cook for 1 minute more. Add the 3 quarts (3 l) water and stir. Cover, bring to a gentle simmer over moderate heat, and cook until the outer shells of the largest beans are tender, about 45 minutes. Add the salt and cook until tender, 15 to 45 minutes more. Stir from time to time to make sure the beans are not sticking to the bottom of the stockpot. (Cooking time will vary according to the size and freshness of the beans.)

3. To serve, remove the herb bundle and ladle the soup—piping hot—into warmed shallow soup bowls. Pass a cruet of extra-virgin olive oil, drizzling directly into each bowl. Pass the pepper mill. (The soup, of course, may be reheated several times over a period of several days. It will thicken. Simply thin with water each time you reheat.)

■ Y i e l d : 6 t o 8 s e r v i n g s ■

Spicy Tomato-Mussel Soup

Zuppa di Cozze

Although the Italians traditionally call this a *zuppa*, or soup, this dish is really a cross between a soup and mussels coated with thick, garlic-rich tomato sauce. I sampled this version in Florence, at the family fish restaurant La Capannina di Sante. Chef and owner Sante Collestano served the mussels still in their shells, topped with the fragrant sauce. He tucked rustic slices of toasted Tuscan garlic bread into the bowls before serving so that they began soaking up the marvelous sauce. For a more elegant presentation, remove the mussels from the shells and serve floating in the fragrant tomato sauce. Be sure to use the freshest, smallest, most tender mussels you can find. This is a hearty dish, which can be served as a main course.

THE SAUCE

6 tablespoons extra-virgin olive oil

12 plump fresh garlic cloves, peeled

¾ teaspoon crushed red peppers (hot red pepper flakes), or to taste

One 28-ounce (765-g) can imported Italian plum tomatoes in juice or one 28-ounce (765-g) can crushed tomatoes in purée

Sea salt to taste

THE MUSSELS

4 pounds (2 kg) small fresh mussels, in their shells

3 tablespoons extra-virgin olive oil

1 small onion, minced

A handful of fresh flat-leaf parsley stems, tied in a bundle with cotton twine

1 cup (250 ml) dry white wine, such as a Chardonnay

Freshly ground black pepper to taste

8 thick slices country bread, toasted and rubbed with fresh garlic

A handful of fresh flat-leaf parsley leaves, snipped with a scissors

1. Prepare the sauce: In a heavy saucepan, combine the oil, garlic, and crushed red peppers over moderate heat. Sauté just until the garlic becomes fragrant and the pepper begins to color the oil, 2 to 3 minutes. If using whole canned tomatoes, place a food mill over the saucepan and purée the tomatoes directly into it. Crushed tomatoes can be added directly from the can. Season with salt, and simmer, uncovered, just until the sauce begins to thicken, 10 to 12 minutes. Set aside and keep warm.

2. Meanwhile, thoroughly scrub the mussels and rinse them in several changes of water. If an open mussel closes when you press on it, it is good. If it stays open, the mussel should be discarded. Note that in some markets, mussels are pre-prepared, in that the small black beard that hangs from the mussel has been clipped but not entirely removed. These mussels need only be rinsed before cooking. If the beards have not been clipped, beard the mussels by gently pulling, removing, and discarding the stringy black beard. Do not beard the mussels in advance or they will die and spoil.

3. In a large covered skillet, combine the oil, onion, parsley stems, and wine, and bring to a boil over high heat. Boil for 2 minutes. Add the prepared mussels, sprinkle generously with pepper, and stir. Cook, covered, just until the mussels open, about 5 minutes. Remove the mussels as they open. Do not overcook. Discard any mussels that do not open.

4. Place 2 slices each of toasted garlic bread at an angle at the edge of 4 warmed shallow soup bowls. With a large slotted spoon, transfer the mussels to the soup bowls. Line a fine-mesh sieve with moistened cheesecloth, place the sieve over the saucepan with the tomato sauce, and strain the mussel-cooking liquid through the cheesecloth and into the saucepan. Simmer for 1 to 2 minutes to blend the flavors. Taste for seasoning. Spoon the sauce over the mussels, and sprinkle each serving with snipped parsley leaves. Serve immediately.

■ Y i e l d :   4   s e r v i n g s   ■

WINE SUGGESTION: Any young, crisp, chilled white would be fine here: Try a Tuscan white—bianco di Toscana—from Antinori, Brolio, or Castello di Volpaia.

Knowing Your Beans

Dried beans can be made tender and flavorful by following just a few simple rules:

■ Consider freshness. Beans may be dried, but that does not make them immortal. When stored in a cool, dark, dry spot in an airtight container, dried beans remain in good form for up to one year. Beyond that, they dry out and toughen. There is no way to make a tough old bean tender. So buy from a reputable shop with quick turnover, and put your own "freshness" date on the package.

■ Salt added to dried beans at the beginning of the cooking period retards tenderness. Once the outer shell is tender—about halfway through the cooking time—salt can no longer inhibit the bean's cooking and softening, so add it then. If you wait until the beans are thoroughly cooked, no amount of salt will season them properly.

■ Acids—such as tomatoes and vinegar—affect bean tenderness. So add acidic ingredients only once the outer shell is tender, about halfway through the cooking time.

■ Hard, mineral-rich water can interfere with the texture of beans. Soft rain water, or filtered water, is ideal for cooking beans.

Pasta and Bean Soup

Pasta e Fagioli

There are about as many versions of pasta and bean soup as there are cooks. This soup—found in almost every region of Italy—varies from a broth-like bean soup to a creamy bean purée gently punctuated with whole beans and tiny pasta to a thick bean paste. I prefer the creamy variety, a satisfying soup that is neither too thin nor too thick, enhanced by a fragrant drizzle of extra-virgin olive oil at serving time. The flavor of the beans is quite delicate and benefits from the company of pancetta, olive oil, herbs, and vegetables. Almost any kind of small dried beans can be used here, such as dried cranberry (borlotti) beans or white (cannellini) beans. I'd advise against using dark red kidney beans: The authenticity would certainly be questionable. Likewise, any tiny pasta—broken bits of vermicelli or spaghetti, tiny elbow macaroni, or tiny stars—is suitable. When adding the pasta, be sure to stir the soup well, for it has a tendency to burn at this point. Note that the soup can be heated and reheated, and like most soups such as this, tastes even better the next day.

I enjoy this soup as a meal unto itself: All one need add is some good, crusty bread, perhaps a bit of cheese afterwards, and a dependable red wine.

(continued)

2½ cups (1 pound; 500 g) dried cranberry beans

3 tablespoons extra-virgin olive oil

½ cup (2 ounces; 60 g) minced pancetta (see Note)

1 medium onion, diced

1 medium carrot, diced

1 large rib celery with leaves, diced

4 plump fresh garlic cloves, minced

Several sprigs of fresh parsley, bay leaves, and celery leaves, tied in a bundle with cotton twine

3 quarts (3 l) water

Sea salt to taste

½ cup (3 ounces; 90 g) tiny dried Italian pasta, such as ditalini, broken spaghetti, or tiny elbow macaroni

Freshly ground black pepper to taste

Extra-virgin olive oil, for the table

1. Rinse the beans, picking them over to remove any pebbles. Place the beans in a large bowl, add boiling water to cover, and set aside for 1 hour. Drain and rinse the beans, discarding the water. Set aside.

2. In a 6-quart (6-l) heavy-bottomed stockpot, combine the oil, pancetta, onion, carrot, celery, garlic, and herb bundle, and stir to coat with the oil. Cook over moderate heat until the vegetables are fragrant and soft, about 5 minutes. Add the drained beans and the 3 quarts (3 l) water. Cover, bring to a simmer over moderate heat, and simmer gently for 30 minutes. Add the salt and continue simmering until the beans are softened, 30 to 60 minutes more. Stir from time to time to make sure the beans do not stick to the bottom of the stockpot. (Cooking time will vary according to the freshness of the beans.)

3. Remove the stockpot from the heat. With a slotted spoon, remove a large ladleful of the beans and vegetables and set aside. Remove and discard the herb bundle. Using a hand blender or immersion mixer, roughly purée the remaining soup directly in the stockpot. (Alternatively, pass the soup through the coarse blade of a food mill and return it to the stockpot.) The soup should have a creamy, but not totally smooth, consistency. Return the reserved beans and vegetables to the stockpot. Return to the

heat and bring the soup back to a simmer over moderate heat. Add the pasta, stir, and cook just until the pasta is tender, about 10 minutes more. Stir from time to time to make sure the pasta does not stick to the bottom of the stockpot. Taste for seasoning.

4. To serve, ladle the soup—piping hot—into warmed shallow soup bowls. Pass a cruet of extra-virgin olive oil, drizzling a swirl of oil directly into each bowl of soup. (The soup may be reheated several times over a period of several days. It will thicken. Simply thin with hot water each time you reheat the soup.)

■ Yield: 6 to 8 servings ■

NOTE: If unsmoked Italian pancetta is unavailable, use a lean, top-quality bacon. Blanch it for 1 minute in boiling water, then drain thoroughly. Blanching will remove the smoked flavor from the bacon without cooking it.

That Handy Little Blender

One of the most efficient and practical of modern gadgets is the hand blender (also called an immersion mixer). The hand blender—which resembles an electric hand mixer with a long, thin wand and a rotary blade at the end—is particularly useful for anyone who prepares soups regularly. For best results:

■ Note that a hand blender does its work in seconds, not minutes. Avoid over-blending to maintain the texture of the food.

■ Take the hand blender to the food, not the food to the blender.

■ To prevent splashing, first immerse the blender in the liquid, then turn it on.

Tuscan Bean and Wheat Berry Soup

Gran Farro

Farro is a delicious variety of soft Tuscan wheat berry, a rustic, mottled grain found in tones of wheat and cream. (The grain is also sometimes called spelt.) I first sampled Le Gran Farro—a fragrant soup of beans and wheat berries—at the popular Tuscan trattoria La Mora, in Ponte a Moriano, north of Lucca, a restaurant devoted to continuing regional gastronomic traditions in Italy. The soup is thinner than the traditional bean soup served all over Tuscany, and thus a bit more elegant. It's a favorite in my house: My husband even takes it in his "lunch box" for late nights at the office. With it, serve a bit of red wine, thick slices of homemade bread, and friendship.

1 cup (6 ounces; 180 g) dried small white (navy) beans (cannellini or toscanelli)

1 cup (6 ounces; 180 g) soft whole wheat berries (spelt)

3 tablespoons extra-virgin olive oil

1 medium onion, minced

1 medium carrot, diced

1 rib celery, diced

2 plump fresh garlic cloves, minced

Several sprigs of fresh thyme, bay leaves, and celery leaves, tied in a bundle with cotton twine

2 quarts (2 l) water

Sea salt to taste

Several tablespoons extra-virgin olive oil, for the table

1. Rinse and drain the beans, picking them over to remove any pebbles. Place the beans in a large bowl, add boiling water to cover, and set aside for 1 hour. Drain and rinse the beans, discarding the water. Set aside.

2. Rinse and drain the wheat berries, place them in a small bowl, and add boiling water to cover. Set aside until ready to add to the soup in Step 5 (for a total soaking time of about 1½ hours).

3. In a 6-quart (6-l) heavy-bottomed stockpot, combine the oil, onion, carrot, celery, garlic, and herb bundle, and stir to coat with the oil. Cook over moderate heat until the vegetables are fragrant and soft, about 5 minutes. Add the drained beans, stir to coat with oil, and cook for 1 minute. Add the 2 quarts (2 l) water and stir. Cover, bring to a simmer over moderate heat, and simmer for 30 minutes. Add the salt and continue simmering until the beans are tender, 30 to 60 minutes more, stirring from time to time to make sure the beans do not stick to the bottom of the stockpot. (Cooking time will vary according to the freshness of the beans.)

4. Remove the stockpot from the heat. With a slotted spoon, remove a large ladleful of the beans and vegetables and set aside. Remove and discard the herb bundle. Using a hand blender or immersion mixer, purée the remaining soup directly in the stockpot. (Alternatively, pass the soup through the coarse blade of a food mill and return it to the stockpot.) The soup should have a broth-like, and almost smooth, consistency.

5. Return the reserved beans and vegetables to the stockpot. Return to the heat and bring the soup back to a simmer over moderate heat. Drain and rinse the wheat berries, discarding the water, and add to the soup. Cook just until the wheat berries are swollen and tender, about 1½ hours more. (Cooking time will vary according to the freshness of the wheat berries.) Stir from time to time to make sure the wheat berries do not stick to the bottom of the stockpot. If the soup appears too thick, add a little lukewarm water to thin it out. Taste for seasoning.

6. To serve, ladle the soup—piping hot—into warmed shallow soup bowls. Pass a cruet of extra-virgin olive oil, drizzling a swirl of oil directly into each bowl of soup. (The soup may be reheated several times over a period of several days. It will thicken. Simply thin with lukewarm water each time you reheat the soup.)

■ Y i e l d : 6 t o 8 s e r v i n g s ■

WINE SUGGESTION: A simple red is ideal here, such as a young Chianti Classico or Valpolicella Classico Superiore.

■ ■ ■

Milanese Vegetable Soup

Minestrone alla Milanese

A minestrone is simply a full-flavored vegetable soup, with few limits to variations and interpretations. What all recipes share are an abundance of fresh vegetables, some type of dried beans, and a starch, either pasta or rice, depending upon the region. This version, sampled at the Antica Trattoria della Pesa in Milan, includes the famed Arborio rice of the region. With soups such as this, wine is not recommended. Since the success of the soup does depend upon proper proportions—for perfection of flavor and color—I have included weights for the ingredients in this recipe.

1 cup (6 ounces; 180 g) dried small white (navy) beans (cannellini or toscanelli)

4 tablespoons (2 ounces; 60 g) unsalted butter

½ cup (2 ounces; 60 g) minced pancetta (see Note)

2 medium onions, minced

Sea salt to taste

2 medium carrots, diced

5 to 6 ribs celery hearts with leaves, cut into thin crosswise pieces

1 cup (4 ounces; 125 g) trimmed and diced green beans

½ small white cabbage (12 ounces; 375 g), shredded

2 medium boiling potatoes (12 ounces; 375 g), peeled and diced

2 quarts (2 l) water

One 16-ounce (480-g) can imported Italian plum tomatoes, with their juice

Freshly ground black pepper to taste

1 cup (6 ounces; 180 g) Italian Arborio rice

About 1 cup (4 ounces; 125 g) freshly grated Italian Parmigiano-Reggiano cheese

1. Rinse the beans, picking them over to remove any pebbles. Place the beans in a large bowl, add boiling water to cover, and set aside for 1 hour. Drain the beans, discarding the water. Set aside.

2. In a 6-quart (6-l) heavy-bottomed stockpot, melt the butter over low heat. Add the pancetta, onions, and salt, and stir to coat with the fat. Cook until the onions are soft and translucent, 3 to 4 minutes. Add the carrots, celery, and drained white beans, stir to coat with the fat, and cook for 5 minutes more. Add the green beans, cabbage, potatoes, and the 2 quarts (2 l) water. Place a food mill over the stockpot and purée the tomatoes directly into it. Cover, bring to a simmer over moderate heat, and simmer for 30 minutes. Season to taste with salt and pepper, and continue simmering until the beans are softened and tender, about 30 to 60 minutes more. (Cooking time will vary according to the freshness of the beans.) Add the rice, and simmer just until the rice is tender but still firm to the bite, about 20 minutes more. Taste for seasoning.

3. To serve, stir several tablespoons of the cheese into the soup. Ladle the soup—piping hot—into warmed shallow soup bowls, and pass the remaining cheese separately. (The soup, of course, may be reheated several times over a period of several days. The soup will thicken. Simply add additional water each time you reheat the soup.)

■ Yield: 4 to 6 servings ■

NOTE: If unsmoked Italian pancetta is not available, use a lean top-quality bacon. Blanch it for 1 minute in boiling water, then drain thoroughly. Blanching will remove the smoked flavor from the bacon without cooking it.

Pasta and Chick Pea Soup

Pasta e Ceci

T he Italians are great soup eaters, and one of the truly classic trattoria soups is this simple blend of chick peas—also known as garbanzo beans—simmered in an aromatic broth, punctuated by bits of pasta, and seasoned at table with best-quality olive oil. The soup should be thick and porridge-like, almost thick enough to hold a spoon upright! Since it's so rich, serve it in small portions, accompanied, at most, by a green salad or simple grilled poultry or fish. It's also a great treat when preceded by a platter of raw vegetables dipped in olive oil, just as I sampled one spring evening at Trattoria Omero, a lively spot with a marvelous view of the hills of Florence. Some foods are simply an excuse for eating something else, and I often think of this golden, harvest-like soup as an excuse for garlic and oil, two favorite foods that always put me in a happy frame of mind.

3 cups (1 pound; 500 g) dried chick peas (garbanzo beans)

3 tablespoons extra-virgin olive oil

1 medium onion, diced

1 medium carrot, diced

1 rib celery, thinly sliced

4 plump fresh garlic cloves, crushed

Several sprigs of fresh parsley, sprigs of sage, bay leaves, and celery leaves, tied in a bundle with cotton twine

2 to 3 quarts (2 to 3 l) cold water

Fine sea salt to taste

½ cup (3 ounces; 90 g) tiny dried Italian pasta, such as ditalini, broken spaghetti, or tiny elbow macaroni

Extra-virgin olive oil, for the table

1. Rinse and drain the chick peas, picking them over to remove any pebbles. Place the chick peas in a large bowl, add boiling water to cover, and set aside for 1 hour. Drain and rinse the chick peas, discarding the water. Set aside.

2. In a 6-quart (6-l) heavy-bottomed stockpot, combine the olive oil, onion, carrot, celery, garlic, and the herb bundle, and stir to coat with the oil. Cook over moderate heat until the vegetables are fragrant and soft, about 5 minutes. Add the chick peas, stir to coat with oil, and cook for 1 minute more. Add 2 quarts (2 l) water and stir. Cover, bring to a simmer over moderate heat, and simmer for 1 hour. Add the salt and continue simmering until the chick peas are tender, about 1 hour more, stirring from time to time to make sure they are not sticking to the bottom of the stockpot. Add additional water if the soup becomes too thick. (Cooking time will vary according to the freshness of the chick peas.)

3. Remove and discard the herb bundle. Using an immersion mixer, roughly purée the soup directly in the stockpot. (Alternatively, pass the soup through the coarse blade of a food mill or purée in batches in a food processor, and return it to the stockpot.) The soup should have a creamy, but not totally smooth, consistency. It should be very thick, almost porridge-like. Season with salt to taste. Add the pasta, stir, and cook just until the pasta is tender, about 10 minutes more, stirring frequently to keep the pasta from sticking. Taste for seasoning.

4. To serve, ladle the soup—piping hot—into warmed shallow soup bowls. Pass a cruet of extra-virgin olive oil, drizzling a swirl of oil directly into each bowl of soup. (The soup, of course, may be reheated several times over a period of several days. If it thickens, simply thin with water each time you reheat the soup.)

■ Y i e l d : 8 t o 10 s e r v i n g s ■

Roasted Yellow Pepper Soup

Passato di Peperoni

Sunset-golden peppers in a delicate broth of vegetables and poultry, steaming hot in pristine white soup bowls. Drizzle with the finest extra-virgin olive oil, grill a few slices of thick and crusty homemade bread, and you've got it made. This is the signature soup of Cibrèo, a modern-day Florentine trattoria, where Fabio and Benedetta Picchi serve up full-flavored, imaginative fare based on the country food of their Tuscan youth. Serve this in small portions as a first course, followed by a more substantial main course, such as roast chicken, grilled lamb chops, or osso bucco. If yellow peppers are not to be found, bright red peppers are a far from shabby substitute. Note that cooking the roasted strips of pepper in the oil with the vegetables gives them a richer flavor. And don't skimp when you drizzle on the olive oil: That's what gives this soup its rich and unctuous flavor.

2 tablespoons extra-virgin olive oil

1 large carrot, minced

1 rib celery, minced

1 medium onion, minced

6 (about 2 pounds; 1 kg) yellow bell peppers, roasted and sliced (see box)

Sea salt to taste

2 medium-size potatoes, peeled and diced

1 quart (1 l) water

2 cups (500 ml) chicken stock, preferably homemade (page 272)

Extra-virgin olive oil, for the table

1. In a large stockpot, combine the olive oil, carrot, celery, and onion, and cook over moderate heat until the vegetables are soft and fragrant, about 10 minutes. Add the sliced peppers and cook for 3 to 4 minutes more, for greater flavor intensity. Season with salt. Add the potatoes, water, and chicken stock, cover, and cook over moderate heat until the potatoes are soft, about 20 minutes.

2. Purée in batches in the food processor or blender, or with an immersion mixer. Taste for seasoning. Serve in warmed shallow soup bowls, drizzling each portion with a generous amount of the best olive oil you can find.

▪ Y i e l d : 6 t o 8 s e r v i n g s ▪

For Better Roasted Peppers

Grilled and roasted peppers are understandably popular today, but like many popular items, they easily soon become the subject of abuse or misunderstanding. Grilled and roasted peppers should be just that, not charred shadows of their former selves. Too often peppers are burnt to a crisp, losing all their fragrant and flavorful essence.

Here are some tips:

■ Select thick-fleshed, thick-skinned peppers. They have more flavor and will better withstand the heat.

■ The best way to grill peppers is to place them at least 3 inches (8 cm) from the heat of the broiler, so they do not come in direct contact with the intense heat and both roast and steam at the same time, making for more moist and tender peppers. Peppers can also be roasted on a grill, over a gas flame, or in a very hot (500°F; 260°C; gas mark 9) oven.

■ Do not pierce the peppers. You want to save that beautifully oily liquid within.

■ Watch the peppers carefully as they cook. Turn them often, using tongs that won't puncture the flesh. The skin should blister, but not burn. (If the skin turns black and charred long before it begins to pull away from the pepper, the heat is too intense.)

■ Once the skin shrinks and peels away from the peppers on all sides, remove the peppers from the heat and seal them in a paper bag or place in a bowl and cover the bowl with plastic wrap. Allow them to cool thoroughly. Remove them from the bag or bowl, being careful not to lose any of the juices. Remove the charred skin from the peppers, carefully remove the seeds, and slice the peppers lengthwise into strips. Do not rinse or wash the peppers once they are peeled, or you will lose the flavorful juices.

DRIED PASTA

Penne with Spicy Tomato Sauce

Penne all'Arrabbiata

How can one simple dish give so much pleasure? Sometimes I think I could eat this every day, with the hint of spice from the red peppers, the bite of the garlic, and the flicker of green from the chopped parsley to add a note of freshness. Like many pasta dishes, this one reminds me of the Italian flag, with its proud red, green, and white. *Arrabbiata,* by the way, means "furious" or "angry," which describes the character of the spicy sauce. Traditionally, cheese is not served with this dish. If you begin boiling the water and preparing the sauce at the same time, the dish will take less than thirty minutes to prepare.

¼ *cup (60 ml) extra-virgin olive oil*

6 *plump fresh garlic cloves, minced*

½ *teaspoon crushed red peppers (hot red pepper flakes), or to taste*

Sea salt

One 28-ounce (765-g) can peeled Italian plum tomatoes in juice or one 28-ounce (765-g) can crushed tomatoes in purée

1 *pound (500 g) dried Italian tubular pasta, such as penne*

1 *cup (250 ml) fresh flat-leaf parsley leaves, snipped with a scissors*

1. In an unheated skillet large enough to hold the pasta later on, combine the oil, garlic, crushed red peppers, and a pinch of salt, stirring to coat with the oil. Cook over moderate heat just until the garlic turns golden but does not brown, 2 to 3 minutes. If using whole canned tomatoes, place a food mill over the skillet and purée the tomatoes directly into it. Crushed tomatoes can be added directly from the can. Stir to blend, and simmer, uncovered, until the sauce begins to thicken, about 15 minutes. Taste for seasoning.

2. Meanwhile, in a large pot, bring 6 quarts (6 l) of water to a rolling boil. Add 3 tablespoons salt and the penne, stirring to prevent the pasta from sticking. Cook until tender but firm to the bite. Drain thoroughly.

3. Add the drained pasta to the skillet with the tomato sauce. Toss, cover, and let rest over low heat for 1 to 2 minutes to allow the pasta to absorb the sauce. Add the parsley and toss again. Transfer to warmed shallow soup bowls and serve immediately.

■ Y i e l d :   6   s e r v i n g s ■

WINE SUGGESTION: A young Italian red table wine such as a Castelli Romani, from the area just southeast of Rome.

Getting the Most out of Parsley

Parsley is an ingredient in its own right, much more than a simple garnish added for a touch of green. Here, as in many Italian dishes, parsley is essential. To get the most flavor from fresh parsley, stem it first, leaving only the leaves. Place the leaves in a large glass or a deep bowl, and snip the leaves with a sharp scissors. Snipped in this manner, the parsley will be coarsely chopped but won't turn to mush as is often the case when chopped with a knife or in a food processor. Note that whenever one measures the volume of minced, chopped, or snipped herbs, they should be loosely packed.

Pay Attention to Salt

I can't argue enough for the use of top-quality sea salt (not what's known as "kosher salt") in the kitchen. Although sea salt may cost a bit more than traditional table salt, it is well worth the investment in flavor.

Sea salt—both fine and coarse—has a bright, clean, distinct flavor and imparts a truly subtle flavor to foods. Common table salt masks flavors: Rather than make foods taste seasoned, it only makes them taste salty.

I use coarse salt for most cooking (when seasoning sauces, soups, or water for cooking pasta). Fine sea salt, or coarse salt that is ground in a salt mill, is preferable for baking, for the table, and for the last-minute seasoning of a dish.

Always remember to cook and season as you go. Many dishes—such as pastas and beans—cannot successfully be seasoned at the end.

Spaghetti with Red Pesto Sauce

Spaghetti con Pesto Rosso

I f you've ever thought of sun-dried tomatoes as a cliché that's passé, try this sauce out on your family and friends and your mind will be changed forever. Sauce the spaghetti very lightly—½ cup (125 ml) of sauce per pound (500 g) of pasta will do—pass the Parmigiano-Reggiano and a bottle of red wine, and live it up!

1 pound (500 g) dried Italian spaghetti

Sea salt

About ½ cup (125 ml) Red Pesto Sauce (page 264)

¼ cup (60 ml) fresh flat-leaf parsley leaves, snipped with a scissors

Freshly grated Italian Parmigiano-Reggiano cheese, for the table (optional)

1. In a large pot, bring 6 quarts (6 l) of water to a rolling boil. As the water is heating, place a large serving bowl over the pot to warm the bowl. When the water is boiling, add 3 tablespoons salt and the spaghetti, stirring to prevent the pasta from sticking. Cook until tender but firm to the bite. Carefully drain the pasta, leaving a few drops of water clinging to the spaghetti so that the sauce will adhere.

2. Add the pasta to the warmed bowl, and toss with the red pesto sauce to blend. Add the parsley and toss again. Transfer to warmed shallow soup bowls and pass the cheese, if desired.

■ Yield: 6 servings ■

WINE SUGGESTION: An everyday red is ideal here, such as a Chianti Classico.

···

Penne with Vodka and Spicy Tomato-Cream Sauce

Penne alla Bettola

This is my husband's favorite pasta dish. I know that if I want to make him happy, I just say "vodka pasta," and a broad smile fills his face. There is something wonderfully satisfying about thick tubes of pasta, such as penne, sauced with a mixture of lightly spiced tomatoes and cream. The addition of vodka makes for a very intriguing dish. I'm sure only one out of a thousand people would guess that vodka is the secret ingredient. The recipe comes from La Vecchia Betolla, a lively, elbows-on-the-table trattoria in Florence, where you squeeze onto rough wooden benches and ultimately share in conversation with your neighbors, always close at hand.

¼ *cup (60 ml) extra-virgin olive oil*

4 *plump fresh garlic cloves, minced*

½ *teaspoon crushed red peppers (hot red pepper flakes), or to taste*

Sea salt

One 28-ounce (765-g) can peeled Italian plum tomatoes in juice or one 28-ounce (765-g) can crushed tomatoes in purée

1 *pound (500 g) dried Italian tubular pasta, such as penne*

2 *tablespoons vodka*

½ *cup (125 ml) heavy cream*

¼ *cup (60 ml) fresh flat-leaf parsley leaves, snipped with a scissors*

1. In an unheated skillet large enough to hold the pasta later on, combine the oil, garlic, crushed red peppers, and a pinch of salt, stirring to coat with the oil. Cook over moderate heat just until the garlic turns golden but does not brown, 2 to 3 minutes. If using whole canned tomatoes, place a food mill over the skillet and purée the tomatoes directly into it. Crushed tomatoes can be added directly from the can. Stir to blend, and simmer, uncovered, until the sauce begins to thicken, about 15 minutes. Taste for seasoning.

2. Meanwhile, in a large pot, bring 6 quarts (6 l) of water to a rolling boil. Add 3 tablespoons salt and the penne, stirring to prevent the pasta from sticking. Cook until tender but firm to the bite. Drain thoroughly.

3. Add the drained pasta to the skillet with the tomato sauce. Toss. Add the vodka, toss again, then add the cream and toss. Cover, reduce the heat to low, and let rest for 1 to 2 minutes to allow the pasta to absorb the sauce. Add the parsley and toss again. Transfer to warmed shallow soup bowls and serve immediately. (Traditionally, cheese is not served with this dish.)

■ Y i e l d : 6 t o 8 s e r v i n g s ■

WINE SUGGESTION: A good-quality red that can stand up to the spice and cream is ideal here, such as a 2- or 3-year-old Chianti Classico from Tuscany or a California Zinfandel.

Spaghetti with Capers, Olives, Tomatoes, and Hot Peppers

Spaghetti alla Puttanesca

"Spaghetti can be eaten successfully if you inhale it like a vacuum cleaner."

SOPHIA LOREN

S paghetti alla puttanesca, or "whore's pasta," is said to have originally been a favorite dish of Italian prostitutes, who could prepare it quickly when they had precious few moments to spend in the kitchen. Today, it's found in trattorias throughout Italy, although it is particularly popular in Rome, where I sampled a pleasantly spiced version at La Campana, a simple restaurant that attracts a glittery and hungry crowd. This is an ideal pasta dish for those who have little in the pantry and little time to spare. When preparing this pasta, don't skimp on the fresh parsley, for it's what adds a great fresh flavor, not to mention a lively color.

¼ cup (60 ml) extra-virgin olive oil

4 flat anchovy fillets cured in salt (see page 279) or in olive oil, drained (if in oil) and minced

3 plump fresh garlic cloves, minced

½ teaspoon crushed red peppers (hot red pepper flakes), or to taste

Sea salt

One 28-ounce (765-g) can peeled Italian plum tomatoes in juice or one 28-ounce (765-g) can crushed tomatoes in purée

15 salt-cured black olives, such as Italian Gaeta or French Nyons olives (see page 280), pitted and halved

2 tablespoons capers, drained and rinsed

1 pound (500 g) dried Italian spaghetti

1 cup (250 ml) fresh flat-leaf parsley leaves, snipped with a scissors

1. In an unheated skillet large enough to hold the pasta later on, combine the oil, anchovies, garlic, crushed red peppers, and a pinch of salt, stirring to coat with the oil. Cook over moderate heat just until the garlic turns golden but does not brown, 2 to 3 minutes. If using whole canned tomatoes, place a food mill over the skillet and purée the tomatoes directly into it. Crushed tomatoes can be added directly from the can. Add the olives and capers. Stir to blend, and simmer, uncovered, until the sauce begins to thicken, about 15 minutes. Taste for seasoning.

2. Meanwhile, in a large pot, bring 6 quarts (6 l) of water to a rolling boil. Add 3 tablespoons salt and the spaghetti, stirring to prevent the pasta from sticking. Cook until tender but firm to the bite. Drain thoroughly.

3. Add the drained pasta to the skillet with the sauce. Toss, cover, and let rest off the heat for 1 to 2 minutes to allow the pasta to absorb the sauce. Add the parsley and toss again. Transfer to warmed shallow soup bowls and serve immediately. (Traditionally, cheese is not served with this dish.)

■ Yield: 6 servings ■

WINE SUGGESTION: A dependable Chianti, such as one from the Antinori or Ricasoli estates.

Spaghetti with Garlic, Oil, and Hot Peppers

Spaghetti con Aglio, Olio, e Peperoncini

"Everything you see I owe to spaghetti."

Sophia Loren

Spaghetti coated with oil, a profusion of garlic, and a hit of pepper is one of the Italy's most universally popular dishes. You'll find variations served in just about every part of the country, sometimes without the hot peppers or without the usual parsley; at other times the herb of choice might be basil, mint, oregano, or rosemary. I adore this version, with a healthy amount of both garlic and hot peppers. It always seems to put me and my guests in a cheery, energetic mood. When preparing this dish at home, be sure to watch the garlic carefully as it cooks. Burnt garlic becomes bitter at once, and turns a sublime dish into one that's thoroughly indigestible. The trick here is to combine the oil, garlic, and hot pepper in an unheated pan, and then heat them together so the garlic does not have a chance to burn. Likewise, adding a touch of oil at the end helps make for a pasta that is evenly and smoothly coated with sauce. Although you will sometimes see this dish served with cheese, that's a mistake: The pasta and sauce are already rich enough, and the cheese is just a lot of lily-gilding!

Sea salt

1 pound (500 g) dried Italian spaghetti

½ cup (125 ml) plus 2 tablespoons extra-virgin olive oil

6 plump fresh garlic cloves, minced

½ teaspoon crushed red peppers (hot red pepper flakes), or to taste

½ cup (125 ml) fresh flat-leaf parsley leaves, snipped with a scissors

1. In a large pot, bring 6 quarts (6 l) of water to a rolling boil over high heat. Add 3 tablespoons salt and the spaghetti, stirring to prevent the pasta from sticking. Cook until tender but firm to the bite. Drain thoroughly.

2. Meanwhile, in an unheated skillet large enough to hold the pasta later on, combine ½ cup (125 ml) of the oil, the garlic, the crushed red peppers, and a pinch of salt. Toss to thoroughly coat the garlic and pepper flakes, and cook over moderate heat just until the garlic turns golden but does not brown, 2 to 3 minutes.

3. Add the drained pasta to the skillet with the sauce. Toss, add the remaining 2 tablespoons of oil, toss thoroughly, and cover. Let rest off the heat for 1 to 2 minutes to allow the pasta to absorb the sauce. Add the parsley and toss again. Transfer to warmed shallow soup bowls and serve immediately. (Traditionally, cheese is not served with this dish.)

▪ Y i e l d :   6   s e r v i n g s ▪

WINE SUGGESTION: I like a good "daily-drinking" Italian red with this assertive dish, such as a Chianti Classico.

• • •

Penne with Zucchini and Spicy Pizza Sauce

Penne con Zucchine alla Pizzaiola

When I'm sad, crabby, or in need of a bit of cheer, this is the pasta dish I turn to for solace. One bite, and I'm in a better mood. The success of this dish depends upon securing very fresh, tender, firm zucchini. Pizzaiola, by the way, is a tomato sauce that tastes a bit like a traditional pizza topping—that is, made with tomatoes, oregano, and garlic. I sampled this version at a little side-street trattoria in Siena. The addition of balsamic vinegar is my own pick-me-up touch, inspired by a recipe from Marcella Hazan. Season with hot pepper according to your taste.

7 *tablespoons extra-virgin olive oil*

3 *tablespoons fresh rosemary leaves, minced*

½ *teaspoon crushed red peppers (hot red pepper flakes), or to taste*

10 *plump fresh garlic cloves, slivered*

Sea salt

One 28-ounce (765-g) can peeled Italian plum tomatoes in juice or one 28-ounce (765-g) can crushed tomatoes in purée

7 *ounces (210 g) firm, fresh zucchini, scrubbed, trimmed, and thinly sliced (do not peel)*

½ *teaspoon dried leaf oregano*

1 *pound (500 g) dried Italian tubular pasta, such as penne*

2 *tablespoons balsamic vinegar*

1. In an unheated skillet large enough to hold the pasta later on, heat 6 tablespoons of the oil, the rosemary, crushed red peppers, garlic, and a pinch of salt. Cook over moderate heat just until the garlic turns golden but does not brown, 2 to 3 minutes. If using whole canned tomatoes, place a food mill over the skillet and purée the tomatoes directly into it. Crushed tomatoes can be added directly from the can. Stir to blend, and simmer, uncovered, until the sauce begins to thicken, about 15 minutes.

2. While the sauce is simmering, prepare the zucchini: In a large nonstick skillet, heat the remaining 1 tablespoon oil over moderately high heat. When the oil is hot but not smoking, add the zucchini and sauté just until golden, 2 to 3 minutes. Transfer to a colander to drain any excess oil, season with salt, and toss with the oregano. Set aside.

3. Meanwhile, in a large pot, bring 6 quarts (6 l) of water to a rolling boil. Add 3 tablespoons salt and the penne, stirring to prevent the pasta from sticking. Cook until tender but firm to the bite. Drain thoroughly.

4. Add the drained pasta to the skillet with the tomato sauce. Add the balsamic vinegar and toss. Add the zucchini and toss again. Cover, and let rest over low heat for 1 to 2 minutes to allow the pasta to absorb the sauce. Toss again, transfer to warmed shallow soup bowls, and serve immediately. (Traditionally, cheese is not served with this dish.)

■   Y i e l d :   6   s e r v i n g s   ■

WINE SUGGESTION: Either a young Italian red, such as a Barbera d'Alba, or a white, such as a Pinot Grigio.

Gemelli with Eggplant, Tomatoes, and Mozzarella

Gemelli alla Siciliana

On a cool fall day, there are few pastas that warm the soul as this one does. While eggplants are fresh, firm, shiny, and still at their peak, take advantage of this versatile vegetable, which blends so well with the heartiness of the pasta and the richness of a full-flavored tomato sauce. It's in this sort of dish that eggplant takes a starring role, tasting so much like meat you can't believe it isn't. (And whatever you do, don't peel the eggplant: The skin is the source of tremendous flavor.) Be sure to cut the eggplant and cheese into small, even cubes. When you reach into the bowl of pasta, "build" the pasta, sauce, and mozzarella on your fork for a harmonious blending of flavors and textures. A variety of dried pastas might be used here: Although rigatoni is traditional, I find it too bulky and cumbersome and prefer gemelli, ziti, fusilli, or the old standby, penne. While this dish is Sicilian in origin, I've seen it served throughout Italy.

¾ cup (185 ml) extra-virgin olive oil

1 small onion, minced

2 plump fresh garlic cloves, minced

Sea salt

One 28-ounce (765-g) can peeled Italian plum tomatoes in juice or one 28-ounce (765-g) can crushed tomatoes in purée

1 firm medium eggplant (1 pound; 500 g), cubed (do not peel)

1 pound (500 g) dried Italian tubular pasta, such as gemelli, ziti, fusilli, or penne

2 cups (10 ounces; 300 g) cubed whole-milk mozzarella

1. In an unheated skillet large enough to hold the pasta later on, combine ¼ cup (60 ml) of the oil, the onion, garlic, and a pinch of salt, stirring to coat with the oil. Cook over moderate heat just until the garlic turns golden but does not brown, 2 to 3 minutes. If using whole canned tomatoes, place a food mill over the skillet and purée the tomatoes directly into it. Crushed tomatoes can be added directly from the can. Stir to blend, and simmer, uncovered, until the sauce begins to thicken, about 15 minutes. Taste for seasoning.

2. While the sauce is simmering, cook the eggplant: In a large deep skillet, heat the remaining ½ cup (125 ml) oil over moderately high heat. When the oil is hot but not smoking, add the eggplant and cook until lightly colored, about 5 minutes. (The eggplant will soak up the oil immediately, but allow it to cook without added oil, keeping the pan moving to avoid scorching.) Season generously with salt.

3. Add the eggplant to the tomato sauce and keep warm over very low heat. (Neither the sauce nor the eggplant needs additional cooking, but the eggplant should have time to absorb some of the tomato sauce.)

4. Meanwhile, in a large pot, bring 6 quarts (6 l) of water to a rolling boil. Add 3 tablespoons salt and the pasta, stirring to prevent the pasta from sticking. Cook until tender but firm to the bite. Drain thoroughly.

5. Add the drained pasta to the skillet with the tomato sauce. Toss to blend. Cover and let rest off the heat for 1 to 2 minutes to allow the pasta to absorb the sauce. Transfer the pasta to warmed shallow soup bowls and sprinkle each serving with the cubed mozzarella. Serve immediately.

■ Yield: 6 servings ■

WINE SUGGESTION: With this, try a full-bodied red, such as a Montepulciano d'Abruzzo.

Spaghetti with Pecorino and Pepper

Spaghetti al Cacio e Pepe

The Romans are great eaters of spaghetti as well as of that deliciously piquant sheep's milk cheese known as pecorino. This simple but sublime dish combines the two, as well as a healthy dose of coarse, freshly ground black pepper. Prepare it for one or for many, serving a sturdy Italian red alongside.

Sea salt

1 pound (500 g) dried Italian spaghetti

¼ cup (60 ml) extra-virgin olive oil

2 cups (8 ounces; 250 g) freshly grated Italian sheep's milk cheese (pecorino), such as Romano

Coarse freshly ground black pepper to taste

1. In a large pot, bring 6 quarts (6 l) of water to a rolling boil. As the water is heating, place a large serving bowl over the pot to warm the bowl. When the water is boiling, add 3 tablespoons salt and the spaghetti, stirring to prevent the pasta from sticking. Cook until tender but firm to the bite. Carefully drain the pasta, leaving a few drops of water clinging to the spaghetti so that the sauce will adhere.

2. Pour the oil into the warmed bowl. Add the pasta, cheese, and plenty of coarse black pepper. Using 2 forks, toss to blend. Transfer to warmed shallow soup bowls and serve immediately.

■ Yield: 4 to 6 servings ■

WINE SUGGESTION: I enjoy this with a sturdy, full-bodied red, such as Barbaresco, Barbera, or a Badia a Coltibuono Riserva.

Tips for Better Pasta

Pasta is a universally loved ingredient, and deserves the best treatment we can give it. Respect your pasta and reward your guests by following these simple rules:

- Cook pasta in plenty of rapidly boiling water—at least 1 quart (1 l) of water for every 3½ ounces (100 g) of pasta.

- Give the water plenty of salt. Use a minimum of 1 teaspoon per quart (liter) of water. Pasta cooked in unsalted water will taste flat and lifeless, no matter how well you salt and flavor the sauce.

- Stir the pasta as it cooks.

- Don't overcook it. Unless you have X-ray vision, "al dente" is not something you can see. You must taste! Both dried pasta and risotto should be cooked al dente, meaning firm to the bite, with no chalkiness in the center. Fresh pasta cooks very quickly, and should be cooked just until tender. Again, taste!

- Drain pasta as soon as it is cooked, but don't overdrain it.

- Sauce pasta as soon as it is drained. Time your cooking so that the sauce is ready when the pasta is. The hotter the pasta, the better it will absorb the sauce.

- Don't oversauce it. When you're done, there should be no sauce left in the bowl.

- Do think about marrying the right sauce to the right pasta.

- Keep it simple. Less is almost always more where pasta is concerned. Let the pasta be the star.

Bucatini with Pancetta, Pecorino, and Black Pepper

Bucatini alla Gricia

A typically Roman preparation, this simple and zesty dish marries the tang of an assertive, aged sheep's milk cheese, the bite of freshly ground black pepper, and the mildly cured flavor of fresh, high-quality pancetta. Traditionally, bucatini alla gricia is made with guanciale, a Roman-style bacon prepared with pork jowls, but a lean, high-quality pancetta is a practical and worthy substitute. Like many Italian pasta sauces, this is more a coating or moistener than a sauce that drowns the pasta, and it can be prepared in the time it takes to get the pasta cooking and uncork a chilled bottle of white wine. The recipe comes from Ninetta Ceccacci Mariani, owner and cook of Rome's family-run Trattoria Checchino dal 1887. Bucatini is a thin, hollow, tubular pasta that's just slightly thicker than traditional spaghetti but thinner than macaroni. I've also successfully prepared this dish with percialetti, a small pierced macaroni that's just slightly thicker than bucatini. Since this is a hearty, substantial dish, a small serving should be sufficient. The recipe can easily be doubled, to serve four.

Sea salt

8 ounces (250 g) dried Italian bucatini, or thick spaghetti

½ cup (2 ounces; 60 g) pancetta, cut into matchsticks (see box)

1 tablespoon extra-virgin olive oil

1 cup (4 ounces; 125 g) freshly grated Italian sheep's milk cheese (pecorino), such as Romano

Coarse freshly ground black pepper to taste

1. In a large pot, bring 3 quarts (3 l) of water to a rolling boil. Add 1½ tablespoons salt and the bucatini, stirring to prevent the pasta from sticking. Cook until tender but firm to the bite. Carefully drain the pasta, leaving a few drops of water clinging to the bucatini so that the sauce will adhere.

2. Meanwhile, in a skillet large enough to hold the pasta later on, combine the pancetta and oil over moderate heat. Sauté until the pancetta is a rosy color but not crisp, 2 to 3 minutes.

3. Add the drained pasta to the skillet and, using 2 forks, toss quickly and thoroughly with the pancetta. Add the cheese, sprinkle generously with coarse black pepper, and toss again. Cover and let rest over low heat for 1 minute to allow the pasta to absorb the sauce. Transfer to warmed shallow soup bowls and serve immediately, passing the pepper mill.

■ Yield: 2 servings as a main course, ■
4 servings as a first course

WINE SUGGESTION: A good white table wine would be nice here. If you can find it, sample one from the Latium region of Rome, such as a Castelli Romani or Colli Albani. Or try a young Orvieto Classico from a reputable bottler, such as Antinori or Ruffino.

What, You Have No Pancetta?

There is no American equivalent for pancetta, the unsmoked Italian bacon that is cured with salt and mild spices and rolled. Pancetta is prized for its subtle, delicate flavor and can be found in most Italian specialty shops. If you cannot find it, substitute a very lean, top-quality bacon. Blanch it for 1 minute in boiling water, then drain thoroughly. Blanching will remove the smoked flavor from the bacon without cooking it.

Rigatoni with Pecorino and Two Peppers

Rigatoni della Casa

This lusty, quick, and satisfying dish is one of what I call the "Summer House Repertoire." You know, those times when you're in a vacation house kitchen equipped with one or two pots, maybe a bowl or none at all—the bare minimalist *cucina*. The only equipment you'll need for this dish is a pot for boiling pasta and a bowl in which to toss it. To make things even more efficient, place the pasta bowl on top of the pasta pot as the rigatoni cooks, so the bowl is nice and warm at serving time. If you're making this for a crowd, and it's going to be served as a main-dish pasta, count on about 4 ounces (125 g) of pasta and 2 ounces (60 g) of freshly grated sheep's milk cheese, or pecorino, per person. The addition of both red pepper and black pepper makes for a great contrast of flavors. Go easy on the hot red peppers, though, for the fire here should be subtle. Save this recipe for a good Italian sheep's milk cheese, one that is not too dried out nor overly pungent.

Sea salt

1 pound (500 g) dried Italian tubular pasta, such as rigatoni

2 cups (8 ounces; 250 g) freshly grated Italian sheep's milk cheese (pecorino), such as Romano, plus additional for the table

½ teaspoon crushed red peppers (hot red pepper flakes), or to taste

Freshly ground black pepper to taste

1. In a large pot, bring 6 quarts (6 l) of water to a rolling boil. As the water is heating, place a large serving bowl over the pot to warm the bowl. When the water is boiling, add 3 tablespoons salt and the rigatoni, stirring to prevent the pasta from sticking. Cook until tender but firm to the bite. Drain thoroughly.

2. Transfer the drained pasta to the warmed bowl. Add the cheese, crushed red peppers, and a generous amount of black pepper, and toss. Cover and let rest for 1 minute to allow the pasta to absorb the cheese and seasoning. Transfer to warmed shallow soup bowls and serve immediately, with additional grated cheese and red and black pepper, if desired.

■ Yield: 6 servings ■

WINE SUGGESTION: Serve this with a sturdy Italian red, such as a Barbera or Brunello di Montalcino.

Toss, Toss, and Toss Again

How often have you been presented a potentially fabulous pasta dish, only to find the sauce dumped carelessly on top? When this happens, the pasta invariably sticks together in dry clumps, and the sauce becomes little more than an afterthought. In the ideal world, pasta and its accompanying sauce should create a marriage of flavors, not serve simply as neighbors on the same block! And, much like a great salad, a great pasta should be tossed, tossed, and tossed again, so the sauce is thoroughly absorbed into the pasta. Tossing (and a moment's resting time to allow for absorption) is particularly important for thick, dense, tubular pastas—such as penne, gemelli, ziti, or rigatoni.

Saffron Butterflies

Farfalle allo Zafferano

"Italy, the paradise of earth and the epicure's heaven."

THOMAS NASHE,
THE UNFORTUNATE TRAVELLER, *1594*

I don't know which I like best: looking at the brilliant, happy colors of this dish, savoring the luxurious aroma of the saffron and butter sauce, or devouring it by the mouthful. Farfalle, or little pasta shaped like a butterfly, seems to be tailor-made to the elegance of the sauce. Yes, saffron is expensive, but please do use pure Spanish saffron. You'll only need a teaspoon, and you're worth it! (I enjoy using a mix of saffron here: saffron threads for flecks of elegance, powdered saffron for rich color.) Since the sauce is very rich, serve the saffron butterflies as a first-course pasta, followed by a light main course, such as a whole Baked Sea Bass with Artichokes (page 210). A dusting of freshly grated cheese here is nice, but go easy—you don't want to mask the saffron's distinctive flavor.

Sea salt

8 ounces (250 g) dried Italian farfalle, or butterfly-shaped pasta

2 tablespoons (1 ounce; 30 g) unsalted butter, at room temperature

½ cup (125 ml) heavy cream

1 teaspoon saffron threads (see Mail Order Sources, page 325)

*Freshly grated Italian Parmigiano-Reggiano cheese, for the table
(optional)*

1. In a large pot, bring 3 quarts (3 l) of water to a rolling boil. As the water is heating, place a large serving bowl over the pot to warm the bowl. When the water is boiling, add 1½ tablespoons salt and the farfalle, stirring to prevent the pasta from sticking. Cook the pasta until tender but firm to the bite. Drain thoroughly.

2. Transfer the drained pasta to the warmed bowl, add the butter, cream, and saffron, and toss. Cover and let rest for 1 minute to allow the pasta to absorb the sauce. Transfer to warmed shallow soup bowls and serve immediately, passing cheese if desired.

■ Y i e l d : 4 s e r v i n g s ■

WINE SUGGESTION: A Gattinara or Chianti Riserva remain favorites with this dish.

O n   S a ff r o n

Saffron—with the powerful name of *zafferano*—has been grown in Italy since the fifteenth century, near Aquila in the Abruzzi. Then, its price equaled that of silver. Today, it's as expensive, as rare, and as fragrantly delicious as truffles. You understand, once you realize it takes 224,000 handpicked stigmas of a crocus flower to make 1 pound (500 grams). In the international market, the most readily available top-quality saffron comes from Spain.

Fusilli with Walnut and Garlic Sauce

Fusilli Salsa di Noci

R ich and fragrant, and elegant as an "all white" dish that reminds me of wintry evenings, this delicious pasta is perfect as a very hearty first course or a main course served with a light salad and fruit gelato to follow. I first sampled this one memorable evening on the terrace of a waterside trattoria in the village of Lazise, along the southern edge of Lake Garda, near Verona in northern Italy. Be sure to toast the walnuts, to bring out their flavor. And go easy on the garlic: The hint should be faint but not overpowering. The little corkscrew pasta know as fusilli is perfect for this sauce, for the tiny flecks of walnuts cling to the pasta, giving you even amounts of sauce and pasta with each bite.

2 plump fresh garlic cloves, degermed and minced

Sea salt

1 cup (4 ounces; 125 g) walnut halves, toasted and cooled

1 cup (250 ml) heavy cream

1 pound (500 g) dried Italian pasta, such as fusilli

½ cup (2 ounces; 60 g) freshly grated Italian Parmigiano-Reggiano cheese

Freshly ground black pepper to taste

1. In a food processor, combine the garlic, a pinch of salt, and the nuts, and process just to coarsely chop the nuts. Add the cream, and process to a fairly smooth sauce. Taste for seasoning. Transfer to a large serving bowl.

2. In a large pot, bring 6 quarts (6 l) of water to a rolling boil. As the water is heating, place the serving bowl over the pot to warm the bowl. When the water is boiling, add 3 tablespoons salt and the fusilli, stirring to prevent the pasta from sticking. Cook the pasta until tender but firm to the bite. Drain thoroughly.

3. Transfer the drained pasta to the warmed bowl, and toss to blend thoroughly. Add the cheese and toss to blend. Season with salt and pepper. Transfer to warmed shallow soup bowls and serve immediately, passing the pepper mill.

■ Yield: 4 to 6 servings ■

WINE SUGGESTION: I like a distinctive white with this, such as Teruzzi & Puthod's Vernaccia di San Gimignano.

Pasta Etiquette

Proper Italian pasta-eating etiquette suggests eating pastas with a fork, not a fork and a spoon. Ideally, all pastas and rice should be served in warm, shallow bowls, rather than on plates. Warm food served in warmed bowls stays hot longer, for the sides of the bowl serve to preserve the heat. The sides of the bowl also come in handy when eating spaghetti or other long pastas: The curve of the bowl serves as a pivoting point for twirling spaghetti on the fork.

Rigatoni with Meat and Celery Sauce

Rigatoni Strasciati

"Everything about Florence seems to be colored with a mild violet, like diluted wine."

HENRY JAMES, LETTER TO HENRY JAMES, SR., 26 OCTOBER 1869

Lean meat sauces lightly bathing spirals of pasta are among my favorite trattoria memories: images of chunky white china bowls mounded with fragrant and steaming pasta tossed quickly and ever-so-lightly with a hearty vermilion-tinged sauce. This particular version is found all over Florence, where several trattorias—including the legendary Antico Fattore and the smaller, less well known Quattro Stagioni—make it one of their regular specials. The secret of this sauce, sampled on Wednesdays at Antico Fattore, is lots of celery, good-quality meat (you can use a variety, including bits of prosciutto or pancetta for added intensity), and just the right amount of cooking (about thirty minutes total). *Strasciati* means "to drag," which is what you do with the thick, stubby pasta, dragging it through the sauce to coat it. While rigatoni is classic here, you might also use penne or large pasta shells.

¼ cup (60 ml) extra-virgin olive
oil

1 small onion, minced

1 cup (250 ml) minced celery

¼ cup (60 ml) minced fresh
flat-leaf parsley leaves

Sea salt

8 ounces (250 g) beef ground
round or a mix of lean
chopped beef, pork, and/or
veal or prosciutto or pancetta

One 28-ounce (765-g) can peeled
Italian plum tomatoes in juice
or one 28-ounce (765-g) can
crushed tomatoes in purée

Several sprigs of fresh parsley, bay
leaves, and celery leaves, tied in
a bundle with cotton twine

1 pound (500 g) dried Italian
rigatoni, penne, or large shell
pasta

Freshly grated Italian
Parmigiano-Reggiano cheese,
for the table

1. In an unheated skillet large enough to hold the pasta later on, combine the oil, onion, celery, parsley, and a pinch of salt, stirring to coat with the oil. Cook over moderate heat until the mixture is soft and fragrant, 4 to 5 minutes. Add the meat, and toss to blend. Reduce the heat to low and cook, making sure to break the meat up into small bits with a spatula, until the meat changes color, about 5 minutes more. If using whole canned tomatoes, place a food mill over the skillet and purée the tomatoes directly into it. Crushed tomatoes can be added directly from the can. Stir to blend. Add the herb bundle and cook, uncovered, until the sauce begins to thicken, about 20 minutes more. Taste for seasoning. Remove and discard the herb bundle.

2. Meanwhile, in a large pot, bring 6 quarts (6 l) of water to a rolling boil. Add 3 tablespoons salt and the pasta, stirring to prevent the pasta from sticking. Cook until tender but firm to the bite. Drain thoroughly.

3. Add the drained pasta to the skillet with the sauce and toss to blend. Cover and let rest for 1 to 2 minutes, off the heat, to allow the pasta to thoroughly absorb the sauce. Transfer to warmed shallow soup bowls and serve immediately, passing freshly grated cheese.

■ Yield: 4 to 6 servings ■

WINE SUGGESTION: I enjoy this with a light Tuscan red, so why not Chianti Classico?

Spaghetti with Spicy Meat Sauce

Spaghetti alla Giannetto

"It is axiomatic in spaghetti cookery that the pasta must boil freely and loosely in plenty of water so that the surface covering of starch may be washed away. Where this is not done, the result is a thick, sticky, starchy mess that no amount of sauce can redeem."

ANGELO PELLEGRINI, THE UNPREJUDICED PALATE

What could seemingly be more banal than spaghetti and tomato sauce? But once the cheery waitress arrives with a heavy skillet fresh from the kitchen, sets it down at your elbow, and begins to dish out a piping hot portion of spaghetti, you know you're onto something special. This was the scene one cool spring afternoon at Da Giannetto, the bustling trattoria set on the Badia a Coltibuono wine-growing estate in Tuscany.

Beyond the Italian borders, the pasta is often an afterthought, and the sauce is the real star. But at Da Giannetto, the tomato and meat sauce appeared as an almost imperceptible veil, just a whisper of moisture laced with hot pepper, weeping with a suggestion of oil and tiny tidbits of meat. For this simple spaghetti dish, I like to prepare the meat sauce with plenty of red pepper. At the final moment, add a touch of parsley, then freshly grated Parmesan for embellishment. Need one ask for more?

Sea salt

1 pound (500 g) dried Italian spaghetti

2 cups (500 ml) Meat Sauce (page 268)

½ cup (125 ml) fresh flat-leaf parsley leaves, snipped with a scissors

Freshly grated Italian Parmigiano-Reggiano cheese, for the table

1. In a large pot, bring 6 quarts (6 l) of water to a rolling boil. Add 3 tablespoons salt and the spaghetti, stirring to prevent the pasta from sticking. Cook until tender but firm to the bite. Drain thoroughly.

2. Meanwhile, in a skillet large enough to hold the pasta later on, warm the meat sauce.

3. Add the drained spaghetti to the skillet, and use 2 large forks to toss to coat the pasta. Add the parsley and toss again. Cover and let rest for 1 to 2 minutes, off the heat, to allow the pasta to thoroughly absorb the sauce. Transfer the pasta to warmed shallow soup bowls and serve immediately, passing freshly grated cheese.

■ Y i e l d :   4   t o   6   s e r v i n g s ■

WINE SUGGESTION: It would only be fitting to serve a Chianti Classico from the Badia a Coltibuono estate.

For Cleaner Clams

Since most clams grow in sandy areas, they tend to be sandy themselves. Nothing is more unpleasant than biting into a tender little clam to find a mouthful of grit. To test if your clams are sandy, steam a few open and taste. If they're gritty, purge them in salt water: Thoroughly dissolve 1 tablespoon salt per quart (liter) of cold water needed. Scrub the shells under cold running water, then purge in the salt water for three hours at room temperature. Scoop up the clams with your fingers, leaving behind the grit and sand. You will be amazed at the amount of sand they give up.

Spaghetti with Shrimp, Clams, and Mussels in Tomato Sauce

Spaghetti alla Sante

Robust as well as beautiful, this rustic main dish combines spaghetti and a lusty tomato sauce laced with plump whole cloves of garlic and a hint of hot peppers, all topped off with generous portions of steamed clams, mussels, and shrimp. I sampled this one cool August night in Florence, at the family-run fish restaurant La Capannina di Sante, a pleasant, pine-paneled spot set right along the banks of the Arno, southeast of the center of town. The menu is rudimentary (some might even say limited), but of the half-dozen dishes we sampled that evening, everything was delightfully fresh and energetically seasoned.

The antipasto misto was made up of an almost endless procession of creations, including a full-flavored combination of squid, steamed mussels and clams, and rosy shrimp, all seasoned with lemon juice, basil, and parsley, as well as a platter of breaded and panfried whole anchovies, set on a bed of whole, fresh bay leaves.

But my favorite of all was this spaghetti dish. At La Capannina di Sante the mussels and clams are served in the shell, for a dish that's both pretty to look at and made for casual, hands-on eating. For a more formal presentation, remove the mussels and clams from the shell, and toss the shellfish in with the pasta at the very last minute.

(*continued*)

¼ cup (60 ml) extra-virgin olive oil

12 plump fresh garlic cloves, peeled

½ teaspoon crushed red peppers (hot red pepper flakes), or to taste

Sea salt

One 28-ounce (765-g) can peeled Italian plum tomatoes in juice or one 28-ounce (765-g) can crushed tomatoes in purée

1 pound (500 g) fresh mussels

1 cup (250 ml) dry white wine, such as a Pinot Grigio

Handful of fresh flat-leaf parsley stems, tied in a bundle with cotton twine

Freshly ground black pepper to taste

1 pound (500 g) fresh littleneck or Manila clams, purged if necessary (see box)

8 ounces (250 g) fresh medium shrimp, shelled

8 ounces (250 g) dried Italian spaghetti

Handful of fresh flat-leaf parsley leaves, snipped with a scissors

1. In a large unheated skillet, combine the oil, garlic, crushed red peppers, and a pinch of salt, stirring to coat with the oil. Cook over moderate heat just until the garlic begins to turn golden but does not brown, 2 to 3 minutes. If using whole canned tomatoes, place a food mill over the skillet and purée the tomatoes directly into it. Crushed tomatoes can be added directly from the can. Stir to blend, and simmer, uncovered, just until the sauce thickens and the garlic offers no resistance when pierced with a knife, about 20 minutes.

2. Meanwhile, thoroughly scrub the mussels, and rinse with several changes of water. If an open mussel closes when you press on it, it is good; if it stays open, the mussel should be discarded. Beard the mussels. (Do not beard the mussels in advance or they will die and spoil. Note that in some markets mussels are pre–prepared, in that the small black beard that hangs from the mussel has been clipped, but not entirely removed. These mussels do not need further attention.)

3. In a very large skillet, combine the wine, parsley stems, and mussels. Sprinkle generously with pepper, cover, and cook just until the mussels open, about 5 minutes. Remove the mussels as they open. Do not overcook. Discard any that do not open.

4. Transfer the mussels, still in their shells, to a large warmed serving bowl. Cover loosely with foil. Set aside and keep warm. Line a sieve with moistened cheesecloth and strain the mussel liquor into the simmering tomato sauce.

5. Using a stiff brush, scrub the clams thoroughly under cold running water. Discard any with broken shells or shells that do not close when tapped.

6. Prepare a large steamer: Fill the steamer pot with 1 cup of water and bring to a boil. Place the clams in the steamer basket, and season generously with freshly ground pepper. Cover and steam the clams over high heat, removing the clams as they open and adding them to the bowl of mussels. (The entire process should take less than 10 minutes.) Discard any shells that do not open. Line a sieve with moistened cheesecloth and strain the clam liquor into the tomato sauce.

7. Taste the tomato sauce. If it is thin, reduce it slightly over low heat. The flavors of the shellfish broths should be distinctive. Toss the cooked clams and mussels, as well as the shrimp, with half of the tomato sauce and keep warm, covered, over low heat. (The shrimp will cook as the pasta is prepared.)

8. Cook the pasta: In a large pot, bring 3 quarts (3 l) of water to a rolling boil. Add 1½ tablespoons salt and the spaghetti, stirring to prevent the pasta from sticking. Cook until tender but firm. Drain thoroughly.

9. Arrange the pasta on a large warmed serving platter and toss with the remaining tomato sauce. Spoon the shellfish and sauce over the pasta, sprinkle with the parsley, and serve immediately. Serve this dish with finger bowls, as well as a large bowl for the mussel and clam shells.

■ Yield: 4 servings ■

WINE SUGGESTION: A crisp white Pinot Grigio is my choice here.

. . .

Spaghetti with Marinated Baby Artichokes and Parmesan

Pasta Bianca

"Adapt your dish of spaghetti to circumstances and your state of mind."

G IUSEPPE M AROTTA (N EAPOLITAN WRITER)

One evening, with nothing but hunger on my mind, I created this simple and satisfying spaghetti dish, using what I had on hand at the moment: a box of spaghetti, a jar of homemade marinated baby artichokes, and a touch of parsley, red peppers, and Parmesan. It's a recipe that can accommodate a single diner or a crowd. The dish might be prepared with purchased marinated artichokes, but the flavor will be less fresh and less intense. I like the pale ivory tones of the dish, flecked with a touch of green and of red, and so I call it white pasta, or *pasta bianca*.

2 cups (500 ml) Marinated Baby Artichokes Preserved in Oil (page 18), drained and thinly sliced, marinating oil reserved

¼ teaspoon crushed red peppers (hot red pepper flakes), or to taste

Sea salt

1 pound (500 g) dried Italian spaghetti

¼ cup (60 ml) fresh flat-leaf parsley leaves, snipped with a scissors

1 cup (4 ounces; 125 g) freshly grated Italian Parmigiano-Reggiano cheese

1. In a skillet large enough to hold the pasta later on, combine the sliced artichokes, the reserved oil, and the crushed red peppers. Set aside.

2. In a large pot, bring 6 quarts (6 l) of water to a rolling boil. Add 3 tablespoons salt and the spaghetti, stirring to prevent the pasta from sticking. Cook until tender but firm. Drain thoroughly.

3. While the pasta is cooking, gently warm the artichokes over low heat.

4. Add the drained pasta to the artichokes and toss to blend. Toss in the parsley and about half of the cheese. Transfer to warmed shallow soup bowls and serve immediately, passing the remaining cheese.

■ Yield: 4 to 6 servings ■

WINE SUGGESTION: A fresh white Sauvignon Blanc nicely complements this dish.

Speedy Lasagne

Lasagne Rapide

One evening—having tested various fresh pasta recipes the previous day—I found myself with a few sheets of leftover pasta that I had cut into odd-shaped triangles and left to dry. I had a hunger for the flavors of lasagne, as my palate yearned for that beloved Italian trinity: pasta, tomatoes, and cheese. Time was short, so I improvised, and came up with a light dish that quickly satisfied my craving. I now call it "speedy lasagne," for it cooks quickly atop the stove and requires no special, hard-to-find ingredients. I particularly relish the crunch and character that the onions add to the sauce, while the ricotta adds the sensation of the richness of cream and of cheese, without making the dish the least bit heavy. I like to prepare this with an egg pasta, just slightly extravagant and a bit more satisfying than the eggless variety. I prefer factory-made pappardelle, fettuccine, or tagliatelle.

2 medium onions (about 10 ounces; 300 g), peeled

¼ cup (60 ml) extra-virgin olive oil

¼ teaspoon crushed red peppers (hot red pepper flakes), or to taste

Sea salt

Several sprigs of fresh parsley, bay leaves, sprigs of fresh rosemary, and celery leaves, tied in a bundle with cotton twine

One 28-ounce (765-g) can peeled Italian plum tomatoes in juice or one 28-ounce (765-g) can crushed tomatoes in purée

1 pound (500 g) dried Italian egg noodles, such as pappardelle, fettuccine, or tagliatelle

10 ounces (300 g) whole-milk ricotta, drained

3 tablespoons fresh flat-leaf parsley leaves, snipped with a scissors

1. Slice 1 of the onions in half lengthwise. Place each half, cut side down, on a cutting board, and cut crosswise into very thin slices. Slice the remaining onion in this manner, for about 2 cups (500 ml) sliced onions.

2. In a skillet large enough to hold the pasta later on, combine the sliced onions, oil, crushed red peppers, a pinch of salt, and the herb bundle, stirring to coat with the oil. Cook, uncovered, over very low heat, stirring from time to time, until the onions are very soft and glazed, about 10 minutes.

3. If using whole canned tomatoes, place a food mill over the skillet and purée the tomatoes directly into it. Crushed tomatoes can be added directly from the can. Stir to blend, and simmer, uncovered, until the sauce begins to thicken, about 15 minutes. Taste for seasoning. Remove the herb bundle.

4. Meanwhile, in a large pot, bring 6 quarts (6 l) of water to a rolling boil. Add 3 tablespoons sea salt and the pasta, stirring to prevent the pasta from sticking. Cook until tender but firm to the bite. Drain thoroughly.

5. Add the drained pasta to the skillet with the sauce. Toss. Add about three-quarters of the ricotta, in small spoonfuls, toss again, and cover. Let rest off the heat for 1 to 2 minutes to allow the pasta to absorb the sauce. Toss again and transfer to warmed shallow soup bowls. Garnish with spoonfuls of the remaining ricotta and the parsley. Serve immediately.

■ Yield: 4 to 6 servings ■

WINE SUGGESTION: Serve with a dependable, daily-drinking red wine, such as a Chianti Classico.

■ ■ ■

Angel's Hair Pasta with Pungent Parsley Sauce

Capellini d'Angelo al Prezzemolo

Delicate angel's hair pasta—capellini—tossed with a pungent blend of parsley, garlic, anchovies, and lemon juice is one of my favorite no-fuss, quick-fix dishes. The sauce knows no season, for parsley can be found in markets year-round. Be sure to prepare the sauce at the last minute, for the anchovy has a tendency to dominate the sauce as it "matures."

Sea salt

*1 pound (500 g) dried Italian pasta,
such as capellini or other thin spaghetti*

1 recipe freshly prepared Pungent Parsley Sauce (page 260)

1 to 2 tablespoons extra-virgin olive oil

1. In a large pot, bring 6 quarts (6 l) of water to a rolling boil. As the water is heating, place a large serving bowl over the pot to warm the bowl. When the water is boiling, add 3 tablespoons salt and the capellini, stirring to prevent the pasta from sticking. Cook until tender but firm to the bite. Drain thoroughly.

2. Transfer the drained pasta to the warmed bowl, add about three-quarters of the parsley sauce, and toss to evenly coat the pasta with the sauce. Cover for 1 minute, to allow the pasta to absorb the sauce. Toss again, and add the oil, to additionally moisten the pasta and to reinforce the fresh flavor of the sauce. Transfer the pasta to warmed shallow soup bowls, adding a dollop of the remaining parsley sauce to each bowl. Serve immediately.

■ Yield: 4 to 6 servings ■

WINE SUGGESTION: With this peppy sauce, drink a nicely chilled crisp white, such as a Pinot Grigio.

FRESH PASTA

■ ■ ■

Fresh Egg Pasta

Pasta all'Uovo

Because fresh pasta is so readily available almost everywhere, many of us, myself included, have all but abandoned a once-favorite pastime of making our own homemade pasta. But there are many dishes—lasagne for one—and many sauces—tangy lemon sauce for example—that cry out for the very best you can give. Here is a simple, traditional recipe that should bring you back into the kitchen (if you ever left!).

2 cups (265 g) unbleached all-purpose flour

3 large eggs, at room temperature, lightly beaten

BY HAND: Sift the flour onto a clean work surface and make a well in the center. Pour the beaten eggs into the well. With a fork, mix the flour and eggs together until the dough is soft and begins to stick together, about 3 minutes. When the dough forms a mass, transfer it to a lightly floured clean surface and knead until satiny and resilient, 10 to 15 minutes. Cover with a clean cloth and set aside for 1 hour.

IN A FOOD PROCESSOR: Sift the flour into the bowl of a food processor. Pulse the machine, slowly adding the beaten eggs (you may not need all the eggs), until the mixture forms clumps the size of small peas. Do not let the dough form a ball. Turn out onto a lightly floured surface and knead until satiny and resilient, about 10 minutes. Cover with a clean cloth and set aside for 1 hour.

Knead the pasta dough in the pasta machine: Divide the dough into 4 equal portions, covering the unused portions with a clean cloth. Set the rollers of the pasta machine at the widest setting. Flour one-quarter of the dough very lightly, and pass it once through the rollers. Fold the dough in thirds, like a business letter. Press the dough down with your fingertips to fuse the layers and push any air from between them. Turn the dough so that an open end feeds into the roller, and repeat the rolling and folding process (lightly flouring only when necessary) 8 more times.

Reset the rollers for the next thinnest setting. Lightly flour the dough but do not fold it. Pass the dough through the machine again, repeating the process on each remaining setting until the dough is as thin as desired (generally the next-to-last or the last setting on most machines).

Repeat the entire process with the remaining pieces of dough. Let the dough rest on towels until it is taut but not dry, about 15 minutes. Cut into desired lengths by machine or by hand.

■ Yield: 1 pound (500 g) dough ■

Tonnarelli with Arugula, Tomatoes, and Shaved Parmesan

Tonnarelli alla Rughetta

There is no way you can go wrong with such a winning quartet: fresh homemade pasta, leaves of pungent arugula, chunks of sun-kissed ripe tomatoes, and generous shavings of Parmigiano-Reggiano. Just make certain that everything is of top, top quality, as usual! This recipe comes from Arancio d'Oro, a popular trattoria near Rome's Via Condotti, a spot that's a favorite with journalists and neighborhood office workers. Even though this uncooked "sauce" seems like typical summer fare, I sampled it on a blustery day in December, and it warmed me to the tip of my toes. At Arancio d'Oro the dish was prepared with tonnarelli, the square-shaped homemade spaghetti better known as maccheroni alla chitarra. Use any fresh pasta noodle, such as the more finely cut tagliarini, the larger tagliatelle, or ribbons of fettuccine. If arugula cannot be found in the market, substitute very fresh leaves of watercress.

One 2-ounce (60-g) chunk of Italian Parmigiano-Reggiano cheese

4 cups (2 bunches, or about 3 ounces; 100 g) stemmed arugula leaves, washed and dried, coarsely chopped or torn

¼ cup (60 ml) extra-virgin olive oil

4 ripe plum tomatoes (8 ounces; 125 g), cored and coarsely chopped

3 tablespoons coarse sea salt

1 pound (500 g) fresh pasta, such as tonnarelli, fettuccine, or tagliatelle (page 126)

Fine sea salt and freshly ground black pepper to taste

1. In a large pot, bring 6 quarts (6 l) of water to a rolling boil. As the water is heating, place a large serving bowl over the pot to warm the bowl.

2. Using a vegetable peeler, shave the cheese into long, thick strips. (If the chunk of cheese become too small to shave, grate the remaining cheese and add to the bowl.) Place half of the cheese directly into the bowl. Add the arugula, oil, and tomatoes, and toss to blend.

3. Add the coarse sea salt to the boiling water, then add the pasta, stirring to prevent the pasta from sticking. Cook until tender. Drain thoroughly.

4. Add the drained pasta to the bowl, toss, and season generously with fine sea salt and pepper. Divide the pasta among warmed shallow soup bowls. Top with the remaining cheese. Serve immediately, passing the pepper mill.

■   Y i e l d :   4   t o   6   s e r v i n g s   ■

WINE SUGGESTION: With this pasta, we drank a young Dolcetto d'Alba, from the Piedmont. Its smoothness provided a perfect match for a dish that is quite delicate, despite the peppery flavor of the arugula.

Tagliarini with Lemon Sauce

Tagliarini al Limone

"The point of drinking wine is to get in touch with one of the major influences of Western civilization, to taste the sunlight trapped in a bottle, to remember some stony slope in Tuscany. . . ."

JOHN MORTIMER, RUMPOLE AND THE BLIND TASTING

All golden yellow with flecks of green, this dish always reminds me of sunshine and springtime. I first sampled it at the very aristocratic table of the Grand Hotel e la Pace in Montecatini Terme, the old-fashioned spa hotel in the hills of northern Tuscany. Since then, I've ordered it many times in restaurants and trattorias all over Italy. At home, I often make a single portion for myself as a quick, uplifting lunch or dinner, especially on a gray winter's day when it seems that one will never again see spring. The addition of parsley is essential, while cheese is optional. This is one pasta dish that demands good, fresh noodles, such as tagliarini, long homemade pasta that is slightly thinner than tagliatelle. Even the best-quality dried pasta won't do justice to the simple, elegant sauce.

4 tablespoons (2 ounces; 60 g) unsalted butter, at room temperature

1 cup (250 ml) heavy cream

¼ cup (60 ml) freshly squeezed lemon juice

Sea salt

1 pound (500 g) fresh tagliarini, tagliatelle, or fettuccine (page 126)

Grated zest (yellow peel) of 3 lemons

3 tablespoons fresh flat-leaf parsley leaves, snipped with a scissors

Freshly grated Italian Parmigiano-Reggiano cheese, for the table (optional)

1. In a skillet large enough to hold the pasta later on, combine the butter, cream, and lemon juice over low heat. As soon as the butter is melted, remove the skillet from the heat, cover, and set aside.

2. Meanwhile, in a large pot, bring 6 quarts (6 l) of water to a rolling boil. Add 3 tablespoons salt and the pasta, stirring to prevent the pasta from sticking. Cook until tender. Drain, leaving a few drops of water clinging to the pasta so that the sauce will adhere.

3. Transfer the pasta to the skillet, off the heat, and toss to blend. Add the lemon zest, and toss once more. Cover and let rest for 1 to 2 minutes to allow the pasta to thoroughly absorb the sauce. Transfer to warmed shallow soup bowls, shower with the parsley leaves, and serve immediately. Pass freshly grated cheese if desired.

■ Yield: 4 to 6 servings ■

WINE SUGGESTION: Although lemon is the dominant flavor here, it is a fresh flavor, and one that won't fight wine. Either white (a Sauvignon Blanc or an Orvieto) or red (Nebbiolo or Chianti) would be fine with this dish.

The Zest of Life

Zest is the dimpled paper-thin outer rind of any citrus fruit—lemon, orange, grapefruit, or lime—and contains the fruit's essential oils. Distinct from the thick white bitter peel that separates the zest from the fruit, zest is one of the world's most refreshing and versatile flavorings.

Lemons are the Italians' favorite citrus, and the bright, sparkling lemon flavor turns up regularly in pastas, desserts, and ices. While the majority of lemons come from the sunny southern climates, such as Sicily, lemons can be found as far north as Lake Garda, not far from the Swiss border. The appropriately named Lake Garda village of Limone boasts of terraced citrus groves stretched along the lake's shores, where the lemons grow under huge glass structures.

There are several ways to remove the zest of a citrus fruit, and each requires attentiveness, to avoid including the bitter white portion of the rind. Add zest to your cooking by:

■ scrubbing the whole fruit against the tiny holes of a small hand grater;

■ paring the outer rind from the fruit with a vegetable peeler and cutting the rind into very thin strips; or

■ using a zester, a tiny hand-held gadget the size of a vegetable peeler. A zester—my preference—shaves the outer rind in extremely thin, fine strips that result in an even, delicate flavoring.

Citrus should be zested just before it is added to other ingredients, for the flavorful oils will dry out as the zest comes in contact with the air.

■ ■ ■

Lasagne with Basil, Garlic, and Tomato Sauce

Liguria is the home of one of Italy's most famous sauces, pesto, that vibrant blend dominated by basil, garlic, and oil. And one of the sauce's most traditional uses is in this dish of lasagne, a far cry from the heavy, layered, baked version most of us are used to. Here, palm-sized rectangles of fresh or dried pasta are simply interlayered with the pungent sauce, making for a dish that's heavenly and oh so simple. I sampled this version one evening in a harborside trattoria in Santa Margherita.

Sea salt

6 ounces (180 g) fresh lasagne (page 126) (or substitute dried Italian lasagne—about 6 sheets)

1 recipe Basil, Garlic, and Tomato Sauce (page 262)

1. In a large pot, bring 6 quarts (6 l) of water to a rolling boil. Add 3 tablespoons salt and the lasagne, stirring gently to prevent the pasta from sticking. Cook fresh pasta until tender, dried pasta until tender but firm to the bite. (Dried lasagne will take 10 to 15 minutes cooking time.) Drain thoroughly but carefully, so the lasagne noodles do not break.

2. Place the drained lasagne on a cutting board and cut each piece in half crosswise. Place a rectangle of pasta in a warmed shallow soup bowl. Whisk the pesto to blend. Top the lasagne with a spoonful of the pesto and smooth out the sauce with the back the spoon. Add 2 more layers of pasta, topping each layer with a spoonful of pesto. Repeat for additional servings, until all the pasta and pesto have been used. Serve immediately.

■ Yield: 6 servings ■

WINE SUGGESTION: With pesto, I enjoy a simple Italian white, such as a Pinot Grigio, or, for a change of pace, a Tyrolean Riesling.

Tajarin with Rosemary-Infused Butter

Tajarin al Burro Aromatizzato

Endlessly soothing, this is a pasta I dream about when I'm really, really hungry. My husband and I sampled this one sunny day in May, at the Tre Gallini (Three Hens) trattoria in Turin. *Tajarin* is the Piemontese name for the delicate, tagliatelle-like strands of homemade pasta found all over the region. The sauce here is so simple and tastes so rich, it is totally deceiving. You really can't imagine that you are eating a sauce of nothing but a bit of butter and a pleasant dose of fresh rosemary. At Tre Gallini, they infuse the butter with rosemary and then strain the butter, making for a pasta that looks as though it has no sauce at all. After experimenting with several variations, I decided I liked the look and ease of the unstrained sauce. This is one recipe designed to stimulate your own creative juices: Try saucing the pasta with other fresh herbs, such as fresh summer savory or sage. Whichever herbs you use, mince them by hand: Machine-minced herbs never have the same fresh, vibrant flavor as those minced carefully by hand. Since the fresh pasta is the star here, be sure that it is top quality, be sure to cook it right, and don't overdrain it! Cheese is optional: Sometimes I prefer the sheer simplicity of the pasta, butter, and herbs. Other times, a light touch of freshly grated Parmesan is totally welcome. (Proportions can easily be adjusted for a dish that serves from one to eight people.)

5 tablespoons (2½ ounces; 75 g) unsalted butter

3 to 4 tablespoons minced fresh rosemary leaves (to taste)

Sea salt

1 pound (500 g) fresh tagliatelle or fettuccine (page 126)

*Freshly grated Italian Parmigiano-Reggiano cheese, for the table
(optional)*

1. In a skillet large enough to hold the pasta later on, combine the butter and rosemary over low heat. As soon as the butter is melted, remove the skillet from the heat and cover. Set aside to infuse for 5 minutes.

2. Meanwhile, in a large pot, bring 6 quarts (6 l) of water to a rolling boil. Add 3 tablespoons salt and the pasta, stirring to prevent the pasta from sticking. Cook until tender. Drain, leaving a few drops of water clinging to the pasta so that the sauce will adhere.

3. Transfer the pasta to the skillet, off the heat, and toss to blend. Cover and let rest for 1 to 2 minutes to allow the pasta to thoroughly absorb the sauce. Transfer to warmed shallow soup bowls and serve immediately, with cheese if desired.

■ Yield: 4 to 6 servings ■

WINE SUGGESTION: A dry white Gavi di Gavi or a smooth, young red Dolcetto d'Alba both are excellent matches for this elegant pasta dish.

Tagliatelle with Tricolor Peppers and Basil

Tagliatelle con Peperoni e Basilico

"Italy is so tender, like cooked macaroni—yards and yards of soft tenderness—ravelled round everything."

D. H. LAWRENCE, SEA AND SARDINIA, 1923

I sampled this dish one sunny Sunday July afternoon in Venice, at the charming neighborhood trattoria Antica Besseta. The small dining room was filled with a large family tucking into platters of fish and pasta, and the room was overflowing with sounds of happy times. I love the purity and simplicity of this colorful dish: golden pasta tossed with a festival of peppers, red, yellow, and green. The spiciness of the hot peppers adds a nice surprise. While the assortment of three colors of peppers is ideal, a mix of green and red peppers will do if yellow ones are not in the market. Whatever you use, the proportions should be half peppers, half pasta, with a gentle nudge of spiciness. This is a terrific first course for a dinner that might include roast poultry or meat.

2 red bell peppers

2 green bell peppers

2 yellow bell peppers

6 tablespoons extra-virgin olive oil

½ teaspoon crushed red peppers (hot red pepper flakes), or to taste

Sea salt

12 ounces (375 g) fresh tagliatelle or fettuccine (page 126)

¼ cup (60 ml) loosely packed fresh basil leaves

Freshly grated Italian Parmigiano-Reggiano cheese, for the table (optional)

1. Prepare the sauce: Wash the peppers, core them, halve them lengthwise, and remove the seeds and membranes. Cut each half lengthwise into pencil-thin slices. If the slices are extra long, halve them. Pour the oil into a covered deep 12-inch (30-cm) skillet. Place the pepper slices and crushed red peppers in the skillet, toss with the oil, and season lightly with salt. Cook, covered, over very low heat until very soft, about 40 minutes, stirring from time to time. You may need to cook these over diffused heat. The peppers should not burn or toughen. Be careful not to allow the juices to cook away: You want to retain as much cooking liquid as possible, for an unctuous sauce. (The peppers can be prepared several hours in advance and reheated at serving time.)

2. Meanwhile, in a large pot, bring 6 quarts (6 l) of water to a rolling boil. Add 3 tablespoons salt and the pasta, stirring to prevent the pasta from sticking. Cook until tender. Drain thoroughly.

3. Transfer the pasta to the skillet, off the heat, and toss to blend. Cover and let rest for 1 to 2 minutes to allow the pasta to thoroughly absorb the sauce. Transfer to warmed shallow soup bowls. Snip the basil with a scissors, sprinkling it over the pasta. Serve immediately. Pass freshly grated cheese if desired.

■　Yield:　4　to　6　servings　■

WINE SUGGESTION: At Antica Besseta we drank a local Venetian white. At home, try a good Soave Classico.

Tagliatelle with Tomato Sauce and Butter

Tagliatelle al Pomodoro e Burro

What could be simpler—or more universally appealing—than fresh pasta in tomato sauce? I sampled this soothing version one evening at Milan's small family restaurant Antica Trattoria Della Pesa. The dish leaves the realm of the ordinary by way of the very high quality of the fresh ingredients used. Guests are invited to give the pasta a last toss, allowing the sweet butter to melt into the tomato sauce, enriching the flavor and the fragrance. Since butter is the final touch here, make sure that it is fresh and hasn't been sitting around in the refrigerator absorbing assorted odors.

¼ cup (60 ml) extra-virgin olive oil

2 plump fresh garlic cloves, minced

Sea salt

One 28-ounce (765-g) can peeled Italian plum tomatoes in juice or one 28-ounce (765-g) can crushed tomatoes in purée

1 pound (500 g) fresh tagliatelle or fettuccine (page 126)

4 tablespoons (2 ounces; 60 g) unsalted butter, at room temperature

¼ cup (60 ml) fresh flat-leaf parsley leaves, snipped with a scissors

Freshly grated Italian Parmigiano-Reggiano cheese, for the table (optional)

1. Prepare the sauce: In an unheated skillet large enough to hold the pasta later on, combine the oil, garlic, and a pinch of salt, stirring to coat with the oil. Cook over moderate heat just until the garlic turns golden but does not brown, 2 to 3 minutes. If using whole canned tomatoes, place a food mill over the skillet and purée the tomatoes directly into it. Crushed tomatoes can be added directly from the can. Stir to blend, and simmer, uncovered, until the sauce begins to thicken, about 15 minutes.

2. Meanwhile, in a large pot, bring 6 quarts (6 l) of water to a rolling boil. Add 3 tablespoons salt and the pasta, stirring to prevent the pasta from sticking. Cook until tender. Drain thoroughly.

3. Transfer the pasta to the skillet, off the heat, and toss to blend. Cover and let rest for 1 to 2 minutes to allow the pasta to thoroughly absorb the sauce. Transfer to warmed shallow soup bowls, placing 1 tablespoon of the butter on top of each serving. Shower with the parsley and serve immediately. Pass freshly grated cheese if desired.

■　Y i e l d :　4　t o　6　s e r v i n g s　■

WINE SUGGESTION: Serve a full-flavored red that will enjoy the company of the tomato sauce, a good Chianti or Montepulciano d'Abruzzo.

Tagliatelle with Prosciutto and Artichokes

Tagliatelle al Prosciutto con Carciofi

A quick, substantial fresh pasta dish, this luxurious mixture of top-quality egg pasta, great ham and cheese, and just a hint of artichokes is one that always seems to take me out of a rut of serving the same, traditional pasta sauces. As with many pasta dishes, the sauce here is almost a background note to the delicious fresh egg pasta, homemade or store-bought. We sampled this one warm evening in May at the fourteenth-century Certosa di Maggiano, just outside of Siena.

2 tablespoons extra-virgin olive oil

1 medium tomato, peeled, cored, quartered, and cut into thin strips

Sea salt

2½ ounces (75 g) thinly sliced prosciutto, cut into matchsticks

2 Marinated Baby Artichokes Preserved in Oil (page 18), drained and cut into matchsticks

8 ounces (250 g) fresh tagliatelle or fettuccine (page 126)

About ¼ cup (1 ounce; 25 g) freshly grated Italian Parmigiano-Reggiano cheese, plus additional for the table

Freshly ground black pepper to taste

¼ cup (60 ml) fresh flat-leaf parsley leaves, snipped with a scissors

1. In a skillet large enough to hold the pasta later on, heat the oil over moderately high heat. When hot, add the tomato and a pinch of salt and cook until most of the liquid has evaporated, about 2 minutes. Add the prosciutto and artichoke hearts and cook just until the prosciutto begins to brown, about 2 minutes more.

2. Meanwhile, in a large pot, bring 3 quarts (3 l) of water to a rolling boil. Add 1½ tablespoons salt and the pasta, stirring to prevent the pasta from sticking. Cook until tender. Drain thoroughly.

3. Transfer the drained pasta to the skillet, tossing quickly and gently with 2 forks. Add the cheese, season generously with pepper, and toss again. Shower with the parsley and toss once more. Transfer to warmed shallow soup bowls and serve immediately, with additional cheese and freshly ground pepper.

■ Yield: Serves 4 as a first course, ■
2 as a main course

WINE SUGGESTION: Any good all-purpose red table wine—such as a Chianti Classico from Tuscany—would be good here.

Tagliatelle with Zucchini and Fresh Parsley

Tagliatelle con Zucchini al Prezzemolo

Golden egg noodles, set off with the contrasting color of bright, spring green zucchini and parsley—this dish makes me want to don white linen slacks and a big straw hat, in anticipation of a sparkling sunny day. This is one preparation that demands your complete last-minute attention—so that the pasta is perfectly cooked and drained, then immediately tossed with the zucchini so the zucchini doesn't turn soggy on the way to the dinner table. That said, the dish is a snap, and a marvelously quick first course, one that would go well with grilled baby lamb chops or a simple roast chicken. I sampled this one spring day at a back-street trattoria in Siena, La Vecchia Taverna di Bacco, where it was served with golden, fresh pasta.

1½ pounds (750 g) firm, fresh zucchini,
scrubbed and trimmed (do not peel)

⅓ cup (80 ml) extra-virgin olive oil

Sea salt

Freshly ground black pepper to taste

12 ounces (375 g) fresh tagliatelle or fettuccine (page 126)

1 cup (250 ml) fresh flat-leaf parsley leaves, snipped with a scissors

Freshly grated Italian Parmigiano-Reggiano cheese, for the table
(optional)

1. Quarter the zucchini lengthwise, then cut into thin slices.

2. In a 12-inch (30-cm) skillet, heat the oil over moderately high heat. When the oil is hot but not smoking, add the zucchini and sauté, shaking the pan vigorously to toss the zucchini, until the slices are lightly golden, 3 to 4 minutes. The zucchini should remain firm and crisp and should not turn soggy. Season generously with salt and pepper, and keep warm.

3. Meanwhile, in a large pot, bring 6 quarts (6 l) of water to a rolling boil. Add 3 tablespoons salt and the pasta, stirring to prevent the pasta from sticking. Cook until tender. Drain thoroughly.

4. Transfer the drained pasta to the skillet with the zucchini, and, using 2 forks, thoroughly toss the pasta to blend. Add the parsley and gently toss again. Taste for seasoning, transfer to warmed shallow soup bowls, and serve immediately. Pass freshly grated cheese if desired.

■ Yield: 4 to 6 servings ■

WINE SUGGESTION: A light white, such as a Sauvignon Blanc, a Soave, or a Verdicchio.

Tagliatelle with Fresh Crabmeat

Tagliatelle al Granchio

Rich, elegant, and sophisticated, this ivory-toned dish is hardly what one thinks of as typical trattoria fare. But when you consider I sampled it in Venice, the most elegant of Italian cities, it makes sense. This is a specialty of Nereo Volpe, owner of the Antica Besseta, a tiny, old-fashioned family trattoria filled with local folks with hearty appetites. I am amazed at the simplicity of this preparation, which requires just three main ingredients: great crabmeat, great pasta, great cream! It's exceptionally rich, so I find that two ounces of pasta satisfies, particularly served as a first course or a delicate main course.

Sea salt

8 ounces (250 g) fresh tagliatelle or fettuccine (page 126)

1 cup (250 ml) heavy cream

8 ounces (250 g) fresh lump crabmeat, drained, picked over, and flaked into generous bite-size pieces

¼ cup (60 ml) fresh flat-leaf parsley leaves or ¼ cup fresh basil leaves, snipped with a scissors

Freshly ground black pepper to taste

1. In a large pot, bring 3 quarts (3 l) of water to a rolling boil. Add 1½ tablespoons salt and the pasta, stirring to prevent the pasta from sticking. Cook until tender but firm. Drain thoroughly.

2. Meanwhile, in a saucepan large enough to hold the pasta later on, warm the cream over low heat. Add the crabmeat and stir gently. Heat just until the crabmeat is warmed through, about 1 minute.

3. Add the drained pasta to the saucepan. With 2 forks, toss the pasta gently over low heat to coat with the sauce. Transfer to warmed shallow soup bowls, sprinkle with the parsley or basil, and serve immediately, passing the pepper mill. (Traditionally, cheese is not served with this pasta.)

■ Yield: 4 servings ■

WINE SUGGESTION: This dish calls for a soft and golden copper-colored white from the Veneto, such as a Pinot Grigio, or a good Chardonnay.

In Search of the Perfect Crab

"Fresh" prepared crabmeat—as opposed to canned or frozen—comes from hard-shell crabs that have usually been steamed whole, in the shell. The meat is then picked from the shell and packed in containers to be sold as refrigerated fresh crabmeat. The prized morsel of crab is the backfin lump meat, often sold simply as lump crabmeat. While crab is generally an expensive delicacy, it's sweet in flavor, and about as "instant" a fresh food as you're likely to find. Many supermarkets and specialty shops now offer pasteurized fresh lump crabmeat that has an amazing six-month shelf life, assuming it's kept carefully refrigerated. Do not opt for canned crabmeat, which is almost as expensive as the fresh or fresh-pasteurized version, but usually rougher in texture and blander in flavor.

Tagliatelle with Arugula and Garlic Sauce

Tagliatelle con Rughetta

O ne warm summer evening in August, I wandered all over the little Lake Garda village of Lazise in search of the perfect spot for dinner. It became a challenge, sort of a test to prove whether or not I could divine a good restaurant simply by examining each spot from the exterior. I narrowed the choice down to three restaurants, and finally chose one along the harbor, where our group of four trenchermen made short work of the menu, devouring the dozens of antipasto specialties laid out before us, following up with varied platters of pasta. This was my choice, and one that has remained a favorite at home. Be sure to stem the arugula, or you will end up with a coarse sauce. Note that once "cooked," the normally peppery and pungent arugula flavor softens. Ideally, the dish should be prepared with top-quality fresh homemade pasta. Although the sauce is prepared in the food processor, the garlic should be minced by hand.

4 plump fresh garlic cloves, degermed and minced

Sea salt

2 cups (1 bunch, or about 1½ ounces; 45 g) loosely packed arugula leaves, washed and dried

1 cup (250 ml) heavy cream

1 pound (500 g) fresh tagliatelle or fettuccine (page 126)

½ cup (2 ounces; 60 g) freshly grated Italian Parmigiano-Reggiano cheese

1. In a food processor, combine the minced garlic, a pinch of salt, and the arugula, and process to a rough purée. Add the cream, and process to a rough sauce. Taste for seasoning. Set aside.

2. In a large pot, bring 6 quarts (6 l) of water to a rolling boil. As the water is heating, place a large serving bowl over the pot to warm the bowl. When the water is boiling, add 3 tablespoons salt and the pasta, stirring to prevent the pasta from sticking. Cook until tender but firm. Drain thoroughly.

3. Just before serving, transfer the arugula sauce to the warmed bowl and stir in the cheese, blending thoroughly. Add the drained pasta, and toss to blend thoroughly. Transfer to warmed shallow soup bowls and serve immediately.

■ Yield: 4 to 6 servings ■

WINE SUGGESTION: With this cream-based sauce, I relish an Italian white, such as a Chardonnay, an Orvieto, or a Frascati.

Tagliatelle with Porcini Mushroom Sauce

Tagliatelle alla Boscaiola

T his elegant, rich, woodsy-flavored pasta dish reminds me of a cold winter's night, a roaring fire, and an intimate group of very hungry friends or family. It's an ideal first-course pasta, followed by a simple roasted chicken and a crisp green salad.

1¼ cups (1½ ounces; 45 g) dried porcini mushroom slices

2 cups (500 ml) boiling water

½ cup (2 ounces; 60 g) pancetta or ham, cut into thin strips

1 shallot, peeled and minced

2 tablespoons extra-virgin olive oil

Sea salt

Freshly ground black pepper

1 cup (250 ml) heavy cream

Freshly grated nutmeg to taste

8 ounces (250 g) fresh tagliatelle or fettuccine (page 126)

Freshly grated Italian Parmigiano-Reggiano cheese, for the table (optional)

1. In a small bowl, combine the mushrooms and boiling water. Soak the mushrooms for at least 30 minutes, preferably for 2 hours. Using your hands, lift the mushrooms from the water, squeezing out as much water at possible. Unless they are perfectly clean, rinse the mushrooms under cold running water. If there are still pieces of soil embedded in the mushrooms, use a small knife to scrape off the soil. Pat them dry with paper towels. If the mushroom slices are unusually large, chop them coarsely. Transfer the mushrooms to a small bowl and set aside. Strain the soaking liquid—rich with porcini flavor—through several thicknesses of moistened cheesecloth. Set aside.

2. In a large skillet, combine the pancetta, shallot, oil, and salt and pepper to taste over moderate heat and cook until the shallot is golden and translucent, 3 to 4 minutes. Add the mushrooms and cook until the mushrooms become fragrant, 3 to 4 minutes more. Add the cream and nutmeg, cook for 2 minutes, then add the mushroom liquid. Cook over very low (diffused) heat until the sauce has reduced to the consistency of heavy cream, from 20 to 25 minutes, stirring regularly. Do not overcook, or the sauce will be too thick to coat the pasta.

3. Meanwhile, in a large pot, bring 6 quarts (6 l) of water to a rolling boil. Add 3 tablespoons salt and the pasta, stirring to prevent the pasta from sticking. Cook until tender. Drain thoroughly.

4. Add the drained pasta to the sauce in the skillet, and toss to blend. Remove from the heat, cover, and let rest for 1 to 2 minutes to allow the pasta to absorb the sauce. Transfer to warmed shallow soup bowls and serve immediately, passing freshly grated Parmesan cheese if desired.

■ Yield: 4 servings ■

WINE SUGGESTION: If you're in the mood for a white wine, drink a nicely oaky Chardonnay. If a red, go for a Chianti Riserva.

...

Lasagne with Tomato-Cream Sauce and Mozzarella

Pasta al Forno Trattoria Diva

One spring afternoon, after a long morning of interviews, we arrived at Trattoria Diva in the Tuscan village of Montepulciano in a state of nearly terminal hunger. It was almost 2 P.M., and after a fifteen-minute wait for a table to clear, we proceeded to order nearly every pasta on the menu. The slightly grumpy but always accommodating padróne scurried about, quickly mollifying us with a basket of thickly sliced Tuscan bread and a bottle of 1986 Montepulciano from the Fattoria del Cerro, a wine that's dark, deep, and serious. The daily special was, quite simply, pasta al forno, the most succulent and fresh lasagne imaginable: thin, thin sheets of fresh homemade egg pasta, interlayered with the lightest of tomato and meat sauces, and a simple topping of mozzarella. The dish made me want to rush home and dust off my pasta machine! We thought of opting for seconds, but then we saw the giant bowls of freshly picked cherries and knew it was time to surrender our forks.

After I did get home and dust off my pasta machine, I decided I best loved the version made with a fragrant tomato and cream sauce between the layers of fresh pasta. But any favorite tomato-based sauce can be used.

A few words of advice: This dish is somewhat long in the making, but not difficult and definitely worth the effort. In fifteen years of marriage, this was one dish that made me say to my husband, "You'd better appreciate all the work that went into this." He did, of course, and now there are regular requests for "fresh lasagne." The fact is, this dish just doesn't sing if it's made with thick, dried lasagne. Its charm is the delicate lightness of the pasta, layered with an equally delicate sauce. Note that the pasta will be easier to handle if it is cut into smaller rectangles.

Butter for preparing the baking dish

Grated zest (yellow peel) of 1 lemon

1 tablespoon extra-virgin olive oil

Sea salt

*1 recipe Fresh Egg Pasta (page 126), rolled as thin as possible and cut
into 3½- by 4½-inch (9- by 12-cm) rectangles*

1 recipe Tomato and Cream Sauce (page 259)

8 ounces (250 g) fresh whole-milk mozzarella, thinly sliced

1. Preheat the oven to 350°F (175°C; gas mark 4/5).

2. Butter a 9- by 14-inch (23- by 36-cm) baking dish and sprinkle with the grated zest.

3. Precook the lasagne: In a large bowl, combine 2 quarts (2 l) of cold water and the
oil. In a large pot, bring 6 quarts (6 l) of water to a rolling boil. Add 3 tablespoons salt
and slide 4 to 5 rectangles of pasta into the boiling water. Cover and cook for 1 minute.
Using a slotted spoon, retrieve the pasta rectangles and transfer to the bowl of cold
water for about 30 seconds, just to stop the cooking. (Do not use ice water, or the ice
will make holes in the pasta.) Immediately transfer the pasta squares to a clean, damp
cloth. Continue until all the pasta is cooked.

4. Spoon about ½ cup (125 ml) of the sauce over the bottom of the baking dish. Cover
with 4 slices of precooked pasta. Continue layering the lasagne and sauce in this manner
until all of the sauce and the pasta have been used, ending with a layer of pasta. Cover
the top with the mozzarella slices.

5. Place the baking dish in the center of the oven and bake until the cheese is melted
and the dish is fragrant and bubbling, about 20 minutes. Remove from the oven and
let sit for 10 minutes before cutting. Since this dish tends to release a fair amount of
liquid, it is best to serve with a slotted spoon.

■ Y i e l d : 6 t o 8 s e r v i n g s ■

WINE SUGGESTION: With the tomato and cream sauce, a pleasing white, such as a
Soave Classico, is nice.

Fettuccine with Butter and Parmesan

Fettuccine al Burro e Parmigiano

"Everything should be made as simple as possible, but not simpler."

ALBERT EINSTEIN

When I'm exhausted and hungry as a wolf, yet the pantry and refrigerator are nearly bare, this is the pasta dish that comes to mind. Soothing, filling, quick, and simple, this traditional trattoria dish is a winning late-night supper for one or for a crowd. It's best prepared with fresh pasta, but in a pinch, dried fettuccine or tagliatelle make respectable substitutes.

Sea salt

1 pound (500 g) fresh tagliatelle or fettuccine (page 126) (or substitute dried Italian tagliatelle or fettuccine)

8 tablespoons (4 ounces; 125 g) unsalted butter, at room temperature

2 cups (8 ounces; 250 g) freshly grated Italian Parmigiano-Reggiano cheese

Freshly ground black pepper to taste

1. In a large pot, bring 6 quarts (6 l) of water to a rolling boil. As the water is heating, place a large serving bowl over the pot to warm the bowl. When the water is boiling, add 3 tablespoons salt and the pasta, stirring to prevent the pasta from sticking. Cook fresh pasta until tender, dried pasta until tender but firm to the bite. Drain thoroughly.

2. Transfer the drained pasta to the warmed bowl, add the butter, and toss thoroughly. Add about half the cheese and toss again. Transfer the pasta to warmed shallow soup bowls and sprinkle with the rest of the cheese. Serve immediately, passing the pepper mill.

▪ Yield: 4 to 6 servings ▪

WINE SUGGESTION: I enjoy this dish with a full-bodied white, such as a Vernaccia di San Gimignano from Teruzzi & Puthod, or with a quality Sauvignon Blanc.

▪ ▪ ▪

Citrus-Infused Baked Tagliatelle

Pasta al Forno

Nine times out of ten, baked pasta is a big disappointment. Why? It's inevitably too dry, with burnt or overcooked sauce and dried-out pasta on the top, and a layer of undersauced and often undercooked pasta below. To ensure a deliciously moist baked pasta—a dish that can't be beat when it's fragrant and warm—do what you should always do in the kitchen: Pay attention to details! There's no secret to success here. Just be sure to take care to make a perfect white sauce, be certain that your sauce is not too thick, and don't overdrain the pasta once it's cooked. The best baked pasta—pasta al forno—I've ever sampled came from the kitchen of Pierro Giannacci at Le Quattro Stagioni ("the four seasons") in Florence.

I spent a morning with him and his staff in his tiny, super-busy kitchen, where varied pastas were boiling away, a chef was frying a mix of zucchini and artichokes, and coming from the oven was the warming fragrance of giant veal chops, roasting away. One of the day's specials was oven-baked pasta. Chef Giannacci's twist is to use fresh tagliolini (thin tagliatelle), layered in a large rectangular pan with a flavorful white sauce and a lovely meat sauce, all topped with freshly grated cheese. The finer egg pasta—either fresh or dried—takes better to baking and dries out less than traditional lasagne or penne.

The end result: a lovely, layered "sandwich" of pasta, moist with an herb-rich white sauce, rich with meat sauce, all accented by the wholesomeness of the Parmesan cheese.

Butter for preparing the baking dish

Grated zest (orange peel) of 1 orange

Sea salt

1 pound (500 g) fresh tagliatelle or fettuccine (page 126) (or substitute dried Italian tagliatelle or fettuccine)

3 cups (750 ml) warm Meat Sauce (page 268)

2 cups (500 ml) warm White Sauce (page 270)

2 cups (8 ounces; 250 g) freshly grated Italian Parmigiano-Reggiano cheese

1. Preheat the oven to 350°F (175°C; gas mark 4/5).

2. Butter a 9- by 14-inch (23- by 36-cm) baking dish and sprinkle with the grated zest. Set aside.

3. In a large pot bring 6 quarts (6 l) of water to a rolling boil. Add 3 tablespoons salt and the pasta, stirring to prevent the pasta from sticking. Cook until tender. Drain, leaving a few drops of water clinging to the pasta.

4. Add about one-third of the drained pasta to the baking dish in an even layer. Cover evenly with half of the meat sauce. Add another one-third of the pasta, and cover with all of the white sauce and about half of the cheese. Add the rest of the pasta and cover with the rest of the meat sauce. Sprinkle with the rest of the cheese.

5. Place the baking dish in the center of the oven and bake until the cheese is melted and the dish is fragrant and bubbling, 15 to 20 minutes. Remove from the oven. Serve immediately, spooning out the pasta with a very large serving spoon.

▪ Yield: 6 to 8 servings ▪

WINE SUGGESTION: A crisp white, such as Pinot Grigio.

For Citrus-Infused Baked Pasta or Rice

I crave the deep, lingering flavor of citrus zest, whether it be lemon, lime, or orange. One day while paging through an Italian cooking magazine, I found this tip on the letters-to-the-editor page: For more flavorful baked pasta dishes, rub your baking pan with butter, then sprinkle with grated lemon or orange zest. The final dish will be infused with the welcoming citrus flavor, giving a special twist to new dishes, as well as old favorites. Now, whenever I bake pasta or rice, lemon or orange comes first!

HOMAGE TO ITALIAN RICE

■

Creamy Italian Arborio rice deserves a menu of its own—a soup, a risotto, a dessert. Try a mature Gattinara or a Chianti Riserva with this menu.

MILANESE VEGETABLE SOUP
OSSO BUCO (BRAISED VEAL SHANKS WITH LEMON AND PARSLEY GARNISH)
SAFFRON RISOTTO
RISOTTO ICE CREAM

RICE AND

POLENTA

• • •

Lemon Risotto

Risotto al Limone

Creamy, pale yellow risotto is appealing cool weather fare, and the addition of flecks of fresh green herbs and lemon make for a dish that's very spring-like and refreshing. This version was inspired by Roberto Fontana at Milan's Casa Fontana, where twenty-three different risottos can be found on the menu at any given time. Remember three important rules for making perfect risotto: Do not add too much liquid at once; do not add more liquid until the previous addition has been absorbed; and stir, stir, stir.

About 5 cups (1.25 l) chicken stock, preferably homemade (page 272)

Sprig of fresh mint

Sprig of fresh rosemary

Sprig of fresh sage

Grated zest (yellow peel) of 1 lemon

4 tablespoons (2 ounces; 60 g) unsalted butter

1 tablespoon extra-virgin olive oil

2 shallots, minced

Sea salt to taste

1½ cups (270 g) Italian Arborio rice

3 tablespoons freshly squeezed lemon juice

½ cup (2 ounces; 60 g) freshly grated Italian Parmigiano-Reggiano cheese, plus additional for the table

1. In a large saucepan, heat the stock and keep it simmering, at barely a whisper, while you prepare the risotto.

2. Stem the fresh herbs. Combine the leaves with the lemon zest and, with a large chef's knife, chop finely. Set aside.

3. In a large heavy-bottomed saucepan, combine 2 tablespoons of the butter, the oil, shallots, and salt over moderate heat. Cook, stirring, until the shallots are soft and translucent, about 3 minutes. (Do not let the shallots brown.) Add the rice, and stir until the rice is well coated with the fats, glistening and semitranslucent, 1 to 2 minutes. (This step is important for good risotto: The heat and fat will help separate the grains of rice, ensuring a creamy consistency in the end.)

4. When the rice becomes shiny and partly translucent, add a ladleful of the stock. Cook, stirring constantly, until the rice has absorbed most of the stock, 1 to 2 minutes. Add another ladleful of the simmering stock, and stir regularly until all of the broth is absorbed. Adjust the heat as necessary to maintain a gentle simmer. The rice should cook slowly and should always be covered with a veil of stock. Continue adding ladlefuls of stock, stirring frequently and tasting regularly, until the rice is almost tender but firm to the bite, about 17 minutes total. The risotto should have a creamy, porridge-like consistency.

5. Remove the saucepan from the heat and stir in the remaining 2 tablespoons butter, the lemon zest and herbs, lemon juice, and the Parmesan. Cover and let stand off the heat for 2 minutes, to allow the flavors to blend. Taste for seasoning. Transfer to warmed shallow soup bowls, and serve immediately, passing additional cheese. Risotto waits for no one.

■ Y i e l d : 4 t o 6 s e r v i n g s ■

WINE SUGGESTION: Serve this with a pale, golden Vernaccia from the hilltop village of San Gimignano in Tuscany.

Risotto with Tomatoes and Parmesan

Risotto alla Cardinale

Festive, bright, and restorative, this is a perfect main-dish rice meal, named after the red color of the cardinal's robes. The recipe was shared with me by Chef Walter Tripodi of the restored monastery-inn La Frateria di Padre Eligio, in Cetona, in Tuscany.

About 4 cups (1 l) vegetable broth or chicken stock, preferably homemade (pages 274 and 272)

2 cups (500 ml) Tomato Sauce (page 256)

4 tablespoons (2 ounces; 60 g) unsalted butter

2 tablespoons extra-virgin olive oil

1 shallot, minced

4 bay leaves, preferably fresh

Fine sea salt to taste

2 cups (360 g) Italian Arborio rice

½ cup (2 ounces; 60 g) freshly grated Parmigiano-Reggiano cheese, plus additional for the table

1. In a large saucepan, combine the broth or stock and tomato sauce and keep the liquid simmering, at barely a whisper, while you prepare the risotto.

2. In a large heavy-bottomed saucepan, combine 2 tablespoons of the butter, the oil, shallot, bay leaves, and salt over moderate heat. Cook, stirring, until the shallot is soft and translucent, about 3 minutes. (Do not let the shallot brown.) Add the rice, and stir until the rice is well coated with the fats, glistening and semitranslucent, 1 to 2 minutes. (This step is important for good risotto: The heat and fat will help separate the grains of rice, ensuring a creamy consistency in the end.)

3. When the rice becomes shiny and somewhat translucent, add a ladleful of the simmering liquid. (The pan will sizzle as you add the liquid.) Stirring constantly, cook until the rice has absorbed most of the liquid, 1 to 2 minutes. Add another ladleful of the liquid, and stir constantly until all of the liquid is absorbed. Adjust the heat as necessary to maintain a gentle simmer. The rice should cook slowly and should always be covered with a veil of liquid. Continue adding ladlefuls of warm stock, stirring constantly and tasting regularly, until the rice is almost tender but firm to the bite, about 17 minutes total. The risotto should have a creamy, porridge-like consistency.

4. Remove the saucepan from the heat and stir in the remaining 2 tablespoons butter and the cheese. Cover and let stand off the heat for 2 minutes, to allow the flavors to blend and the rice to finish cooking. Taste for seasoning. Remove and discard the bay leaves. Transfer to warmed shallow soup bowls, and serve immediately, passing additional cheese.

■ Yield: 6 to 8 servings ■

WINE SUGGESTION: I like a mature red with this dish, such as a Gattinara, Barbaresco, or Chianti Riserva.

Eating Risotto

If you thought there was ritual involved in making risotto, just wait until you eat it! Italian etiquette even covers proper risotto consumption. The cooked risotto should always be mounded, steaming hot, in the center of warmed individual shallow bowls. As you eat the risotto, use a fork to push the grains of cooked rice out slightly toward the edge of the bowl, eating from the thinned-out ring of rice. Continue spreading from the center and eating around the edges in a circle. The mound in the middle will keep the risotto hot as you savor the just-right risotto around the rim. Some Milanese risotto-eating purists even advocate spoons instead of forks.

Saffron Risotto

Risotto alla Milanese

The traditional accompaniment to the delicately flavored osso buco, braised veal shanks, saffron risotto is one of the world's most elegantly beautiful dishes, seductive with its creamy texture, joyful with its hopeful golden hues. For simple meals, I often serve it as a main dish, the better to savor it all on its own. Here, go easy on the saffron: The color should be golden, the flavor faint with saffron. And be sure to use the best-quality saffron you can find.

About 5 cups (1.25 l) chicken stock, preferably homemade (page 272)

A pinch (about ¼ teaspoon) saffron threads

4 tablespoons (2 ounces; 60 g) unsalted butter

1 tablespoon extra-virgin olive oil

2 shallots, minced

Sea salt to taste

1½ cups (270 g) Italian Arborio rice

½ cup (2 ounces; 60 g) freshly grated Italian Parmigiano-Reggiano cheese, plus additional for the table

1. In a large saucepan, heat the stock and keep it simmering, at barely a whisper, while you prepare the risotto.

2. In a measuring cup with a spout, combine ½ cup (125 ml) of the hot stock and the saffron. Stir to infuse and set aside.

3. In a large heavy-bottomed saucepan, combine 2 tablespoons of the butter, the oil, shallots, and salt over moderate heat. Cook, stirring, until the shallots are soft and translucent, about 3 minutes. (Do not let the shallots brown.) Add the rice, and stir until the rice is well coated with the fats, glistening and semitranslucent, 1 to 2 minutes. (This step is important for good risotto: The heat and fat will help separate the grains of rice, ensuring a creamy consistency in the end.)

4. When the rice becomes shiny and partly translucent, add a ladleful of the stock. Cook, stirring constantly, until the rice has absorbed most of the stock, 1 to 2 minutes. Add another ladleful of the simmering stock, and stir regularly until all of the broth is absorbed. Adjust the heat as necessary to maintain a gentle simmer. The rice should cook slowly and should always be covered with a veil of stock. Repeat the procedure, stirring frequently and tasting regularly, until the rice is almost tender but firm to the bite, about 17 minutes total. Add the saffron stock at the end. The risotto should have a creamy, porridge-like consistency.

5. Remove the saucepan from the heat and stir in the remaining 2 tablespoons butter and the cheese. Cover and let stand off the heat for 2 minutes, to allow the flavors to blend. Taste for seasoning. Transfer to warmed shallow soup bowls, and serve immediately, passing additional cheese.

■ Yield: 4 to 6 servings ■

WINE SUGGESTION: I serve this, and the osso buco, with a fine Gattinara.

On Leftover Risotto

Should you find yourself with leftover risotto, prepare risotto al salto, a dish historically served in country inns. When travelers in a hurry were unwilling to wait the twenty-five to thirty minutes it took to create a risotto from scratch, innkeepers tossed already prepared risotto into a buttered or oiled frying pan and made it "jump," or *salto*, offering diners a quick, hot meal.

Orange, Sage, and Mushroom Risotto

Risotto Sforzesco

A combination of fresh and woodsy flavors—the orange zest and the wild mushrooms—makes for a dish that's not just zesty and perky from the first bite, but has a depth of flavor that wears well on the palate. Be sure to use fresh sage, and taste it first to make sure it does not have a strong, medicinal flavor. If you can't secure fresh sage, substitute parsley. This recipe was shared with me by Roberto Fontana, owner and chef of Milan's temple to risotto, Casa Fontana.

1 cup (1½ ounces; 45 g) dried porcini mushroom slices

5 cups (1.25 ml) boiling water

Grated zest (orange peel) of 1 orange

¼ cup (60 ml) fresh sage leaves (or substitute fresh flat-leaf parsley leaves)

4 tablespoons (2 ounces; 60 g) unsalted butter

1 tablespoon extra-virgin olive oil

2 shallots, minced

Sea salt to taste

1½ cups (270 g) Italian Arborio rice

3 tablespoons freshly squeezed orange juice

½ cup (2 ounces; 60 g) freshly grated Italian Parmigiano-Reggiano cheese, plus additional for the table

1. In a large bowl, combine the mushrooms and the boiling water. Soak the mushrooms for at least 30 minutes, preferably for 2 hours. Using your hands, lift the mushrooms from the water, squeezing out as much water at possible. Unless they are perfectly clean, rinse the mushrooms under cold running water. If there are still pieces of soil embedded in the mushrooms, use a small knife to scrape off the soil. Pat them dry with paper towels. If the mushroom slices are unusually large, chop them coarsely. Transfer the mushrooms to a small bowl and set aside. Strain the soaking liquid—rich with porcini flavor—through several thicknesses of moistened cheesecloth.

2. In a large saucepan, heat the mushroom liquid and keep it simmering, at barely a whisper, while you prepare the risotto.

3. Combine the orange zest and sage leaves and, with a large chef's knife, chop fine. Set aside.

4. In a large heavy-bottomed saucepan, combine 2 tablespoons of the butter, the oil, shallots, and salt over moderate heat. Cook, stirring, until the shallots are soft and translucent, about 3 minutes. (Do not let the shallots brown.) Add the rice, and stir until the rice is well coated with the fats, glistening and semitranslucent, 1 to 2 minutes. (This step is important for good risotto: The heat and fat will help separate the grains of rice, ensuring a creamy consistency in the end.)

5. When the rice becomes shiny and partly translucent, add a ladleful of the mushroom liquid. Cook, stirring constantly, until the rice has absorbed most of the liquid, 1 to 2 minutes. Add another ladleful of the simmering liquid, and stir regularly until all of the liquid is absorbed. Adjust the heat as necessary to maintain a gentle simmer. The rice should cook slowly and should always be covered with a veil of liquid. Repeat this procedure, stirring frequently and tasting regularly, until the rice is almost tender but firm to the bite, about 17 minutes total. About 2 minutes before the rice is cooked, add the mushrooms along with a ladleful of the liquid. The risotto should have a creamy, porridge-like consistency.

6. Remove the saucepan from the heat and stir in the remaining 2 tablespoons butter, the orange zest and sage, the orange juice, and cheese. Cover and let stand off the heat for 2 minutes, to allow the flavors to blend. Taste for seasoning. Transfer to warmed shallow soup bowls, and serve immediately, passing additional cheese.

▪ Yield: 4 to 6 servings ▪

WINE SUGGESTION: Serve this with a rich, dark Barolo, from the Piedmont.

Baked Risotto with Asparagus, Spinach, and Parmesan

Risotto Verde

I love preparing (as well as eating) this spring-inspired specialty of Ugo Salis, cook and owner of the no-frills Trattoria da Graziella, situated in the hills above Florence, in Maiano. We sampled this verdant, fragrant, and soul-satisfying baked rice as a side dish, part of a huge, multi-course Sunday lunch one warm August afternoon. At home, I usually make it a quick main dish, served with a mixed salad alongside. Note that here both the spinach and the asparagus are added raw. They cook up nicely along with the rice.

1 tablespoon extra-virgin olive oil

1 small onion, minced

Sea salt to taste

1 cup (180 g) Italian Arborio rice

2 cups (500 ml) vegetable broth or chicken stock, preferably homemade (pages 274 and 272)

4 cups (about 3 ounces; 90 g) loosely packed fresh spinach leaves, rinsed, dried, and finely chopped

10 thin spears fresh asparagus, rinsed, trimmed, and cut into thin diagonal slices

¼ teaspoon freshly grated nutmeg

½ cup (2 ounces; 60 g) freshly grated Italian Parmigiano-Reggiano cheese

1. Preheat the oven to 400°F (200°C; gas mark 6/7).

2. In a 1½-quart (1½-liter) saucepan, combine the oil, onion, and salt over moderate heat. Stir to coat with the oil and cook until the onion is soft and translucent, 3 to 4 minutes. Add the rice, stirring to coat with the oil. Add the chicken stock, spinach, asparagus, nutmeg, and salt, and bring just to a simmer over moderate heat. Stir in half the cheese. Transfer to a 1-quart (1-l) soufflé dish, and smooth out the top with the back of a spoon. Sprinkle with the remaining Parmesan. Cover the soufflé dish.

3. Place the soufflé dish in the center of the oven. Bake until the rice is cooked through and has absorbed most of the liquid, 35 to 40 minutes. The baked rice should be moist but not soupy. Serve immediately, as a vegetable side dish or a main dish.

■ Yield: 4 to 6 servings ■

WINE SUGGESTION: With this, sample a crisp Italian white: a Pinot Grigio, Galestro, or Orvieto Secco.

The Secrets of Arborio

The highly glutinous Arborio rice—the quintessential risotto grain—is grown in Italy's Po River Valley, which runs through the Piedmont, Lombardy, Emilia, and Veneto regions. This medium-grain rice produces a risotto that is creamy on the outside and al dente—firm to the bite—on the inside.

During cooking, proper risotto rice releases a starch that helps the grains to cling together without becoming sticky or glutinous, resulting in the characteristic creamy texture. Italian Arborio also has the ability to absorb great quantities of liquid without losing its shape and turning to mush. Even the best American short-grained rice cannot make the same claim.

• • •

Baked Risotto with Tomato Sauce and Pecorino

Risotto Rosso

One evening I found myself with some leftover tomato sauce and a small chunk of top-quality Italian sheep's milk cheese (pecorino). I immediately remembered Ugo Salis—owner of Trattoria da Graziella in the hills of Florence—talking about his baked rice with tomatoes and pecorino, a dish that pays homage to his native Sicily. So, here it is, in all its simple glory, a homey baked rice that goes well with roast chicken, or stands on its own with a mixed salad of greens and vegetables.

1 tablespoon extra-virgin olive oil

1 small onion, minced

Sea salt to taste

1 cup (180 g) Italian Arborio rice

1½ cups (375 ml) vegetable broth or chicken stock, preferably homemade (pages 274 and 272)

½ cup (125 ml) Tomato Sauce (page 256)

¾ cup (3 ounces; 90 g) freshly grated Italian sheep's milk cheese (pecorino), such as Romano

1. Preheat the oven to 400°F (200°C; gas mark 6/7).

2. In a 1-quart (1-l) heatproof baking dish, combine the oil, onion, and salt over moderate heat. Stir to coat the onion with the oil and cook until the onion is soft and translucent, 3 to 4 minutes. Add the rice, stirring to coat with the oil, and cook for 1 minute. Add the chicken stock and tomato sauce, and bring just to a simmer over moderate heat. Stir in half the cheese and smooth out the top with the back of a spoon. Sprinkle with the remaining cheese. Cover the baking dish.

3. Place the baking dish in the center of the oven. Bake until the rice is cooked through and has absorbed most of the liquid, 30 to 35 minutes. The baked rice should be moist but not soupy. Serve immediately, as a vegetable side dish or a main dish.

■　Y i e l d :　4　t o　6　s e r v i n g s　■

WINE SUGGESTION: With this, try a crisp Italian white, such as a Pinot Grigio, Galestro, or Orvieto Secco.

Tips for Better Risotto

■ Rice is highly porous, and quickly absorbs odors, many of them unwanted. Store rice with a few fresh and fragrant bay leaves in an airtight container in a cool location. For best results, use rice within one year.

■ Never rinse rice for risotto: You'll be washing away the highly desirable starch.

■ Allow the raw rice to cook in fat (butter or oil) for at least one minute, so the grains are well coated and nicely flavored, and do not stick.

■ Acid—wine or tomatoes, for example—inhibits rice's ability to take in water. You may need more liquid, and more time, when cooking with acidic ingredients.

Risotto with Bay Leaves and Parmesan

Risotto all'Alloro

I am a bona fide bay leaf lover. I have a huge pot of it growing at all times and use the fragrant, elegant leaf whenever and wherever it seems to make sense. I sampled this risotto at La Frateria di Padre Eligio in Cetona, in Tuscany, where Chef Walter Tripodi oversees the small restaurant on the grounds of the monastery. Rice easily absorbs any odors with which it comes in contact, so I always stuff a few fresh bay leaves into a new bag of rice and seal it carefully, then add another batch of fresh leaves when I prepare this ultimately simple and subtle dish. If you cannot secure fresh bay leaves, use the freshest of dried leaves you can find in your market. This risotto makes a nice first course when served with roast chicken or Parmesan-coated lamb chops (page 238).

About 5 cups (1.25 l) vegetable broth or chicken stock, preferably homemade (pages 274 and 272)

4 tablespoons (2 ounces; 60 g) unsalted butter

2 tablespoons extra-virgin olive oil

1 shallot, minced

4 bay leaves, preferably fresh

Sea salt to taste

2 cups (360 g) Italian Arborio rice

½ cup (125 ml) flowery white wine, such as a Vernaccia di San Gimignano

½ cup (2 ounces; 60 g) freshly grated Italian Parmigiano-Reggiano cheese, plus additional for the table

1. In a large saucepan, heat the broth or stock and keep it simmering, at barely a whisper, while you prepare the risotto.

2. In a large heavy-bottomed saucepan, combine 2 tablespoons of the butter, the oil, shallot, bay leaves, and salt over moderate heat. Cook, stirring, until the shallot is soft and translucent, about 3 minutes. (Do not let the shallot brown.) Add the rice, and stir until the rice is well coated with the fats, glistening and semitranslucent, 1 to 2 minutes. (This step is important for good risotto: The heat and fat will help separate the grains of rice, ensuring a creamy consistency in the end.)

3. When the rice becomes shiny and partly translucent, add the wine. Cook, stirring constantly, until the rice has absorbed most of the wine, 1 to 2 minutes. Add a ladleful of the simmering stock, and stir regularly until all of the liquid is absorbed. Adjust the heat as necessary to maintain a gentle simmer. The rice should cook slowly and should always be covered with a veil of stock. Continue adding ladlefuls of warm stock, stirring frequently and tasting regularly, until the rice is almost tender but firm to the bite, about 17 minutes total. The risotto should have a creamy, porridge-like consistency.

4. Remove the saucepan from the heat and stir in the remaining 2 tablespoons butter and the Parmesan. Cover and let stand off the heat for 2 minutes, to allow the flavors to blend. Taste for seasoning. Remove and discard the bay leaves. Transfer to warmed shallow soup bowls, and serve immediately, passing additional cheese.

■ Yield: 6 to 8 servings ■

WINE SUGGESTION: A pale golden Vernaccia from the hilltop village of San Gimignano in Tuscany.

Polenta

A long with pasta and rice, fluffy, golden cooked cornmeal, or polenta, is Italy's favorite starch. I love to serve it with roast meats and poultry, and never mind having some leftover polenta waiting in the refrigerator, ready to prepare grilled snacks. Here I offer two methods: The first, the traditional method, does require a bit of patience and attention but results in a superior product. The second method, cooking in a double boiler, results in a polenta that is quite delicious and a reasonable compromise.

1 quart (1 l) water

1½ teaspoons fine sea salt

1 cup (150 g) coarse-grained Italian yellow cornmeal

TRADITIONAL METHOD:

1. In a large heavy saucepan, bring the 1 quart (1 l) water to a boil over high heat. Add the salt and stir vigorously to create a vortex in the center of the water. Very slowly add the cornmeal in a thin, steady stream, stirring constantly with a whisk as you add the cornmeal, making sure that the water continues to boil. (Should any lumps form, press them against the side of the pot and they will disappear.)

2. Once all the cornmeal has been added, reduce the heat to low and stir constantly with a long-handled wooden spoon, bringing the mixture up from the bottom and scraping the sides of the pot. Continue to stir until the cornmeal forms a mass that pulls cleanly away from the sides of the pot, 40 to 45 minutes. Remove from the heat.

DOUBLE-BOILER METHOD:

1. Fill the bottom half of a large double boiler with water, adding as much water as will be needed to touch the bottom of the top half of the boiler. Bring to a simmer over moderate heat.

2. Pour the 1 quart (1 l) of water into the top half of the double boiler. On another burner, bring this water to a boil over high heat. Add the salt and stir vigorously to create a vortex in the center of the water. Very slowly add the cornmeal in a thin, steady stream, stirring constantly with a whisk, making sure that the water continues to boil.

3. Once all the cornmeal has been added, reduce the heat to low and stir constantly with a long-handled wooden spoon, bringing the mixture up from the bottom and scraping the sides of the pot, for 2 minutes.

4. Cover the top half of the double boiler and set it over the bottom half of the double boiler. Every 10 minutes, uncover and stir for 1 full minute, cooking until the cornmeal forms a mass that pulls cleanly away from the sides of the pan, about 1 to 1½ hours. (Between stirring times, keep the pot covered.)

SERVING METHODS:

■ To serve the polenta warm, in an attractive mound, rinse the inside of a 1½-quart (1½-l) stainless steel bowl with water. Pour the hot polenta into the bowl and let set for 10 minutes. Turn the bowl out onto a large round platter, and serve.

■ To prepare polenta ahead of time, for cutting into squares and broiling or grilling later on, line a 9- by 5-inch (23- by 13-cm) baking pan with plastic wrap. Pour the hot polenta into the pan and smooth out the top with a spatula. Let cool. Cover and refrigerate for up to 3 days.

To serve, remove the chilled polenta from the refrigerator about an hour before serving. Preheat a broiler or grill. Invert the polenta onto a cutting board and remove the plastic wrap. Cut the polenta into 3- to 4-inch (8- to 10-cm) rectangles or diamonds. To broil, place on a baking sheet and broil until lightly browned on each side, about 3 minutes per side. Alternatively, grill on a gas, electric, or charcoal grill for about 2 minutes per side.

■ Yield: 6 to 8 servings ■

● ● ●

Pilaf with Tomato Sauce, Porcini Mushrooms, and Parmesan

Riso con Funghi Porcini

I think it would actually be a toss-up as to which I could consume every day, rice or pasta. As much as I love risotto, I sometimes revel in the leisure of letting a dish cook away without constant attention, and it's on days like that that I turn to this special rice dish taught to me by Chef Pierro Giannacci at Le Quattro Stagioni in Florence. Here Italian Arborio rice is cooked like a pilaf, in that it is browned lightly in fats, then cooked, covered, atop the stove, with a blend of flavorful liquids. I love the depth of flavors in this dish, and the way the intensity of the dried mushrooms manages to penetrate the rice.

⅓ cup (½ ounce; 15 g) dried porcini mushroom slices

2 cups (500 ml) boiling water

1 tablespoon extra-virgin olive oil

3 tablespoons (1½ ounces; 45 g) unsalted butter

1 shallot, minced

Sea salt to taste

1½ cups (270 g) Italian Arborio rice

3 bay leaves, preferably fresh

1 cup (250 ml) chicken stock, preferably homemade (page 272)

2 cups (500 ml) Tomato Sauce (page 256)

¼ cup (60 ml) fresh flat-leaf parsley leaves, snipped with a scissors

¼ cup (60 ml) fresh basil leaves, snipped with a scissors

1. In a large bowl, combine the mushrooms and the boiling water. Soak the mushrooms for at least 30 minutes, preferably for 2 hours. Using your hands, lift the mushrooms from the water, squeezing out as much water at possible. Unless they are perfectly clean, rinse the mushrooms under cold running water. If there are still pieces of soil embedded in the mushrooms, use a small knife to scrape off the soil. Pat them dry with paper towels. If the mushroom slices are unusually large, chop them coarsely. Transfer the mushrooms to a small bowl and set aside. Strain the soaking liquid—rich with porcini flavor—through several thicknesses of moistened cheesecloth. Set aside.

2. In a large heavy-bottomed saucepan, combine the oil, 1 tablespoon of the butter, the shallot, and salt over moderate heat. Cook, stirring, until the shallot is soft and translucent, about 3 minutes. (Do not let the shallot brown.) Add the rice, and stir until the rice is well coated with the fats, glistening and semitranslucent, 1 to 2 minutes.

3. Add the bay leaves, the mushrooms and reserved mushroom liquid, the chicken stock, and tomato sauce, and bring just to a boil over high heat. Reduce the heat to a gentle simmer, cover, and cook until the rice is almost tender but firm to the bite, about 15 minutes total. The pilaf should have a creamy, porridge-like consistency, and the liquid should not be completely absorbed. Taste for seasoning. Remove the bay leaves.

4. Remove the pan from the heat, and stir in the remaining 2 tablespoons butter, the parsley, and basil. Transfer to warmed shallow soup bowls and serve immediately. (Cheese is not traditionally served with this dish.)

■ Yield: 4 to 6 servings ■

WINE SUGGESTION: With the heartiness of the mushrooms and the tomatoes, I enjoy a big wine, such as a Gattinara, from the Piedmont.

Bay Leaves: Grow Your Own!

I often feel as though I am waging a one-woman campaign to make fresh bay leaves fashionable. Why would anyone ever think that grayish-brown, dead, dried bay leaves could perk up a sauce? Particularly when fresh bay leaves grow so easily indoors, in window boxes, in pots on the balcony, or outdoors, in the earth.

With their distinctively fragrant, almost citrus-like aroma, fresh bay leaves add a singularly herbal, intense flavor to sauces and stews. The essence of the bay lies in its fragrant oils: Just try rubbing a fresh bay leaf between your fingers, then inhale deeply, and you'll become an instant convert.

Since it is the oil that actually infuses the sauce, the bay leaf instantly flavors quick sauces that cook in a matter of minutes. (Once the bay has done its job, the leaf should be removed: You don't want to feed yourself, or your guests, a mouthful of leaves.)

Since antiquity the evergreen shrub sweet bay—known as *laurus nobilis*—has been used to crown the heads of heroes. English myth suggests that bay leaves ward off disease, witchcraft, and lightning. In the Mediterranean region, bay leaf trees—often towering, bushy shrubs—grow to forty feet high. In Italy, bay trees often form a fragrant and protective hedge around country properties.

When grown in pots, the bay leaf plant requires minimal care: The plants are naturally pruned and trimmed by regular harvesting for the kitchen, and demand only a rich, well-drained soil and moderate sunlight. Bay trees will freeze in cold weather, but can be brought indoors during the colder months. While most recipes are miserly with bay, suggesting a single leaf, I often prepare an aromatic herb bundle consisting of a dozen or more bay leaves and thick bunches of thyme.

BREADS AND

PIZZAS

Basic Bread and Pizza Dough

Pasta per Pane e Pizza

This is my basic bread and pizza dough recipe, one I've developed over time, finding that it makes an incomparably moist, flavorful, and dependable dough. The fact that there is a very small amount of yeast, combined with the long, cool rise, makes for pizzas and breads that are not overly yeasty. I almost always have some in my refrigerator, for making last-minute pizza, focaccia, rolls, or bread. For best results, be sure to check the expiration date on your package of yeast and make sure it's still viable. The dough may be prepared with unbleached all-purpose flour, but bread flour will ensure a finer flavor and texture. (If you are in a hurry, the dough can be allowed to rise at room temperature, but the result will be less moist and flavorful.)

1 teaspoon active dry yeast

1 teaspoon sugar

1⅓ cups (330 ml) lukewarm water

2 tablespoons extra-virgin olive oil

1 teaspoon fine sea salt

About 3¾ cups (1 pound; 500 g) bread flour

1. In a large bowl, combine the yeast, sugar, and water, and stir to blend. Let stand until foamy, about 5 minutes. Stir in the oil and salt.

2. Add the flour, a little at a time, stirring until most of the flour has been absorbed and the dough forms a ball. Transfer the dough to a floured work surface and knead until soft and satiny but still firm, 4 to 5 minutes, adding additional flour as needed to keep the dough from sticking.

3. Transfer the dough to a bowl, cover tightly with plastic wrap, and place in the refrigerator. Let the dough rise in the refrigerator until doubled or tripled in bulk, 8 to 12 hours. (The dough can be kept for 2 to 3 days in the refrigerator. Simply punch down the dough as it doubles or triples.)

Proceed with the individual recipes for rolls and pizza.

■ Yield: Enough dough for 15 rolls or 4 small pizzas ■

All-Purpose Versus Bread Flour

While all-purpose flour is suitable for all types of baking, bread flour—with a higher level of protein—is preferred for breads. When the protein in flour is mixed with liquid, it forms gluten. And it is the gluten in flour that gives dough its resiliency and elasticity. Thus the higher the protein, the greater the gluten, and the better the bread.

Tips for Better Bread, a Crustier Loaf

■ Use a minimal amount of yeast: Too much yeast makes for a puffy, bloated loaf.

■ Let the bread rise slowly, two to three times. Each rise will give the bread additional character.

■ Begin baking in a very hot—500°F (260°C; gas mark 9)—oven to create a thick, dense, chewy crust.

■ Use a baking stone: It helps to create a dense and deeply colored loaf.

■ Spray the bottom and sides of the oven with water three to four times during the first six minutes of baking. The steam created by the spray will help give the dough a boost during rising, will improve the crust, and will give the loaf a lovely, finished sheen.

■ Cool the bread on a rack. Circulating air will cool it down more quickly and help maintain a crisp bottom crust.

■ Do not slice the bread until it has cooled for at least one hour. Slicing warm bread makes for a doughy loaf.

Rustic Whole Wheat Bread

Pane Integrale

"The vintage has begun here at San Gimignano. . . . On the roads the heavy farm carts drawn by two oxen are already lumbering from the vineyards to the fattoria, each fully loaded with tubs. It is a festal time. . . . The vineyards, till now so silent and empty, are echoing with laughter and sprinkled with happy people, men and women, boys and girls, and children too, from neighboring poderi, have come to help the gathering, not for pay or wages but in expectations of similar assistance in their turn. The contadino provides these helpers with bread, fruit, and thin wine through the long day."

EDWARD HUTTON,
SIENA AND SOUTHERN TUSCANY, *1955*

T his recipe makes a lovely, moist, and springy whole wheat bread, much like those I sampled all over Italy. Yes, the slow rise overnight in the refrigerator may seem long, but in the end, you'll be rewarded with a healthful, wheaty loaf. The use of a very small amount of yeast makes for a bread with the character of wheat, not yeast.

(continued)

1 teaspoon active dry yeast

1 teaspoon sugar

1⅓ cups (330 ml) lukewarm water

1 teaspoon fine sea salt

1½ cups (225 g) whole wheat flour

About 1½ cups (225 g) bread flour

1. In a large bowl, combine the yeast, sugar, and water, and stir to blend. Let stand until foamy, about 5 minutes. Stir in the salt.

2. Add the whole wheat flour a little at a time, stirring to blend after each addition. Add 1½ cups bread flour a little at a time, stirring until most of the flour has been absorbed and the dough begins to form a ball. Transfer the dough to a lightly floured work surface and knead until soft and satiny, about 5 to 10 minutes, adding additional bread flour as needed to keep the dough from sticking.

3. Return the dough to the bowl, cover tightly with plastic wrap, and refrigerate. Let the bread rise in the refrigerator until doubled in bulk, about 8 hours. (You can let the dough rise and then punch it down several times, for a more flavorful and finely textured loaf.)

4. The next day, remove the dough from the refrigerator, punch it down, and cover again with plastic wrap. Let rise at room temperature until about doubled in size, 2 to 3 hours.

5. Shape the loaf: Punch down the dough and knead it for about 30 seconds. Shape the dough into a tight rectangular loaf by rolling the ball of dough and folding it over itself. Place a large floured cloth in a large loaf pan or rectangular basket and place the dough, smooth side down, in the pan or basket. Loosely fold the cloth over the dough. Let rise at room temperature until doubled in size, about 1 hour and 15 minutes.

6. At least 40 minutes before placing the dough in the oven, preheat the oven to 500°F (260°C; gas mark 9). If using a baking stone, place it in the oven to preheat.

7. Bake the bread: Lightly flour a baking paddle or rimless baking sheet, and turn the dough over onto the paddle or sheet. Slash the top of the dough several times with a razor blade, so it can expand evenly during baking. With a quick jerk of the wrists, slide the dough onto the baking stone. Using a garden mister, generously spray the bottom and sides of the oven with water. Then spray 3 more times during the first 6 minutes of baking. (The steam created will help give the loaf a good crust and will give the dough a boost during rising.) Once the bread is lightly browned—after about 10 minutes—reduce the heat to 400°F (200°C; gas mark 6/7), and rotate the loaf so that it browns evenly. Bake until the crust is a dark golden brown and the loaf sounds hollow when tapped on the bottom, about 10 minutes more, for a total baking time of about 20 minutes. Transfer to a baking rack to cool. Do not slice the bread for at least 1 hour, for it will continue to bake as it cools.

■ Yield: 1 loaf ■

· · ·

Sardinian Parchment Bread

Carta da Musica

ITALIAN PROVERB:

"Give me eggs of an hour, bread of a day, wine of a year, a friend of thirty years."

As with all unleavened bread, this Sardinian flat bread is thin, crunchy, and irresistible. I've sampled this sort of dimpled, bumpy bread at trattorias all over Italy, and always go back for more. I particularly love it as a "salad" antipasto, served on a platter and showered with a mixed salad of cucumbers and tomatoes tossed with olive oil and vinegar. The dough should be rolled as thin as a *carta da musica*, or sheet of music paper. This cracker-like bread (which is also called pane carasau), is an obvious relative of other unleavened breads, such as matzo, Indian flat breads, and Armenian cracker bread. Because it will keep for a long time, it is the traditional bread of the shepherds, who take it with them while tending their flocks of sheep.

I know of few recipes in the world that make a cook feel so accomplished: Guests are always in awe of the fact that the bread is homemade. Actually, it is child's play. I prepare little "bread kits" in advance, mixing the flours and salt and storing them in zipper-lock bags. When I want to make a quick bread, I turn on the oven, prepare the dough, and within an hour's time, we're snacking on these golden, no-fat, crusty cracker breads.

I have baked carta da musica on a baking stone and on baking sheets with equally successful results. Parchment bread baked on a baking stone will puff up a bit more, but will not be measurably better than the bread baked on a baking sheet. A good heavy-duty rolling pin is helpful, though not essential.

2 cups (265 g) unbleached all-purpose flour

1 cup (180 g) fine semolina flour

1½ teaspoons fine sea salt

About 1¼ cups (300 ml) lukewarm water

1. At least 40 minutes before placing the dough in the oven, preheat the oven to 450°F (230°C; gas mark 9). If using a baking stone, place it in the oven to preheat.

2. In a large shallow bowl, combine the flours and salt. With your fingers, mix the ingredients thoroughly. Slowly add the water, stirring with a wooden spoon, until the mixture forms a soft dough. (You may not need to add all the water.) With your hands, work the dough into a ball. Transfer to a clean, floured work surface, and knead gently for about 1 minute. The dough should be firm and pliable, and not sticky.

3. Divide the dough evenly into 12 balls. Place the balls on a lightly floured surface and cover with a clean, damp cloth. Flatten each ball into a thick 4-inch (10-cm) pancake. Generously flour the work surface, and, with a heavy-duty rolling pin, roll each portion of the dough as thin as possible into an 8- to 9-inch (20- to 23-cm) round. These breads are meant to be rather roughly shaped. Thinness is more important than shape here: The dough should be thin enough to see your hand through it.

4. Place several rounds of dough on an ungreased baking sheet and place in the oven, or place on the baking stone with a baker's paddle. Bake just until the top of the bread is firm and lightly browned, 3 to 4 minutes. (Baking time will vary from oven to oven and will depend upon the number of breads placed in the oven. I find variations between 2 and 5 minutes, depending upon the oven. Watch the bread carefully, and don't leave the room to answer the telephone! It helps if you have an oven with a glass window.) With tongs or with your fingers, turn the bread over and bake until the other side is lightly browned, 3 to 4 minutes more. (The bread should be rather bumpy, puffy, and irregular, with occasional huge pockets full of air.) Transfer the bread to a wire rack to cool. Repeat the procedure with the remaining rounds of dough.

5. The bread cools almost instantly and can be served immediately. To serve, stack the breads in the center of the table or in a large basket. (The bread may be stored for 3 to 4 days, in a metal container or zipper-lock bag at room temperature.)

■ Yield: 12 breads ■

Sourdough Bread

Pane Campagnolo

For any cook who also loves bread and baking, there is no joy like perfecting the art of baking natural yeast, or sourdough, bread. It takes time, trial and error, patience and stick-to-itiveness, but the simple, slightly sour aroma of that loaf rising in your hot, steamy oven is enough to make you forgive it any anguish or frustration it may have caused.

This is a recipe I have worked on over the years, and it works for me and for others with whom I have shared the process. But each baker will find that perfecting and keeping the starter, and finding the right flour, the exact oven temperature, even the spot in the oven that produces the best bread, becomes a very personal affair.

My own habits change from month to month. Sometimes I bake this "pure," with just a single type of flour, and the same proportions of salt and water. Other times, I add olives or walnuts for a bread to pair with cheese. Or I add toasted pumpkin seeds, sunflower seeds, sesame seeds, or a bit of whole wheat or rye flour, alone or in tandem with other ingredients.

The point is to make it *your* loaf, *your* bread, the one with which you identify, and the one that fits into your schedule and life-style. I often like to prepare the bread at night, then bake it first thing in the morning, so the oven is heating as I sip my first cup of espresso.

Some helpful tips I've found over the years: Bread flour offers more consistent results than all-purpose flour. The starter remains more active, while with all-purpose flour it turns lifeless. Also, don't be impatient with the rising time. The bread will pay you back with flavor.

And when I slice the bread, toast it, and spread it with tuna mousse or tomato and artichoke sauce, or simply drizzle it with golden freshly pressed olive oil, I know no greater gastronomic high.

SOURDOUGH STARTER

1 cup (125 ml) water, at room
temperature

2 cups (270 g) bread flour, at
room temperature

FOR THE FINAL LOAF

3 cups (750 ml) water, at room
temperature

1 tablespoon fine sea salt

7 to 8 cups (945 g to 1 kg 80 g)
bread flour, at room
temperature

1. DAY 1 THROUGH 4: Prepare the starter: In a small bowl, combine ¼ cup (60 ml) of the water and ½ cup (70 g) of the flour and stir until the water absorbs all of the flour and forms a soft dough. Transfer the dough to a lightly floured work surface and knead into a smooth ball. It should be fairly soft and sticky. Return the starter to the bowl, cover with plastic wrap, and set aside at room temperature for 24 hours. The starter should rise slightly and take on a faintly acidic aroma. Repeat this for 3 days, each day adding an additional ¼ cup (60 ml) water and ½ cup (70 g) flour to the starter. Each day the starter should rise slightly, and it should become more acidic with time. (If it does not progress as described, and turns unpleasantly sour or greyish, toss it out and begin again, until you have a pleasantly fragrant starter.)

2. DAY 5: You are ready to make bread. Transfer the starter to the bowl of a heavy-duty electric mixer fitted with a flat paddle. Add about 1 cup (250 ml) of the water, and mix at the lowest possible speed until the starter is thoroughly blended with the water. Slowly add the remaining 2 cups (500 ml) of water and the 1 tablespoon salt and blend for about 1 minute to thoroughly dissolve the starter. The mixture should be very thin and very bubbly. Add the flour, a bit at a time, mixing at the lowest possible speed all the while. A slow, steady addition of flour will make for a dense, well-constructed loaf. Continue adding flour until the dough begins to form a loose but cohesive ball and the dough pulls away from the sides of the bowl. Knead at the lowest possible speed for about 5 minutes more.

(continued)

3. Form the loaf and reserve the starter: Pinch off a handful of dough, about 8 ounces (250 g), to set aside for the next loaf. Transfer this starter to a medium-size covered container (see Note). Shape the remaining dough into a tight ball by folding it over itself. Place a large floured cloth in a shallow bowl or basket—one about 10 inches (25 cm) in diameter works well—and place the dough, smooth side down, in the cloth-lined bowl or basket. Loosely fold the cloth over the dough. Set aside at room temperature for 6 to 12 hours. (You have a lot of flexibility here. A 6-hour rise is the minimum. The dough will rise very slowly, but a good loaf should just about double in size.

4. At least 40 minutes before placing the dough in the oven, preheat the oven to 500°F (260°C; gas mark 9). If using a baking stone, place it in the oven to preheat.

5. Lightly flour a baking peel or paddle (or a rimless baking sheet). Turn the loaf out onto the peel, and lightly slash the top of the bread several times with a razor blade held at an angle, so it can expand evenly during baking. With a quick jerk of the wrists, shuffle the bread onto the baking stone or onto a baking sheet. Using a garden mister, generously spray the bottom and sides of the oven with water. Then spray 3 more times during the first 6 minutes of baking. (The steam created will help give the loaf a good crust and will give the dough a boost during rising.) The bread will rise slowly, generally rising to its full height during the first 15 minutes of baking. Once the bread begins to brown nicely—after about 15 minutes—reduce the heat to 425°F (220°C; gas mark 8) and continue baking until the crust is a deep golden brown and the loaf sounds hollow when tapped, 30 to 45 minutes more (for a total baking time of 45 minutes to 1 hour). Transfer to a baking rack to cool. Do not slice the bread for at least 1 hour, for it will continue to bake as it rests. The bread should remain deliciously fresh for 3 to 4 days.

■ Yield: 1 loaf ■

NOTE: After you have made your first loaf and have saved the starter, begin at Step 2 for subsequent loaves. Proceed normally through the rest of the recipe, always remembering to save about 8 ounces (250 g) of the starter. The starter may be stored at room temperature (in a covered plastic container) for 1 or 2 days, or refrigerated for up to 1 week. If not using the starter regularly, reactivate it once a week by thoroughly mixing in ¼ cup (60 ml) of water and ½ cup (70 g) of flour. Do not use more than 8 ounces (250 g) of starter per loaf. (If you find you can't bake bread every week and you end up with excess starter, offer the excess to a friend, add it to a yeast dough, or—as a last resort—discard it.) If the starter has been refrigerated, remove it from the refrigerator at least 2 hours before preparing the dough. I successfully freeze the starter, thaw it at room temperature, then reactivate it over a 2-day period.

Italian Slipper Bread

Ciabatta

C iabatta—the flat, airy, puffy, light loaf known as Italian slipper bread—is ideal for those who want great flavor in a hurry. I often make it in the morning and have it ready for lunchtime. Once you've made ciabatta, you'll make it again and again, for it fills a lot of our requirements for a good homemade bread: It's got a golden but light crust, with a soft and moist interior. It's multipurpose in that it's great as is or toasted. The bread itself may not fit the portrait of the picture-perfect loaf, for the dough is so soft and batter-like, it does not resemble other yeast doughs of our acquaintance. And the final loaf may not rise to more than 2 inches (5 cm).

Ciabatta really does need to be made in a heavy-duty mixer, unless you are willing to stand and beat with a wooden spoon for about twenty minutes to get all that gluten working and turn the mixture into a highly elastic dough. Note that the dough is too sticky and soft to let rise in a traditional basket. I prefer to give the dough a single rise on a piece of cornmeal-dusted waxed paper, then turn it onto a baking stone for baking. My favorite memories of this bread come from two weeks we once spent at Lake Garda: Each morning we would walk to town for the makings of lunch, then take the long trek back up the hill home, picking bay leaves from high hedges along the road and clutching our ciabatta under our arms.

Cornmeal for dusting

1 teaspoon active dry yeast

1 teaspoon sugar

2 cups (500 ml) lukewarm water

1½ teaspoons fine sea salt

About 4 cups (530 g) bread flour

1. Place a piece of waxed paper on a baking sheet. Dust it with cornmeal and set aside.

2. In the bowl of a heavy-duty electric mixer fitted with a paddle, combine the yeast, sugar, and water, and stir to blend. Let stand until foamy, 5 to 10 minutes. Stir in salt.

3. Slowly add the flour to the mixing bowl in general additions, stirring well after each addition. Mix until all of the flour has been absorbed, 1 to 2 minutes. (The dough will not form a ball.) Knead at the lowest speed for about 7 minutes, or just until the dough cleans the bowl and forms an elastic mass around the paddle.

4. Using a pastry scraper, transfer the dough (it will be loose, and stringy with gluten) to the waxed paper. Let it spread out in a rectangular mass. Cover with a clean cloth and let rise at room temperature until doubled and puffy, about 2 hours.

5. At least 40 minutes before baking, preheat the oven to 500°F (260°C; gas mark 9). If using a baking stone, place it in the oven to preheat. If you do not have a baking stone, preheat a baking sheet.

6. Using 2 heavy oven mitts, remove the baking stone, or the baking sheet, from the oven. Invert the dough onto the baking stone or baking sheet. Inevitably, some of the moist dough will stick to the waxed paper, despite the cornmeal dusting. Use a pastry scraper to peel away the dough. At this point the dough will look like a rather unpromising mass. Don't despair. Return the baking stone or sheet and dough to the oven. Using a garden mister, generously spray the bottom and sides of the oven with water. Then spray 3 more times during the first 6 minutes of baking. (The steam created will help give the loaf a good crust and will give the dough a boost during rising.) Once the bread has risen slightly and is a nice golden brown—about 10 minutes—reduce the heat to 425°F (220°C; gas mark 8). Continue baking until the crust is a deep, golden brown and the loaf sounds hollow when tapped on the bottom, 25 to 30 minutes total. Transfer to a baking rack to cool. Do not slice the bread for at least 1 hour, for it will continue to bake as it rests. Store the bread in a paper, cloth, or plastic bag for up to 3 days. It is delicious toasted.

▪ Yield: 1 loaf ▪

Individual Olive Rolls

Pane alle Olive

One sunny August afternoon, we lunched on the terrace of Il Vescovino, a white, pristine little restaurant set off a narrow, meandering street in the village of Panzano in Chianti, and luxuriated in the spectacular, slumber-inducing view of the Tuscan hillsides. After an all-morning auto trip, the restaurant offered a welcoming sense of lushness and country calm as we sat on the hazelnut tree–shaded terrace facing a landscape filled with jolts of blue, yellow, green, and red. The inevitable Tuscan haze lent a sense of softness and roundness that was instantly comforting. From the brief handwritten menu we selected a simple homemade pasta dressed with melted butter flavored with lemon, served with delicious homemade rolls, fresh from the oven. To our surprise and delight, they were studded with rich chunks of pitted black olives. I can't offer you that afternoon or the view, but hope that you'll create your own sense of the country when you prepare these at home, enjoying the rich olive flavor that permeates the small golden breads.

1 recipe Basic Bread and Pizza Dough (page 178),
prepared through Step 3

About 30 salt-cured black olives, such as Italian Gaeta or French Nyons
olives (see page 280), pitted and halved

Cornmeal, for dusting

1. Three hours before you plan to bake the rolls, remove the dough from the refrigerator. Punch down the dough and let it rise until about doubled in size, 2 to 3 hours.

2. Preheat the oven to 450°F (230°C; gas mark 9).

3. Divide the dough evenly into 15 portions, each weighing about 2 ounces (60 g). Press several olive halves into each portion of dough and shape each portion into a neat round, pulling the dough around itself to form a tight ball. Place the balls of dough on a baking sheet dusted with cornmeal. Cover with a clean towel and let rise for 30 minutes.

4. Place the rolls on the baking sheet in the center of the oven. Using a garden mister, generously spray the bottom and sides of the oven with water. Then spray 3 more times during the first 6 minutes of baking. (The steam created will give the dough a boost during rising and will help give the roll a good crust.) Bake until the rolls are a deep golden brown, 20 to 25 minutes, turning the baking sheet from time to time for even browning.

5. Remove the rolls from the oven and transfer to a rack to cool. The rolls should be consumed the day they are prepared.

■ Yield: 15 rolls ■

VARIATION: In place of olives, you may wish to fill these light little rolls with freshly chopped rosemary or leaves of fresh thyme.

Pizza with Red Onions, Rosemary, and Hot Pepper

Pizza Fiamma

One Sunday afternoon in January, we reserved a table at the modern, lively, family-style pizzeria Il Mozzo, in Milan. The nondescript pizzeria was bustling with large multigeneration families, all feasting on different fare. The children drank Coke and the parents sipped beer or wine, while salads, pizzas, and steaming bowls of pasta were rushed by. We devoured a variety of luscious pizzas, including this thin-crusted version topped with slices of red onions marinated in oil, rosemary, and hot red pepper flakes. The name—*fiamma*, or flame—comes from the fact that the cooked onions resemble bright red flames. I find that the unleavened dough for Sardinian Parchment Bread works great as a thin-crusted pizza.

4 small red onions (about 10 ounces/300 g total), sliced into very thin rings

½ cup (125 ml) extra-virgin olive oil

¼ teaspoon fine sea salt

½ teaspoon crushed red peppers (hot red pepper flakes), or to taste

¼ cup (60 ml) fresh rosemary leaves, finely minced

1 recipe Sardinian Parchment Bread (page 184)

1. In a large bowl, combine the onions, oil, salt, crushed red peppers, and rosemary. Stir to coat the onions with oil and to distribute the herbs and spices evenly. Set aside to marinate for at least 1 hour, or up to 4 hours. The marinating will soften the flavor of the onions and will give the topping a more finished flavor.

2. At least 40 minutes before placing the pizza in the oven, preheat the oven to 450°F (230°C; gas mark 9). If using a baking stone, place it in the oven to preheat.

3. Divide the dough evenly into 4 balls, and flatten each ball into a thick 4-inch (10-cm) pancake. On a generously floured work surface, roll each portion of the dough into an even 8-inch (20-cm) round.

4. Place the rounds of dough on a baking sheet or a baking stone. Spoon the onion topping onto the dough, spreading it out evenly with the back of the spoon. Bake until the dough is crusty and browned and the onions are sizzling, about 10 minutes. Serve immediately.

■ Yield: 4 servings ■

WINE SUGGESTION: Any drinkable red would do here, such as a good-quality Chianti.

Pizza Five Ways

In traveling throughout Italy, the finest pizzas I sampled were the most classic: thin, moist, flavorful dough topped frugally and simply with top-quality ingredients. The following are suggestions for classic Italian pizza.

Tomato and Mozzarella Pizza/Pizza Margherita

Brush the dough with oil, then top, in concentric circles, with a single, slightly overlapping layer of thin, half-moon slices of tomato and mozzarella. Drizzle with oil and sprinkle with crumbled leaf oregano. After baking, drizzle with oil. A few torn leaves of fresh basil can also be added after baking.

White Pizza/Pizza Bianca

Brush the dough with oil, sprinkle with freshly grated Italian Parmigiano-Reggiano cheese, and top with wedges of drained marinated artichokes. Drizzle with oil before baking.

Vegetarian Pizza/Pizza Vegetariana

Brush the dough with oil, then top, in concentric circles, with a single, slightly overlapping layer of thin slices of tomato, eggplant, and mozzarella. Sprinkle with dried leaf oregano.

Four Seasons' Pizza/Pizza alle Quattro Stagioni

Brush the dough with a thin layer of tomato sauce, and sprinkle with strips of prosciutto and slices of fresh mushrooms tossed in olive oil, slices of marinated artichokes, and halved and pitted black olives.

Tomato, Caper, Olive, and Anchovy Pizza/Pizza Marinara

Brush the dough with a thin layer of tomato sauce, and sprinkle with rinsed and drained capers, halved and pitted black olives, minced anchovies, fine sea salt, and freshly ground black pepper.

TO ASSEMBLE AND BAKE THE PIZZAS:

1 recipe Basic Bread and Pizza Dough (page 178)
Coarse cornmeal for dusting

1. At least 40 minutes before placing the assembled pizzas in the oven, preheat the oven to 500°F (260°C; gas mark 9). If using a baking stone, preheat it.

2. Punch down the prepared dough and divide it evenly into 4 pieces. Shape each piece into a ball. On a lightly floured surface, roll each ball of dough into an 8-inch (20-cm) round.

3. Sprinkle a wooden pizza peel (or a baking sheet) with coarse cornmeal and place the rounds of dough on the peel or sheet. Working quickly to keep the dough from sticking, assemble the pizzas.

4. Slide the pizzas off the peel and onto the baking stone (or place the baking sheet on a rack in the oven). Bake until the dough is crisp and golden, 10 to 15 minutes.

5. Remove from the oven, transfer to a cutting board, and cut into wedges. Serve immediately.

■ Yield: Four 8-inch pizzas ■

Tips for Better Pizza

■ To ensure a fine flavor and better texture, use bread flour when preparing pizza dough. Remember that in pizza, the crust should be the star, the topping simply an accent.

■ For a moist and flavorful dough, let it rise slowly, several times, preferably overnight in the refrigerator. Soft, moist dough makes for a light and crispy crust.

■ Keep the topping simple and light in weight: Try to limit yourself to three to five top-quality ingredients.

■ For an even flavor, coat the dough with a thin layer of either oil or sauce before assembling.

■ Toss any ingredients that tend to dry out in baking—such as sliced fresh mushrooms or strips of prosciutto—with oil a few minutes before assembling the pizza.

■ Be prepared: Arrange all topping ingredients in a series of small bowls, with the ingredients already chopped, sliced, or drained, so that pizza assembly is leisurely and fun, not frantic.

■ Distribute toppings evenly, so that each bite of pizza contains a bit of each flavor. Leave a margin around the edges to form a crust and to keep toppings from seeping out onto the baking stone.

■ Preheat the oven to its highest temperature at least 40 minutes before baking.

■ Bake on a baking stone. Additionally, you may want to use a wooden peel to slide the pizza into the oven, a metal peel for retrieving it from the oven.

■ If you want crisp crust, eat pizza hot. The crust will soften as it sits after baking.

FISH AND
SHELLFISH

Spicy Squid Salad

Insalata di Calamari

V ariations of this spicy, refreshing salad show up often on antipasto tables all over Italy. Personally, I can make a meal out of this, as long as there is plenty of crusty bread for absorbing the sauce, and a chilled white wine, such as a Pinot Grigio or Orvieto. Just make sure your squid is perfectly fresh (it should have almost no odor—only a "fresh" one). And it should be springy and just pleasantly chewy once cooked. Make the salad as hot as you like, but don't let the red pepper overwhelm it. What I love most about this salad is the texture: the pleasant chewiness of the squid, the crunch of the celery, the softness of the green olives. You might even consider this salad a contender for the Italian flag food award: the white of the squid, the red of the peppers, the green of the olives.

⅔ cup (150 ml) extra-virgin olive oil

⅓ cup (80 ml) freshly squeezed lemon juice, or to taste

4 plump fresh garlic cloves, degermed and minced

¾ teaspoon crushed red peppers (hot red pepper flakes), or to taste

4 ribs celery hearts with leaves, minced

20 drained pimento-stuffed green olives, quartered crosswise

2 pounds (1 kg) very fresh squid

Sea salt

1. In a medium-size bowl, stir together the oil, lemon juice, garlic, and crushed red pepper. Stir in the celery and olives. Taste for seasoning. Set aside.

2. Clean the squid: Rinse and drain thoroughly. Slice off the tentacles just above the eyes. Squeeze out and discard the hard little beak just inside the tentacles at the point where they join the head. Pull out the innards and the cuttlebone, or quill, from the body and discard. Do not worry about removing the skin, which is edible. Slice the squid bodies crosswise into ¼-inch rings. Cut the tentacles in half lengthwise. Rinse the squid again and drain thoroughly.

3. In a large saucepan, bring 3 quarts (3 l) of water to a rolling boil. Add 2 tablespoons salt. Add the squid rings and tentacles and cook just until they turn opaque—not more than 1 minute, or they will toughen. (I usually begin tasting the squid about 30 seconds after it has hit the water.) Drain but do not rinse: Hot squid will absorb the sauce better. Transfer the hot squid to the olive dressing and toss to coat. Taste for seasoning. Cover and refrigerate for at least 3 hours, or overnight.

4. At serving time, taste for seasoning. Serve as part of an antipasto platter, or on small salad plates as a first course, accompanied by plenty of crusty bread.

Yield: 6 servings as a
first course

WINE SUGGESTION: With this, try a crisp Italian white, such as Pinot Grigio or Orvieto.

Fried Calamari

Calamari Fritti

A quick and delicious first course, these tiny fried calamari can be found in trattorias all over Italy, and are a particular favorite along the coastline. I like using a light semolina flour here, for it makes a very rustic, crispy, golden coating. If you do not have semolina on hand, use superfine flour for an even more refined coating. Be sure to soak the squid in ice water for at least ten minutes before cooking so the shock of the cold against the heat of the oil stops the squid from absorbing the fat and they remain pure in flavor.

1 pound (500 g) very fresh squid, or calamari

¾ cup (100 g) semolina flour or superfine flour, such as Wondra

Fine sea salt

1 to 1½ quarts (1 to 1.5 l) peanut or sunflower oil, for deep-frying

Lemon wedges, for garnish

1. Clean the squid: Rinse and drain thoroughly. Slice off the tentacles just above the eyes. Squeeze out and discard the hard little beak just inside the tentacles at the point where they join the head. Pull out the innards and the cuttlebone, or quill, from the body and discard. The mottled red skin is edible, though it may be removed if desired. Slice the squid bodies crosswise into ¼-inch (½-cm) rings. Cut the tentacles in half lengthwise. Rinse the squid again and drain thoroughly. Place in a large bowl of ice water for at least 10 minutes before cooking.

2. In a clean paper or plastic bag, combine the flour and 1 teaspoon salt and shake to blend.

3. Preheat the oven to 200°F (100°C; gas mark 1).

4. Pour the oil into a wide 6-quart (6-1) saucepan, or use a deep-fat fryer. (The oil should be at least 2 inches [5 cm] deep.) Place a deep-fry thermometer in the oil and heat the oil to 375°F (190°C).

5. Drain the squid and dry thoroughly with a clean towel. Dip a handful of squid into the bag of flour and shake to coat with flour. Transfer the coated squid to a fine-mesh sieve and shake off excess flour. Carefully drop the squid by small handfuls into the hot oil. Cook until lightly browned, 1 to 2 minutes. With a wire skimmer, lift them from the oil, drain, and transfer to paper towels. Immediately season with sea salt, then place in the oven—with the door slightly ajar—to keep warm. Continue frying until all of the squid are cooked, allowing the oil to return to 375°F (190°F) each time before adding another batch. Serve immediately, with lemon wedges.

■ Yield: 4 servings as a first course ■

WINE SUGGESTION: This dish makes me think of Venice, and so why not a light white Sauvignon Blanc, such as one from Italy's northeast, Friuli-Venezia Giulia?

Shrimp with Garlic, Oil, and Hot Peppers

Scampi alla Veneziana

Venice is a haven for fish and shellfish, and this simple and beautiful dish is typical of the specialties found in waterside trattorias throughout that magic city. Pink, fresh, and glistening, this is a glorious dish, made for sharing at the table, along with crusty bread for soaking up the garlic-rich sauce, and a nicely chilled white wine, such as a Pinot Grigio. I like to serve it as a first course, followed by a simple grilled or roasted chicken with potatoes and Garlic Mayonnaise (page 275).

16 to 20 (about 1 pound; 500 g) large shrimp, in their shells

½ cup (125 ml) extra-virgin olive oil

4 plump fresh garlic cloves, minced

2 teaspoons fresh thyme leaves

¼ teaspoon crushed red peppers (hot red pepper flakes), or to taste

Coarse sea salt

¼ cup (60 ml) fresh flat-leaf parsley leaves, snipped with a scissors

1. Rinse the shrimp, pat them dry, and set aside. In a skillet large enough to hold all the shrimp in a single layer, heat the oil over moderately high heat. When the oil is hot but not smoking, add the garlic, thyme, crushed red peppers, and shrimp. Toss to coat with oil, and cook, stirring occasionally, just until the shrimp are pink, 4 to 5 minutes.

2. Remove the pan from the heat and, with a slotted spoon, transfer the shrimp to a warmed serving platter or to warmed individual plates. Pour the sauce over the shrimp, sprinkle lightly with coarse salt, and shower with the parsley. Serve immediately, offering a finger bowl and an extra napkin for each guest.

■ Yield: 4 servings as a first course ■

WINE SUGGESTION: Try a nicely chilled Pinot Grigio or a Chardonnay.

MEMORIES OF VENICE

■

The elegance and the subtlety of Venice are reflected in the city's food, which displays a great sense of grace and prosperity. Make the wine a crisp white Sauvignon from the Veneto.

MIXED FRIED FISH
TAGLIATELLE WITH FRESH CRABMEAT
TIRAMSÙ (COFFEE AND MASCARPONE LADYFINGER CREAM)

Baked Swordfish with Tomatoes and Green Olives

Pesce Spada alla Marinara

S wordfish—known as *pesce spada* in Italian—is a popular Mediterranean fish, and takes well to baking with tomatoes and salty ingredients such as olives. With its off-white, sometimes pinkish, flesh and fine grain, swordfish is a firm, medium-fat fish most often cut into steaks for grilling or for baking. This uncomplicated, distinctly Italian dish can also be prepared with tuna steaks.

3 tablespoons extra-virgin olive oil

1 fresh swordfish or tuna steak, cut ¾ inch (2 cm) thick (about 1 pound; 500 g)

Sea salt and freshly ground black pepper to taste

1 small onion, minced

1 rib celery, cut into thin slices

One 28-ounce (765-g) can peeled Italian plum tomatoes in juice or one 28-ounce (765-g) can crushed tomatoes in purée

¼ teaspoon crushed red peppers (hot red pepper flakes), or to taste

⅓ cup (80 ml) drained pitted green olives

1. Preheat the oven to 450°F (230°C; gas mark 9).

2. In a large skillet, heat the oil over moderately high heat until hot but not smoking. Add the swordfish and brown lightly, 2 to 3 minutes per side, seasoning each side with salt and pepper after browning. Using a large flat spatula, transfer to a baking dish just large enough to hold the fish. Set aside.

3. In the same skillet, cook the onion and celery over moderate heat until translucent, 4 to 5 minutes. If using whole canned tomatoes, place a food mill over the skillet and purée the tomatoes directly into it. Crushed tomatoes can be added directly from the can. Add the crushed red peppers. Stir to blend, cover, and simmer until the sauce begins to thicken, about 15 minutes. Stir in the olives. Taste for seasoning.

4. Spoon the sauce over the fish. Cover the dish with foil, place in the center of the oven, and bake for 30 minutes. To serve, quarter the fish, remove the skin, and transfer to warmed individual dinner plates. Use a slotted spoon to transfer the sauce to the plates, since the sauce has a tendency to thin out while baking.

Yield: 4 servings as a
main course

WINE SUGGESTION: Swordfish cries out for a dry white, such as a Sauvignon Blanc or Chardonnay.

Sea Bass with Potatoes and Tomatoes in Parchment

Branzino in Cartoccio

O n one trip to Florence, I sampled this lovely baked fish dish—with very minor variations—on two consecutive evenings. This version comes from La Capannina di Sante, where the whole baked fish is brought to the table in its bundle of parchment, allowing diners to enjoy the fragrance of the fresh fish as the package is slit open. While Chef Sante Collesano used branzino, the firm-fleshed sea bass, here you might also use a super-fresh whole snapper. Be sure to peel and slice the potatoes at the last minute or they will discolor.

1 whole sea bass, Alaska snapper, or red snapper (about 2 pounds; 1 kg), scaled and cleaned, but with head and tail on, rinsed, and patted dry

Sea salt and freshly ground black pepper to taste

Several sprigs fresh thyme

4 bay leaves, preferably fresh

2 large potatoes, peeled and sliced paper-thin

1 medium onion, sliced paper-thin

10 cherry tomatoes, halved lengthwise

3 tablespoons extra-virgin olive oil

Lemon wedges, for garnish

Extra-virgin olive oil, for the table

1. Preheat the oven to 450°F (230°C; gas mark 9).

2. Place the fish on one half of a sheet of baking parchment large enough to comfortably wrap the fish. Season the fish inside and out with salt and pepper. Tuck the thyme and bay leaves inside. Spread the potatoes, onion, and tomatoes over and around the fish. Drizzle with the oil.

3. Carefully fold the other half of the paper over the fish, closing it like a book. To seal the package, double-fold the edges and secure each side with several staples.

4. Place the package on a large baking sheet and place in the center of the oven. Bake for 25 minutes.

5. Remove the package from the oven and cut it open with a scissors. Let sit for about 3 minutes to allow the fish to firm up enough to fillet. To serve, fillet the fish and divide it among 4 warmed dinner plates. Arrange several spoonfuls of the potato-tomato mixture alongside. Pass the lemon wedges and a cruet of olive oil.

■ Yield: 4 servings as a ■
main course

WINE SUGGESTION: A white, for sure, such as a Pinot Grigio or Vernaccia di San Gimignano.

▪ ▪ ▪

Baked Sea Bass with Artichokes

Branzino coi Carciofi

I adore whole baked fish and have an equal passion for artichokes, so whenever I see this dish on a trattoria menu, I simply have to have it. It's amazing what an affinity sea bass and artichokes have for one another. The only secret here is to slice the artichokes very thin, so once they are precooked, they take about the same cooking time as the sea bass.

4 globe artichokes

1 lemon

½ cup (125 ml) plus 3 tablespoons extra-virgin olive oil

Sea salt and freshly ground black pepper to taste

1 whole sea bass, Alaska snapper, or red snapper (about 2 pounds; 1 kg), scaled and cleaned, but with head and tail on, rinsed, and patted dry

4 sprigs fresh rosemary

3 tablespoons freshly squeezed lemon juice

Lemon wedges, for garnish

Extra-virgin olive oil, for the table

1. Preheat the oven to 450°F (230°C; gas mark 9).

2. Prepare the artichokes: Halve the lemon, squeeze the juice, and place the halved lemon and the juice in a bowl filled with cold water. Rinse the artichokes under cold running water. Using a stainless steel knife to minimize discoloration, trim the stem of an artichoke to about 1 inch (2.5 cm) from the base. Carefully trim off and discard the stem's fibrous exterior. Bend back the tough outer green leaves one at a time, and snap them off at the base. Continue snapping off the leaves until only the central cone of

yellow leaves with pale green tips remains. Trim the top of the cone of leaves to just below the green tips. Trim any dark green areas from the base. Halve the artichoke lengthwise. With a small spoon, scrape out, and discard, the hairy choke. Cut each artichoke half lengthwise into paper-thin slices, and place immediately in the acidulated water. Repeat with the remaining 3 artichokes.

3. Drain the artichokes. In a large skillet, combine the artichoke slices, ½ cup (125 ml) of the oil, and the salt, and toss to coat the artichokes with the oil. Over moderate heat, sauté the artichoke slices just until soft, 3 to 4 minutes. Taste for seasoning. Set aside.

4. Season the fish generously inside and out with salt and pepper. Place it in a shallow baking dish that will hold it snugly. Stuff the cavity with the sprigs of rosemary and as many artichoke slices as will fit. Scatter the remaining artichokes, as well as the juices, around the fish. Drizzle with the lemon juice and the remaining 3 tablespoons olive oil.

5. Place the baking dish in the center of the oven and bake, uncovered, until the fish is opaque through but not dry, 30 to 40 minutes, basting every 10 minutes. (The baking time will vary according to the size of the fish.)

6. Remove the fish from the oven and let sit for about 3 minutes to allow the fish to firm up enough to fillet.

7. To serve, fillet the fish and divide it among 4 warmed dinner plates. Arrange several spoonfuls of artichokes alongside. Pass the lemon wedges and a cruet of olive oil.

Yield: 4 servings as a
main course

WINE SUGGESTION: With this dish, I've thoroughly enjoyed a chilled white Vernaccia di San Gimignano from the Tuscan hill town of San Gimignano. One of the finest is the oak-aged Terre di Tufo, from Teruzzi & Puthod.

Mixed Fried Fish

Frittura di Pesce

Some of the best fried fish I ever ate was prepared by Cesare Benelli, chef and owner of Venice's small forty-seat restaurant Al Covo. Cesare grew up in a Venetian restaurant family (his father had a trattoria on the Lido) and remembers when, as a child, he could go snorkeling in the area and within a few minutes spear with a kitchen fork more baby sole than the family could possibly consume. Today—due to pollution and overfishing—sole are a sacred delicacy in Venice. But with a combination of rigorous standards and careful shopping Cesare manages to obtain a variety of sparkling fresh fish for Al Covo diners. One of his specialties is delicate first-course servings of mixed fried fish, light as pillows and deliciously crispy and fresh. He confided his personal frying secret: Once the fish is rinsed, he lets it rest in ice water for a few minutes. With the temperature difference between the cold fish and the hot oil, the fish has less of a tendency to absorb the oil.

1 pound (500 g) mixed small fish or shellfish, such as anchovies, sardines, smelt, whitebait, tiny sole fillets, rings or tentacles of small squid, shrimp, or cubed fish fillets

1 cup (135 g) superfine flour, such as Wondra

Fine sea salt and freshly ground black pepper to taste

⅛ teaspoon cayenne pepper

1 to 1½ quarts (1 to 1.5 l) oil, for deep-frying

Lemon wedges, for garnish

1. Rinse the fish or shellfish and soak in ice water for at least 10 minutes before cooking.

2. In a paper or plastic bag, combine the flour, ¼ teaspoon salt, pepper, and cayenne and shake to blend.

3. Preheat the oven 200°F (100°C; gas mark 1).

4. Pour the oil into a wide 6-quart (6-l) saucepan, or use a deep-fat fryer. (The oil should be at least 2 inches [5 cm] deep.) Place a deep-fry thermometer in the oil and heat the oil to 375°F (190°C).

5. Drain the fish or shellfish and dry well. Dip a handful of fish or shellfish into the bag of flour and shake to coat with flour. Transfer the coated fish to a fine-mesh sieve and shake off excess flour. Carefully drop the fish or shellfish by small handfuls into the hot oil. Cook until lightly browned, 1 to 2 minutes. With a wire skimmer, lift from the oil, drain, and transfer to paper towels. Immediately season with sea salt, then place in the oven—with the door slightly ajar—to keep warm. Continue frying until all of the fish or shellfish are cooked, allowing the oil to return to 375°F (190°C) each time before adding another batch. Serve immediately, with lemon wedges.

> ■ Yield: 4 to 6 servings as a ■
> first course

WINE SUGGESTION: Light fried foods suggest a light white Sauvignon Blanc, such as one from Italy's northeast, the Friuli-Venezia-Giulia region.

Small-Fry Fish Tips

- Use any kind of small whole fish, fish fillets, or steaks, but try to keep them small and uniform: no more than 1½ inches (4 cm) thick and no more than 5 to 6 inches (13 to 15 cm) long. (Small fish with bones—such as whitebait, smelt, anchovies, or sardines—can be fried whole, for the deep-frying will soften the bones and make them edible.)

- Use a very light coating of seasoned flour only, to help the fish retain its moisture on the inside and form a nice crispy crust on the outside.

- Preheat the oil to 375°F (190°C). Hotter oil will burn the fish and coating; cooler oil will make for soggy fish that have absorbed the oil.

- Soak the rinsed fish in ice water, and dry thoroughly before coating.

POULTRY AND MEATS

Sautéed Chicken Breasts with Fresh Sage

Petti di Pollo alla Salvia

ITALIAN DICTUM:

"Spring is for looking, autumn for tasting."

Ever since I sampled this ultimately simple chicken preparation one weekday afternoon at Antico Fattore in Florence, it's been a family favorite. I love to "stretch" a whole chicken by reserving the breasts for this recipe and using the remaining bird to prepare chicken stock. The quick marinade of lemon juice, oil, and fresh sage helps infuse the chicken with flavor, and tenderizes it at the same time. Be sure to sample the sage leaves before using: Even fresh sage can taste bitter. Do not use dried sage. Worthy substitutes include fresh rosemary or fresh tarragon. Serve this with Lemon Risotto (page 158) or simple buttered pasta.

4 skinless, boneless chicken breast halves (each 6 ounces; 180 g)

3 tablespoons freshly squeezed lemon juice

5 tablespoons extra-virgin olive oil

28 fresh sage leaves

3 tablespoons (1½ ounces; 45 g) unsalted butter

Sea salt and freshly ground black pepper to taste

2 lemons, halved, for garnish

1. Place the chicken breasts in a glass baking dish. Add the lemon juice, 3 tablespoons of the oil, and the sage leaves. Turn the chicken to coat evenly, cover, and set aside at room temperature for 30 minutes.

2. Remove the chicken from the marinade and pat dry. Strain the marinade into a small bowl; reserve the sage leaves separately.

3. In a large skillet, melt the butter in the remaining 2 tablespoons of oil over moderately high heat until hot and bubbly. Add the chicken breasts, smooth side down, and cook until evenly browned, about 5 minutes. Turn the breasts, and season the cooked side generously with salt and pepper. Tuck the reserved sage leaves around the chicken and cook until the chicken is browned on the bottom and just white throughout but still juicy, 5 to 10 minutes more. Do not scorch the sage.

4. Remove the skillet from the heat. Transfer the chicken to a cutting board and season the bottom side with salt and pepper. Slice the chicken breasts on the diagonal into thick slices, and arrange on a warmed serving platter. Place the sage leaves over the chicken. Cover loosely with foil.

5. Discard the fat from the skillet. Heat the skillet over moderately high heat until hot. Add the reserved marinade and stir with a wooden spoon, scraping up the brown bits from the bottom of the pan. The sauce will boil almost immediately. As soon as it reduces to a brown glaze (less than 1 minute), pour the sauce over the chicken. Garnish with the lemon halves. Serve immediately.

■ Y i e l d :   4   s e r v i n g s ■

WINE SUGGESTION: At the Antico Fattore, we sampled the trattoria's house wine, Ruffino Chianti Riserva Ducale, a worthy local choice from Tuscany.

Chicken Cooked Under Bricks

Pollo al Mattone

T his is the dish that inspired this book. On a trip to Italy some years ago, I sampled this delicious, crispy-skinned chicken at a popular Tuscan trattoria named Da Giulio, in Lucca. I loved it so, I had to have the recipe, and, almost like a sleepwalker, I found myself in the kitchen, pen and notebook in hand. The move to the kitchen was so instinctive and spontaneous, I wasn't even quite sure how I had arrived there. But as I was writing down the details of the preparation of this traditional Italian dish, a light bulb went off in my head, and I knew that trattoria cooking would be the subject of my next book. I now jokingly call the dish "smashed" chicken, for it is really fried chicken that is split and cooked whole, held tight to the skillet and the heat by a heavy weight, usually bricks, or *mattone*. In fact, kitchenware shops in Italy sell special heavy-duty glazed pottery two-piece cookers, with flat, heavy tops, made for cooking the chicken. The weights are not just a gadget or gimmick, but actually help the chicken cook more evenly and make for a very pleasantly crispy but not fatty crust, for all the fat is pressed out of the chicken. The weighting technique can also be used in grilling chicken over medium-hot coals. Cooked whole and on the bone, the chicken has more flavor than chicken parts or boned chicken. I like to serve this with steamed new potatoes and garlic mayonnaise as an accompaniment. The only trick here is to properly regulate the heat as you cook, for you can't actually keep an eye on the chicken skin, but want to make sure it does not burn. I work by aroma and keep the heat beneath the skillet between moderate and moderately high, making sure the chicken cooks evenly but not too quickly.

1 free-range roasting chicken (4 pounds; 2 kg)

½ cup (125 ml) extra-virgin olive oil

Sea salt and freshly ground black pepper to taste

1. Place the chicken breast side down on a flat surface. With a pair of poultry shears, split the bird lengthwise along the backbone. Open it flat, and press down with the heel of your hand to flatten completely. Turn the chicken skin side up, and, with a sharp knife, make slits in the skin near the tail and tuck the wing tips in to secure. The bird should be as flat as possible to ensure even cooking.

2. In a 12-inch skillet, or one large enough to hold the chicken flat, heat the oil over moderately high heat. When the oil is hot but not smoking, place the chicken skin side down in the skillet. Put a lid or another skillet over the chicken, then weight it down with a 10-pound (5-kg) weight. (Use bricks or heavy rocks.) Cook over medium-high heat until the skin is golden brown, about 12 minutes. Remove the lid and weights. Using tongs so that you do not pierce the meat, turn the chicken over, and season generously with salt and pepper. Replace the lid and weights, and cook for 12 minutes more. To test for doneness, pierce the thigh with a skewer. The chicken is done when the juices run clear.

3. Transfer the chicken to a platter and place it at an angle against the edge of an overturned plate, with its head down and tail in the air. (This heightens the flavor by allowing the juices to flow down through the breast meat.) Cover the chicken loosely with foil. Let it rest for at least 10 minutes and up to 30 minutes. (If desired, keep the chicken warm by placing it in a warm oven.)

4. To serve, carve the chicken and arrange it on a warmed platter. (The chicken can also be served at room temperature.)

■ Yield: 4 to 6 servings ■

WINE SUGGESTION: Any good, sturdy wine goes well with this. If you prefer white, try a Vernaccia di San Gimignano; for a red, try a Tuscan Cabernet from Antinori.

Tomatoes: Canned versus Fresh, Whole versus Crushed

For preparing tomato sauce, canned tomatoes are often better than fresh. Fresh tomatoes vary dramatically in quality and price, and are quite labor-intensive, while quality canned tomatoes remain a year-round, dependable pantry staple. Brands of canned tomatoes vary widely, and most markets offer a choice. Do a test at home, preparing the same sauce with several brands of both domestic and imported tomatoes to decide which flavor you prefer. A good canned tomato should produce a rich sauce with a fresh tomato flavor, with no tomato paste aftertaste.

The recipes here offer a choice of peeled plum tomatoes in their juice and crushed tomatoes in purée, since these are the most readily available choices. I prefer whole canned plum tomatoes in juice: They produce a more refined sauce, with a pure tomato flavor. Pass the whole canned tomatoes through a food mill to remove bits of tough pulp as well as most of the seeds, which can turn the sauce bitter. Crushed tomatoes tend to be thicker than whole tomatoes, so adjust cooking times accordingly.

Chicken with a Confit of Red Bell Peppers and Onions

Pollo alla Peperonata

Some dishes become such challenges that a cook can't rest until the result truly sings! One August evening in Florence, at the very simple Osteria del Cinghiale Bianco, I ordered an uncomplicated dish of sautéed chicken with red peppers and onions, a garnish traditionally called a peperonata. The thin strips of red peppers, shining with their own natural oils, were all intertwined with the strands of onions, which had melted away to almost nothing. The entire dish was a symphony of aromatic flavors of the Mediterranean. It was hard to believe these vegetables weren't meat, because they were so serious and stood out on their own. At home, I began to play around with the combination, and, time after time, hit a false chord. Too bland. No life. Nothing special. Finally, I carefully thought it all through, and came up with a dish that, I hope, sings on key as well as the one I sampled that evening in Florence. The trick is to slice the onions very, very thin, so they cook up quickly, taking on a soft, sweet essence. The peppers are cooked separately, just until they wilt and give up their natural oils. The balsamic vinegar at the end gives the final dish a unity and a special boost. I like to serve this with wedges of grilled polenta(page 172), preceded by a salad of tomatoes and mozzarella or a light pasta, finishing off with a bowl of fresh fruit.

(continued)

4 red bell peppers (about 1½ pounds; 750 g), cut into thin lengthwise strips

Sea salt to taste

7 tablespoons extra-virgin olive oil

2 medium onions (about 10 ounces; 300 g), peeled

1 tablespoon finely minced fresh rosemary leaves

1 tablespoon sugar

1 chicken (3 to 4 pounds; 1.5 to 2 kg), at room temperature, cut into 8 serving pieces

Freshly ground black pepper to taste

1 tablespoon unsalted butter

One 16-ounce (480-g) can peeled Italian plum tomatoes in juice or one 16-ounce (480-g) can crushed tomatoes in purée

Several sprigs of fresh parsley, bay leaves, sprigs of fresh rosemary, and celery leaves, tied in a bundle with cotton twine

½ cup (125 ml) chicken stock, preferably homemade (page 272)

1 tablespoon balsamic vinegar

1. In large skillet, combine the peppers, a pinch of salt, and 2 tablespoons of the oil. Toss to coat the peppers with oil and cook, covered, over very low heat, stirring from time to time, until soft and glazed, about 15 minutes. Remove from the heat and set aside.

2. Meanwhile, slice an onion in half lengthwise. Place each half, cut side down, on a cutting board and cut crosswise into very thin slices. Slice the remaining onion in this manner, for about 2 cups (500 ml) sliced onions.

3. In another large skillet, combine the onions, a pinch of salt, the rosemary, sugar, and 2 tablespoons of the oil. Toss to coat the onions with oil and cook, uncovered, over very low heat, stirring from time to time, until the onions are very soft and glazed, about 10 minutes. Remove from the heat and set aside.

4. Season the chicken liberally with salt and pepper. In a third skillet, combine the remaining 3 tablespoons oil and the butter over high heat. When hot, add several pieces of chicken and cook on the skin side until it turns an even golden brown, about 5 minutes. Turn the pieces and brown them on the other side, about 5 minutes more. Do not crowd the pan; brown the chicken in several batches. Carefully regulate the heat to avoid scorching the skin. When all the pieces are browned, return all the chicken to the pan. If using whole canned tomatoes, place a food mill over the skillet and purée the tomatoes directly into it. Crushed tomatoes can be added directly from the can. Add the herb bundle, stir to blend, and simmer for about 5 minutes. Add the chicken stock, onions, and peppers, and simmer, partially covered, until the chicken is cooked through, 25 to 30 minutes more. Remove and discard the herb bundle. Stir in the vinegar and cook for 1 minute more.

5. Transfer the chicken to warmed dinner plates, along with the sauce. Serve immediately.

■ Yield: 4 to 6 servings ■

WINE SUGGESTION: This assertive, acidic dish is not tailor-made for wines, so go with something uncomplicated, such as a young Chianti or Valpolicella.

■ ■ ■

Grilled Chicken with Lemon, Oil, and Black Pepper

Pollo alla Diavola

"Amarone . . . a wine of incredible depth, bouquet, and breed. Forget about that, however, and listen to the name, preferably pronounced by Luciano Pavarotti—Am-mahr-roh-nay; a siren song, a seduction."

LEONARD BERNSTEIN, THE OFFICIAL GUIDE TO WINE SNOBBERY

"**H**ot as the devil," or *alla diavola,* is perhaps the most classic of all Italian trattoria dishes. The fire comes from coarsely ground black peppercorns, which radiate their fire as the chicken marinates, along with extra-virgin olive oil and freshly squeezed lemon juice. Roasting only heightens their flavor, making a superbly intense dish that's great during hot or cold weather. I like to serve this with Seared and Roasted Tomatoes (page 13) and perhaps Panfried Potatoes with Black Olives (page 52).

1 free-range roasting chicken (about 3 pounds; 1.5 kg)

5 tablespoons freshly squeezed lemon juice

3 tablespoons extra-virgin olive oil

About 1 tablespoon whole black peppercorns, coarsely crushed

Fine sea salt to taste

1. Prepare the chicken: Place the chicken breast side down on a flat surface. With a pair of poultry shears, split the bird lengthwise along the backbone. Open it flat, and press down with the heel of your hand to flatten completely. Turn the chicken skin side up, and, with a sharp knife, make slits in the skin near the tail and tuck the wing tips in to secure. The bird should be as flat as possible to ensure even cooking.

2. Place the chicken in a deep dish and add the lemon juice, oil, and 1 tablespoon crushed black peppercorns. Cover and marinate at room temperature for 30 minutes, turning the chicken with tongs from time to time.

3. Preheat the oven broiler. Or prepare a wood or charcoal fire. The fire is ready when the coals glow red and are covered with ash.

4. Season the chicken generously with salt. With the skin side toward the heat, place beneath the broiler or on the grill about 5 inches (13 cm) from the heat so that the poultry cooks evenly without burning. Cook until the skin is evenly browned, basting occasionally with the marinade, about 15 minutes. Using tongs so you do not pierce the meat, turn and cook the other side, basting occasionally, about 15 minutes more. To test for doneness, pierce the thigh with a skewer. The chicken is done when the juices run clear.

5. Remove the chicken from the heat and season once more with salt and with additional cracked pepper if desired. To serve, quarter the chicken and slice the breast meat, arranging it on a warmed serving platter.

■ Y i e l d :   4   t o   6   s e r v i n g s   ■

WINE SUGGESTION: A full-bodied white, such as a Chardonnay, or a soft red, such as Recioto della Valpolicella Amarone.

Poached Chicken with Fresh Herb Sauce

Pollo Bollito in Salsa Verde

T ender, moist poached chicken and the vibrant herb sauce known as salsa verde seem to be made for one another. The delicate flavor of the chicken takes well to the strength and freshness of the tangy herb sauce. Poaching a chicken is the age-old way of preparing chicken broth and dinner at the same time.

1 *chicken (3 to 4 pounds; 1.5 to 2 kg), at room temperature, trussed*

2 *large onions, halved and stuck with 2 whole cloves*

3 *plump fresh garlic cloves*

Several parsley stems, celery leaves, and sprigs of thyme, wrapped in several ribs of celery and tied in a bundle with cotton twine

4 *large carrots, trimmed, peeled, and tied in a bundle*

4 *ribs celery, trimmed and tied in a bundle*

6 *whole black peppercorns*

1 *recipe Fresh Herb Sauce (page 266)*

1. Place all the ingredients except the herb sauce in an 8-quart (8-l) stockpot. Add cold water to cover and bring just to a simmer over high heat. Skim off the impurities that rise to the surface. Reduce the heat and simmer very gently for 3 hours, skimming as necessary.

2. To serve: Remove the chicken and set aside to drain. With a slotted spoon, remove the vegetables. Discard the herb bundle and the garlic. Untie the chicken and vegetables. Carve the chicken and place on a large warmed platter. Surround the chicken with the vegetables. Serve immediately, with the herb sauce.

3. To prepare chicken broth from the remaining liquid: Line a fine-mesh sieve with dampened cheesecloth and set over a large bowl. Ladle—do not pour—the liquid into the bowl. The broth can be stored, covered, in the refrigerator for up to 3 days or frozen for up to 1 month.

■ Yield: 6 servings of chicken, and ■
about 3 ½ quarts (3.5 l) chicken broth

WINE SUGGESTION: I like red with this dish, a good Chianti Classico or Barbera d'Alba.

For Quick Crushed Peppercorns

Although one can purchase crushed or cracked peppercorns, home-crushed pepper will have a far superior, fresher, more pungent flavor. Here's how: On a work surface, carefully crush the peppercorns with a heavy mallet or with the bottom of a heavy skillet. Alternatively, crush the peppercorns in a mortar with a pestle.

Chicken Cacciatora

Pollo alla Cacciatora

Is there a chicken dish more universal and more universally loved than chicken cacciatora? When I was a child, this was one of my favorite dishes, and I can still smell my mother's chicken simmering in her ever-sturdy skillet on the stove. Today, all I have to say is "chicken cacciatora," and everyone's in a cheery mood. Like many dishes in the book, this version is a personal composite of many I sampled along the trattoria trail, and shows off to good advantage one of the Italian national vegetables, celery. Be sure to buy the best chicken you can find: It will make all the difference between an everyday dish and one that's really special. I like to serve this on its own as a main course, but you may want to accompany it with steamed or boiled potatoes.

1 chicken (3 to 4 pounds; 1.5 to 2 kg), at room temperature, cut into 8 serving pieces

Sea salt and freshly ground black pepper to taste

3 tablespoons extra-virgin olive oil

1 tablespoon unsalted butter

1 small onion, minced

2 ribs celery, thinly sliced

¼ teaspoon crushed red peppers (hot red pepper flakes), or to taste

One 28-ounce (765-g) can peeled Italian plum tomatoes in juice or one 28-ounce (765-g) can crushed tomatoes in purée

Several sprigs of fresh parsley, bay leaves, sprigs of fresh rosemary, and celery leaves, tied in a bundle with cotton twine

1. Season the chicken liberally with salt and pepper. In a large skillet, combine the oil and butter over high heat. When hot, add several pieces of chicken and cook on the skin side until it turns an even golden brown, about 5 minutes. Turn the pieces and brown them on the other side, about 5 minutes more. Do not crowd the pan; brown the chicken in several batches. Carefully regulate the heat to avoid scorching the skin. When all the pieces are browned, transfer them to a platter.

2. Add the onion, celery, crushed red peppers, and salt to the fat in the pan and cook over moderate heat until the onion and celery are soft and translucent, 4 to 5 minutes. If using whole canned tomatoes, place a food mill over the skillet and purée the tomatoes directly into it. Crushed tomatoes can be added directly from the can. Add the herb bundle, stir to blend, and simmer for about 5 minutes. Bury the chicken in the sauce, and simmer, partially covered, until the chicken is cooked through, 25 to 30 minutes more. Remove and discard the herb bundle.

3. Transfer the chicken to warmed dinner plates, along with the sauce. Serve immediately.

■ Yield: 4 to 6 servings ■

WINE SUGGESTION: For a favorite dish, drink your favorite red, such as a simple Chianti Classico.

> *"There was one more formative experience, and that was Italy. It was still a country where wine was a part of life—we picked the grapes from the roadside vineyard to quench our thirst as the Eighth Army clanked and rumbled its way northwards in a cloud of dust—and where men grew wine as a matter of course, and put grimy carafes of it on the table at every meal, equally a matter of course."*
>
> CYRIL RAY, RAY ON WINE

Peperoncini: Trip to Hell!

The Italians call them *peperoncini;* we know the dried, fiery red spice as chile peppers. On one visit to the large indoor fruit and vegetable market in Florence, I spied a merchant who sold baskets of whole, cayenne-like peperoncini with a sign in English warning: "Trip to Hell!" Hot peppers are used sparingly in most Italian cooking, generally in stews and sauces, or to flavor olives or oil. Chile peppers not only make a dish fiery, but also serve as subtle flavor enhancers, adding a stimulating layer of flavor. Since the intensity of hot peppers varies, the recipes here suggest quantities for crushed red peppers, readily found packed in glass jars and sold in supermarket spice departments. Internationally, the intensity of peppers is rated on a Scoville heat indicator scale, and these crushed red peppers range from 25,000 to 50,000 heat units. (As a point of comparison, cayenne pepper is rated at 40,000 heat units, jalapeño peppers at 55,000 heat units. On the scale, a pepper rated at 20,000 heat units is half as hot as a pepper rated at 40,000.) Bottled crushed red peppers may come from China, India, Pakistan, or all three. Generally the entire pepper is dried and then crushed, with the stem and cap removed. Dried chile peppers—capsicum—should be refrigerated, to maintain their shiny, fresh color. Crushed red peppers have a shelf life of about two years. Discard any dried peppers that have become cloudy or dark red, for they can turn a dish harshly bitter. When traveling in Italy, purchase whole dried peperoncini, and use to taste in any recipe calling for crushed red peppers. Just be sure to remove the whole peppers at serving time!

Rabbit with Red Peppers and Polenta

Coniglio alla Cacciatora

Even though I first sampled this dish one golden, sunny evening in May in the Piedmont, it always reminds me of Christmastime, especially when the polenta is prepared with a pale ivory-white cornmeal. The reddish hues of the cacciatora—a brilliant red sauce of red peppers punctuated with a touch of tomatoes and an avalanche of herbs—are gorgeous alongside a little "fence" of steaming polenta. The recipe was shared with me by the hard-working, enthusiastic Claudia Verro. Along with her husband, Tonino, she runs one of Italy's more charming and romantic restaurants, La Contea, in the hamlet of Neive. When preparing this dish, be sure that you carefully stem the thyme and finely chop the rosemary beforehand, or you're likely to feed your guests, and yourself, sticks of herbs.

(*continued*)

1 whole fresh rabbit (about 3
  pounds; 1.5 kg), cut into serving
  pieces

9 tablespoons extra-virgin olive
  oil

5 tablespoons freshly squeezed
  lemon juice

2 tablespoons fresh thyme leaves

2 tablespoons fresh rosemary
  leaves, finely chopped

3 bay leaves, preferably fresh

4 red bell peppers, thinly sliced

One 16-ounce (480-g) can peeled
  Italian plum tomatoes in juice
  or one 16-ounce (480-g) can
  crushed tomatoes in purée

Sea salt and freshly ground black
  pepper to taste

1 recipe freshly made Polenta
  (page 172), served warm in a
  mound

1. In a large shallow dish, marinate the rabbit pieces in 3 tablespoons of the oil, the lemon juice, and the herbs at room temperature for at least 1 hour, and up to 3 hours, turning from time to time.

2. In a skillet large enough to hold the rabbit later on, heat 3 tablespoons of the oil until hot but not smoking. Add the sliced peppers, toss to coat with oil, and reduce the heat to low. Cover and cook until soft, stirring from time to time, about 10 minutes. Do not let the peppers burn. If using whole canned tomatoes, place a food mill over the skillet and purée the tomatoes directly into it. Crushed tomatoes can be added directly from the can. Season with salt and pepper, stir to blend, cover, and continue cooking for 30 minutes more, stirring from time to time.

3. Meanwhile, cook the rabbit: Pat the rabbit pieces dry and season with salt and pepper. Reserve the marinade. In a very large skillet, heat the remaining 3 tablespoons oil over moderately high heat. When hot but not smoking, add the rabbit pieces. Reduce the heat immediately to low (to keep the rabbit meat from drying out), cover, and cook, shaking the pan from time to time, until the rabbit is lightly browned but still moist, about 5 minutes per side. (Cooking time will vary according to the size of the pieces.)

4. Add the rabbit pieces to the simmering pepper mixture, burying the rabbit in the sauce. Deglaze the pan in which the rabbit was cooked with the reserved marinade, scraping up any bits that cling to the bottom. Add this liquid to the pepper and rabbit mixture. Stir, cover, and cook for 30 minutes more. Remove and discard the bay leaves.

5. To serve, place the rabbit pieces on warmed dinner plates, cover with the pepper-tomato sauce, and place a dollop of polenta alongside. Serve immediately.

▪ Y i e l d :   4   t o   6   s e r v i n g s ▪

WINE SUGGESTION: With this meal, we sampled a spectacular old Barolo, and you should do so if your pocketbook can afford it. Otherwise, any robust red would go well with this brilliant dish.

Cutting up a Rabbit

To cut up a whole rabbit for cooking: Place the rabbit belly side down on a clean work surface. Trim off the flaps of skin, the tops of the forelegs, and any excess bone. With a cleaver or a heavy knife, divide the carcass crosswise into three sections: hind legs, saddle, and forelegs, including the rib cage. Cut between the hind legs to separate them into two pieces. Split the front carcass into two pieces to separate the forelegs. Split the saddle crosswise into three even pieces.

• • •

Cubed Pork with Garlic, Spinach, and Spicy Chick Peas

Ceciata di Suino della Casa

Bright and colorful, with the spring green of spinach, the mahogany hues of the pork, and the wheaty tones of garbanzo beans, this unusual pork dish is a specialty of Trattoria Cammillo, a popular Florentine trattoria that's been a gathering spot since 1946. Then, Cammillo Masiero ran a little one-room trattoria where people came to drink, play cards, and eat whatever was being served that day. Today, Cammillo's grandson, Francesco Masiero, runs a bustling, multiroom spot filled with an equal mix of tourists and locals. On my last visit, I spent part of the evening in the tiny kitchen that's open to view, and the cooks kindly walked me through this dish, which has been a family favorite ever since. This dish is equally delicious prepared with cubed lamb.

1½ cups (8 ounces; 250 g) dried chick peas (garbanzo beans)

6 tablespoons extra-virgin olive oil

Several parsley stems, several sprigs of thyme, a bay leaf, and several celery leaves, tied in a bundle with cotton twine

Sea salt to taste

1 pound (500 g) fresh spinach, washed and stemmed

1 pound (500 g) pork loin, cut into 1-inch (2.9-cm) cubes

8 to 12 plump fresh garlic cloves, cut into slivers, or to taste

½ teaspoon crushed red peppers (hot red pepper flakes), or to taste

Freshly ground black pepper to taste

1. Rinse and drain the chick peas, picking them over to remove any pebbles. Place the beans in a large bowl, add boiling water to cover, and set aside for 1 hour. Drain and rinse the beans, discarding the water.

2. Transfer the chick peas to a medium-size saucepan. Add 2 tablespoons of the oil and the herb bundle, cover with fresh cold water, and bring to a simmer over moderate heat. Reduce the heat to low, cover, and simmer for 1 hour. Add the salt and continue simmering until tender, about 1 hour more. (Check the water level in the pan every half hour, adding water as needed.) Once cooked, taste for seasoning, then drain. Remove and discard the herb bundle. Set aside.

3. In a large deep skillet, combine the spinach and salt, cover, and steam the leaves over moderate heat, tossing them from time to time, until they wilt, about 5 minutes. Strain and squeeze the spinach, removing every drop of water you can. Using a stainless steel knife to prevent discoloration, chop very fine. Set aside.

4. In another large deep skillet, combine the pork, the remaining 4 tablespoons olive oil, the garlic, and the crushed red peppers, tossing to coat with oil. Sauté the pork over moderate heat, adjusting the heat as necessary so the garlic does not scorch. The small cubes of pork should cook in 5 to 7 minutes. Season to taste with salt and pepper. Add the chick peas, then the spinach, and cook just until warmed through. Taste for seasoning. Transfer to warmed dinner plates and serve immediately.

■ Yield: 4 to 6 servings ■

WINE SUGGESTION: With this dish, sample an equally energetic wine, such as a Vino Nobile di Montepulciano.

Rosemary Roast Loin of Pork

Arista

"The roast, flavored with herbs and larded with olive oil, mounts to the nostrils and invites to the feast."

ANGELO PELLEGRINI, THE UNPREJUDICED PALATE

The secret to this succulent roast pork is to begin roasting at high heat—to sear and brown the surface and help seal in the juices—then continue to roast gently at a lower heat, to cook it slowly without drying out. Don't cheat and cook the roast without the bones: They add essential flavor to the meat. But do not forget to ask your butcher to crack the bones, to make it easy for you to slice the roast into thick chops at serving time. I always serve this Florentine specialty with oven-roasted potatoes. An incredible version of this pork roast can be found at Florence's Coco Lezzone, an elbow-to-elbow trattoria where one sits at long, shared tables. The waiter there confided that their secret was to cook the meat on the bone, using the high-heat/low-heat method for a crusty exterior and moist interior. As an extra touch, the roast is studded with whole sprigs of fragrant, fresh rosemary. Any leftover pork is great the next day, as picnic fare or cold cuts.

1 loin-end pork roast, bones split (about 5 pounds; 2.5 kg)

2 sprigs of fresh rosemary

Sea salt and freshly ground black pepper to taste

About 1½ cups (375 ml) dry white wine, such as a Pinot Grigio

About 1½ cups (375 ml) water

1. Preheat the oven to 400°F (200°C; gas mark 6/7).

2. Using a thick needle or a sharp knife, pierce the meatiest center portion of the pork at either end. Carefully insert a sprig of rosemary in each slit. Season the roast generously with salt and pepper. Place the pork, fat side up, bone portion down, on a roasting rack in a roasting pan. Place in the center of the oven and roast until the skin is crackling and brown and the meat begins to exude fat and juices, about 30 minutes.

3. Reduce the heat to 325°F (160°C; gas mark 3/4) and baste with the juices from the pan, adding about ½ cup (125 ml) each of the white wine and water to the pan juices. Continue to add wine and water as needed, to maintain a thin layer of liquid in the pan at all times, and baste at 20 minute intervals. Roast the pork for about 25 minutes per pound, until an instant-read meat thermometer registers 155°F (85°C). (Alternatively, insert a standard meat thermometer into the roast, making sure it does not touch the bone.) Remove from the oven, season immediately with salt and pepper, and cover loosely with foil. Let stand for 15 minutes, or until the thermometer registers 160°F (90°C). (Since the meat will continue to cook—and eventually dry out—as it rests, do not allow the pork to rest for more than 15 minutes.)

4. Meanwhile, skim the fat from the pan juices, and place the roasting pan over moderate heat, scraping up any bits that cling to the bottom. If necessary, add several tablespoons of cold water to deglaze (hot water would cloud the sauce), and bring to a boil. Cook, scraping and stirring, until the liquid is almost caramelized, 2 to 3 minutes. Do not let it burn. Spoon off and discard any excess fat. Reduce the heat to low and simmer just until thickened, 2 to 3 minutes more. Strain the sauce through a fine-mesh sieve and pour into a warmed sauceboat.

5. Carve the roast into thick chops and serve immediately on warmed dinner plates, passing the sauce.

■ Yield: 6 servings ■

WINE SUGGESTION: This succulent roast calls for a deep ruby red, such as a Vino Nobile di Montepulciano.

Parmesan-Breaded Baby Lamb Chops

Costolettine d'Abbacchio Fritte

"When I am asked, as I sometimes am, what is the bottle of wine I have most enjoyed, I have to answer that it was probably some anonymous Italian 'fiasco' that I drank one starlit Tyrrhenian night under a vine-covered arbor, while a Neapolitan fiddler played 'Come Back to Sorrento' over the veal cutlet of the young woman I had designs on. . . ."

CYRIL RAY, RAY ON WINE

The Italians are true masters at gently coating meats, poultry, and vegetables with beautifully seasoned combinations of ingredients, and the results could convert anyone who thinks that breaded food has to be heavy. There is nothing tricky or complicated about properly breading and panfrying these lamb chops: Simply pay attention, and follow directions to the letter. I love these on a cool day, served with oven-roasted potatoes (page 54) or fried zucchini blossoms or artichokes (page 56). As a first course, serve sautéed red peppers (page 4). These lamb chops actually benefit from being breaded one to two hours in advance so that the coating dries a bit and better adheres to the meat. I sampled these one December evening in Rome.

8 single-rib lamb chops, bone ends trimmed of fat and meat (about ½ inch/1 cm thick; 6 to 9 ounces/180 to 270 g per chop)

¾ cup (3 ounces; 90 g) freshly grated Italian Parmigiano-Reggiano cheese, in a shallow dish

2 large eggs, lightly beaten, in a shallow dish

1 cup (250 ml) very fine fresh bread crumbs, in a shallow dish

About 2 cups (500 ml) peanut oil, for frying

Fine sea salt and freshly ground black pepper to taste

2 lemons, quartered, for garnish

1. With a meat pounder or the side of a heavy cleaver, gently pound the meat of the lamb chops, to form an even chop, not to flatten to a pancake. Hold a lamb chop by the bone and turn each side of the chop in the cheese, shaking off the excess. Immediately turn each side of the chop in the beaten eggs, shaking off the excess. Turn each side of the chop in the bread crumbs, shaking off the excess. Transfer to a platter. Repeat with the remaining lamb chops. (The lamb may be coated up to 1 hour in advance and held at room temperature, or up to 4 hours in advance and refrigerated; remove from the refrigerator 1 hour before preparation.)

2. In a large skillet, heat the oil over moderately high heat until hot but not smoking. Place as many lamb chops as possible in the skillet without crowding. Cook until golden brown, about 4 minutes. Using tongs, carefully turn each chop, trying not to upset the coating, and season the browned side with salt and pepper. Continue cooking until the second side is golden brown, about 4 minutes more. Season the second side and drain briefly on paper towels. Transfer to warmed dinner plates and serve immediately, with the wedges of lemon for squeezing over the lamb chops.

■ Yield: 4 servings ■

WINE SUGGESTION: This sturdy dish deserves a good, tasty red, such as a Montepulciano d'Abruzzo.

Grilled Marinated Lamb Chops with Lemon and Oil

Costolette d'Agnello a Scottadito

The secret of these light, thin chops is to dry-cook them over high heat, producing a crisply golden and crusty exterior, and a tender, meaty interior. For this style of dry-cooking, you need tender meat, such as top-quality lamb chops or slices of leg of lamb. To keep the interior of the meat moist during cooking (and to keep it from sticking to the unoiled pan or grill), the meat is marinated first, in a classic mixture of top-quality olive oil and freshly squeezed lemon juice. Do not salt the meat, or it will draw out the flavorful juices. These thin and dainty lamb chops—meant to be eaten with your hands—are justly called *scottadito*, or "burning fingers." I've sampled them at several trattorias in Rome. My favorite accompaniments are Roasted Rosemary Potatoes (page 54) and Sautéed Spinach with Garlic, Lemon, and Oil (page 62).

8 single-rib lamb chops, bone ends trimmed of fat and meat (about ½ inch/1 cm thick; 6 to 9 ounces/180 to 270 g per chop)

¼ cup (60 ml) extra-virgin olive oil

3 tablespoons freshly squeezed lemon juice

Fine sea salt and freshly ground black pepper to taste

Lemon wedges, for garnish

1. In a large shallow dish, marinate the lamb chops in the oil and lemon juice at room temperature for at least 1 hour, and up to 3 hours, turning from time to time. Pat the meat dry and set aside.

2. Preheat a heavy-duty cast-iron skillet or cast-iron griddle pan over high heat for 5 minutes. Or prepare a wood or charcoal fire. The fire is ready when the coals glow red and are covered with ash.

3. If cooking in a skillet or a griddle, reduce the heat to moderate, add the lamb chops, and cook until nicely browned, about 2 minutes per side for rare. Season each side with salt and pepper after cooking. Transfer to warmed dinner plates and serve immediately, with the wedges of lemon for squeezing over the lamb chops.

■ Yield: 4 servings ■

WINE SUGGESTION: Set aside a fine, tasty red, such as a Montepulciano d'Abruzzo, for these deliciously simple lamb chops.

Testing for Doneness

To test for doneness when cooking lamb chops or other meat, press the meat with the tip of your finger. If the meat is very soft, the lamb chops are rare. If the meat is medium-soft, the lamb chops are medium-rare. If the meat is very firm, the lamb chops are well-done.

Lamb Braised in White Wine, Garlic, and Hot Peppers

Abbàcchio alla Cacciatora

"When in Rome, live as the Romans do; when elsewhere, live as they live elsewhere."

ADVICE TO SAINT AUGUSTINE FROM SAINT AMBROSE,
BISHOP OF MILAN (A.D. 339–397)

Fragrant and bold, with a surprising complexity of flavors, this wintry dish from Trattoria Checchino dal 1887 in Rome is the sort of dish I love to make when I'm at home all day, puttering around the house. The aromatic combination of vinegar, white wine, anchovies, hot peppers, and garlic is an unusual one, but the flavor results are supremely satisfying, as each ingredient manages to have its say. While white wine is traditionally used in this classic dish, I've prepared it with both red and white with equal success. Likewise, the cut of lamb used here should be dictated by your pocketbook. I've prepared the dish with leg of lamb and neck of lamb, and one could also use a good lamb shoulder.

3 tablespoons extra-virgin olive oil

10 flat anchovy fillets in olive oil, drained and minced

¾ teaspoon crushed red peppers (hot red pepper flakes), or to taste

2½ pounds (1.25 kg) lamb (leg of lamb, shoulder, or neck), cut into 3-inch (8-cm) cubes

Sea salt and freshly ground black pepper to taste

1 cup (250 ml) dry white wine, preferably a young Chardonnay

¼ cup (60 ml) best-quality red wine vinegar

3 plump fresh garlic cloves, minced

½ teaspoon dried leaf oregano

1 teaspoon superfine flour, such as Wondra

1. In a 6-quart (6-l) flameproof casserole with a lid, combine the oil, 5 of the anchovy fillets, and ½ teaspoon of the crushed red peppers over moderate heat. Cook just until the peppers begin to color the oil, 2 to 3 minutes. Add the cubed lamb and brown carefully on all sides, about 3 to 4 minutes per side. Do not crowd the pan: The pieces of meat should not touch as they brown. The lamb may need to be browned in batches. Season the lamb generously with salt and pepper. Add the wine, vinegar, and garlic. Cover, reduce the heat to low, and cook until tender, about 1 hour.

2. To serve, remove the pieces of meat to a warmed serving platter. Cover the platter with foil to keep the lamb warm. Leave the sauce in the casserole, keeping it warm over very low heat.

3. Finish the sauce: In a small bowl, combine the oregano, flour, the remaining ¼ teaspoon crushed red peppers, the remaining 5 anchovy fillets, and about 3 tablespoons of the sauce. Stir to blend. Whisk this mixture into the sauce in the casserole, stirring over low heat until the flour is cooked and the sauce begins to thicken, 1 to 2 minutes. Taste the sauce, and adjust the seasoning as necessary. Serve the lamb on warmed dinner plates, spooning the sauce on top of the meat.

■ Y i e l d : 4 t o 6 s e r v i n g s ■

WINE SUGGESTION: This dish deserves an 8- or 9-year-old Chianti Riserva, such as Chianti Ruffino Riserva.

Braised Veal Shanks with Lemon and Parsley Garnish

Osso Buco

A great osso buco can bring you to your knees. With veal that's chewy, meaty, yet pale and tender—braised to perfection—topped by a lively and colorful blend of lemon zest, parsley, and garlic, it is one of the world's great dishes. As an added advantage, the core of the bones of the veal shank is filled with delicious marrow, which can be scooped out with a tiny spoon. But the greatness of an osso buco (literally, "hollow bone") lies in securing top-quality ingredients, then following through with careful and attentive braising. The lemon and parsley garnish—known as *gremolata*—helps transform what could be an ordinary dish into an unforgettable one. Ask your butcher to cut a meaty veal shank crosswise into very thick (3-inch; 8-cm) slices. The hindshank will produce more marrow and meatier pieces of veal. Traditionally, osso buco is served with Saffron Risotto (page 162).

4 tablespoons (2 ounces; 60 g) unsalted butter

3 tablespoons extra-virgin olive oil

Six 3-inch (8-cm) meaty veal shanks (about 6 pounds; 3 kg)

Sea salt and freshly ground black pepper to taste

1 medium onion, minced

1 rib celery, minced

1 carrot, minced

3 to 4 cups (750 ml to 1 l) chicken stock, preferably homemade (page 272)

4 medium tomatoes, peeled, cored, seeded, and chopped

LEMON AND PARSLEY GARNISH

2 plump fresh garlic cloves, degermed and minced

½ cup (125 ml) minced fresh flat-leaf parsley leaves

Grated zest (yellow peel) of 2 lemons

1. In a very large deep skillet, heat the butter and oil until hot. Working in batches, add the veal to the skillet and brown over moderate heat until browned on all sides, about 10 minutes. As the veal pieces are browned, transfer to a platter and season with salt and pepper. Set aside.

2. Add the onion, celery, and carrot to the skillet, and cook until softened but not browned, about 5 minutes. Deglaze with about ½ cup (125 ml) of the stock, using a metal spatula to scrape up any bits that cling to the bottom of the pan. Cook until most of the liquid has evaporated. (This will help begin building the flavor base of the sauce.)

3. Return the veal to the skillet. Add the tomatoes, along with enough stock to almost immerse the veal. Cover the skillet and simmer very gently for 1½ hours, or until the meat is almost falling off the bone. Watch the pan carefully, keeping the heat as low as possible, and adding liquid as necessary to keep the pan moist. The resulting sauce should be thick and gelatinous.

4. As the veal cooks, finely chop together the garlic, parsley, and grated lemon zest to make the gremolata. Five minutes before serving, sprinkle some of the gremolata over the meat, allowing its aromas to penetrate the tender veal.

5. Serve the veal shanks on 4 warmed dinner plates, spooning the sauce over the veal, and garnishing with the remaining gremolata if desired.

■ Yield: 4 servings ■

WINE SUGGESTION: A cold-weather red wine, such as a Gattinara or a Chianti Riserva, is my choice for this wintry dish.

The Art of Braising

Braising is an art unto itself. Proper braising turns tough and fibrous cuts of meat into soft and pleasantly chewy meat. After preliminary browning, the meat is cooked slowly in a bit of liquid, while its natural gelatin helps to form a thick and luxurious sauce. A braise is not a stew: The meat cooks in just enough liquid to keep the meat moist. Since the pan is covered during braising, the steam that rises helps keep the exposed portion of meat moist. Either water, wine, or stock can be used for braising, but remember that it is the braising liquid that will add body to the final sauce.

Beef Braised in Barolo Wine

Brasato al Barolo

ITALIAN PROVERB:

"One barrel of wine can work more miracles than a church full of saints."

This moist, fragrant, and flavorful braised beef is perfect for entertaining. Everything can be prepared a day in advance and reheated at serving time. The whole piece of beef is marinated, then slowly braised, making for meat that is full of a complex combination of flavors, including rosemary and rich red wine. This recipe comes from Angelo Maionchi, chef at Turin's historic Del Cambio. Although Barolo is the traditional wine for this dish, the less-expensive Barbera can be substituted without loss of quality. Traditionally, beef in Barolo is served with slices of polenta alongside (page 172). Other accompaniments might include baked and seasoned rice or pasta tossed with butter and fresh rosemary (page 134).

(continued)

2 pounds (1 kg) boneless braising beef in one piece (such as chuck roast)

1 bottle tannic red wine, preferably a Barolo or Barbera

¼ cup (60 ml) brandy

¼ cup (60 ml) plus 3 tablespoons extra-virgin olive oil

2 carrots, cut into thin rounds

2 bay leaves, preferably fresh

3 ribs celery, cut into thin slices

1 sprig fresh rosemary

1 teaspoon whole black peppercorns, crushed

½ cinnamon stick

4 whole cloves

2 medium onions, peeled and halved

Sea salt and freshly ground black pepper to taste

1. In a 3-quart (3-l) heavy-duty flameproof casserole with a lid, combine the beef, wine, brandy, ¼ cup (60 ml) of the olive oil, the carrots, bay leaves, celery, rosemary, crushed peppercorns, and cinnamon stick. Stick a clove into each of the onion halves and add to the casserole. Cover and refrigerate for at least 12 hours or up to 24 hours. Turn the meat from time to time.

2. At least 2 hours before cooking the meat, remove the casserole from the refrigerator to bring the meat to room temperature.

3. Remove the beef from the marinade and pat dry. Pour the marinade into another container and reserve. Rinse and dry the casserole. Add the remaining 3 tablespoons of olive oil to the casserole and heat the oil over moderately high heat. When the oil is hot but not smoking, add the beef and brown evenly on all sides, 3 to 4 minutes per side. Season the beef generously with salt and pepper. Add the marinade to the casserole. Bring just to a simmer, then reduce heat to very low and cover. Simmer gently until the beef is fork-tender, about 3 hours. Turn the meat from time to time, and do not let much of the liquid evaporate. You should have about 1 cup (250 ml) of liquid remaining for the sauce.

4. To serve: Transfer the beef to a carving board. Cut the beef against the grain into thick slices, and transfer the slices—slightly overlapping them—to a warmed serving platter. Cover with foil to keep warm. Strain the cooking liquid through a fine-mesh sieve and discard the solids. Return the liquid to the casserole, taste for seasoning, and, if necessary, boil until reduced to 1 cup (250 ml). Spoon the sauce over the beef and serve immediately. (Alternatively, the beef may be sliced and refrigerated for 1 more day, along with the sauce. Simply reheat at serving time.)

■ Yield: 4 to 6 servings ■

WINE SUGGESTION: A Barolo or Barbera, both from the Piedmont, are not only traditional but also ideal red wines for this dish. Their acidity, combined with a flavor that's full-bodied and robust, makes for a lovely food and wine marriage.

New Life for a Rich Sauce

Should you have even a few tablespoons of the delicious Barolo sauce left over, use it to add to a flavorful vinaigrette to toss over cold beef or salad greens. If you can't use the sauce right away, freeze in a small container and save for a rainy day.

On Warmed Plates

Nothing is more frustrating than to be served a succulent portion of meat on a cold plate. Since meat tends to cool as it rests, it is rarely piping hot at serving time. To best enjoy a warm meal, be sure to make a practice of warming plates ahead of time. You don't need to install an "official" plate-warming drawer (though if you're planning a kitchen, don't leave it out!). Here are some tips on do-it-yourself plate warmers:

■ Warm plates in a warm oven.

■ Or warm them in a microwave, heated at a low setting.

■ If you have a free sink, you can fill it or a large wash basin with hot tap water, and keep the plates warm in the hot water.

■ If at serving time you find you've forgotten to do any of the above, run very hot tap water over the plates to warm them, and dry before serving.

Braised Oxtail with Tomatoes, Onions, and Celery

Coda alla Vaccinara

Dark, rich, and meaty, this warming, wintry dish is typical of the hearty cold-weather fare served at Checchino dal 1887, near the old Roman stockyards. The restaurant all but put this dish on the map, although it has been changed and lightened over the years. Rather than pork rind and pork fat, only pancetta and olive oil are now used to cook the oxtail. Believe me, there is no loss of flavor, and the dish is a good deal more healthful. To reduce the fat even further, prepare the dish a day or two in advance, chill it, and then remove any solidified fat that has risen to the surface. The final dish should not be swimming in fat, but there should be enough tomato sauce left to use your homemade bread for sopping up! *Coda*, by the way, is Italian for oxtail. *Vaccinara* is the old name for a butcher in the Roman dialect: They worked in the stockyards, often lunching on oxtail stew at a nearby trattoria. This recipe dates from 1887, when Checchino was founded. The inclusion of golden raisins, pine nuts, and a touch of chocolate dates from the original recipe, but is optional. This is the type of main dish that demands no vegetable accompaniment. I like to precede it with Celery Salad with Anchovy Dressing (page 34).

(continued)

3 tablespoons extra-virgin olive oil

½ cup (2 ounces; 60 g) minced pancetta (see Note)

5 pounds (2.5 kg) oxtail, cut into 4-inch (10-cm) pieces (about 15 pieces)

Sea salt and freshly ground black pepper to taste

2 whole cloves

3 small onions, peeled and halved

3 plump fresh garlic cloves, minced

2 cups (500 ml) dry white wine, preferably a Chardonnay

One 28-ounce (785-g) can peeled Italian plum tomatoes in juice or one 28-ounce (785-g) can crushed tomatoes in purée

8 ribs celery, trimmed to 6-inch (15-cm) lengths

1 ounce (30 g) unsweetened chocolate, grated (optional)

2 tablespoons pine nuts (optional)

2 tablespoons golden raisins (optional)

1. In a 6-quart (6-l) flameproof casserole with a lid, combine the oil and pancetta over moderate heat. Cook the pancetta just until browned and crisp, 3 to 4 minutes. Remove the pancetta with a slotted spoon and set aside. Add the oxtail pieces and brown thoroughly on all sides, about 15 minutes. This may have to be done in batches. Do not crowd the meat in the pan, and do not allow the pieces of oxtail to touch. Once the meat is browned, season it generously with salt and pepper. Stick the cloves into two of the onion halves and add to the casserole. Add the remaining onions, the browned pancetta, and the garlic, and cook for 2 to 3 minutes. Add the wine and stir to incorporate. If using whole canned tomatoes, place a food mill over the casserole and purée the tomatoes directly into it. Crushed tomatoes can be added directly from the can. Cover, and bring just to a simmer over moderate heat. Reduce the heat to very low and simmer gently until the oxtail is fork-tender and the meat is falling off the bones, about 4 hours. Turn the meat two or three times during the cooking period. (The stew may be prepared up to this point 1 day in advance. Remove the casserole from the heat and allow to cool for several hours. Cover and refrigerate. At serving time, remove the casserole from the refrigerator and, with a small spoon, remove and discard any fat that has solidified on the surface. Bring to a simmer before proceeding with the recipe.)

2. Add the celery, slipping it under the pieces of oxtail so it cooks in the sauce. Simmer until the celery is tender, about 30 minutes. About 10 minutes before the celery is cooked, stir in the chocolate and add the pine nuts and raisins, if using. Taste the sauce, seasoning it as necessary. To serve, transfer the pieces of oxtail to individual warmed dinner plates. Spoon several tablespoons of the sauce around the meat, and arrange the pieces of celery alongside.

■ Y i e l d : 4 t o 6 s e r v i n g s ■

WINE SUGGESTION: With this dish, we drank a 4-year-old Colle Picchioni, considered one of the best wines of the Castelli Romani area of Rome. Its sturdiness stands up well to the robust flavors of the oxtail.

NOTE: There is no American equivalent for pancetta, the unsmoked Italian bacon that is cured with salt and mild spices and rolled. Pancetta is prized for its subtle, delicate flavor, and can be found in most Italian specialty shops. If you cannot find it, substitute a very lean, top-quality bacon. Blanch it for 1 minute in boiling water, then drain thoroughly. Blanching will remove the smoked flavor from the bacon without cooking it.

HERE'S TO THE

RICCI HERITAGE

.

Thank you Mom, Grandpa Felix, Aunt Ella, and Aunt Flora, for the great taste memories of childhood. The flavors of these trattoria dishes take me back to the days when we crowded around the table—aunts, uncles, and cousins—to share in a family feast. We didn't drink wine back then, but today, I'd opt for a gutsy, ruby Montepulciano d'Abruzzo Rosso, in honor of our Abruzzi ancestry.

AUNT FLORA'S OLIVE SALAD

CHICKEN CACCIATORA

BAKED RISOTTO WITH ASPARAGUS, SPINACH, AND PARMESAN

SOURDOUGH BREAD

FRAGRANT ORANGE AND LEMON CAKE

SAUCES, BROTHS, SPREADS, AND CONDIMENTS

⋅ ⋅ ⋅

Tomato Sauce

Salsa di Pomodoro

Tomato sauce should be rich, elegant, smooth, and redolent of herbs, even if it's to figure as the centerpiece of a basically peasant dish. Here is my everyday favorite. I sometimes make up a double batch, so there's always some in the freezer for those days I don't have time to cook.

¼ cup (60 ml) extra-virgin olive oil

1 small onion, minced

3 plump fresh garlic cloves, minced

Sea salt to taste

One 28-ounce (765 g) can peeled Italian plum tomatoes in juice or one 28-ounce (765 g) can crushed tomatoes in purée

Several sprigs of fresh parsley, bay leaves, and celery leaves, tied in a bundle with cotton twine

In a large unheated saucepan, combine the oil, onion, garlic, and salt, and stir to coat with oil. Cook over moderate heat just until the garlic turns golden but does not brown, 2 to 3 minutes. If using whole canned tomatoes, place a food mill over the skillet and purée the tomatoes directly into it. Crushed tomatoes can be added directly from the can. Add the herb bundle, stir to blend, and simmer, uncovered, until the sauce begins to thicken, about 15 minutes. For a thicker sauce, for pizzas and toppings, cook for 5 minutes more. Taste for seasoning. Remove and discard the herb bundle. The sauce may be used immediately, stored in the refrigerator for up to 2 days, or frozen for up to 2 months. If small quantities of sauce will be needed for pizzas or other toppings, freeze in ice cube trays.

⋅ Yield: About 3 cups (750 ml) sauce ⋅

▪ ▪ ▪

Tomato-Mushroom Sauce

Sugo di Pomodoro e Funghi

This simple tomato and mushroom sauce is ideal for serving alongside Tartra (page 30), the savory, herb-flecked custard from the Piedmont. The sauce can also serve as an all-purpose sauce for pasta or as a vegetarian sauce for a baked pasta dish.

¼ cup (60 ml) extra-virgin olive oil

1 small onion, minced

3 plump fresh garlic cloves, minced

1 small carrot, minced

1 small rib celery, minced

Sea salt to taste

8 ounces (250 g) fresh brown mushrooms, such as cremini, rinsed, dried, and thinly sliced

One 28-ounce (765-g) can peeled Italian plum tomatoes in juice or one 28-ounce (765-g) can crushed tomatoes in purée

Several sprigs of fresh parsley, bay leaves, and celery leaves, tied in a bundle with cotton twine

In a large unheated saucepan, combine the oil, onion, garlic, carrot, celery, and salt, and stir to coat with oil. Cook over low heat just until the vegetables are soft but not brown, 5 to 6 minutes. Add the mushrooms and cook until soft, 3 to 4 minutes more. If using whole canned tomatoes, place a food mill over the skillet and purée the tomatoes directly into it. Crushed tomatoes can be added directly from the can. Add the herb bundle, stir to blend, and increase the heat to moderate. Simmer, uncovered, until the sauce begins to thicken, about 15 minutes. Taste for seasoning. Remove and discard the herb bundle. The sauce may used immediately, refrigerated for 1 to 2 days, or frozen for up to 1 month.

▪ Yield: About 3 cups (750 ml) sauce ▪

Fantastic Tomato-Artichoke Sauce

Salsa Fantastica

On one of my trips to Italy, I picked up a little jar of this orange-red sauce, partially because I loved the name. Of course, the fact that it included two of my favorite foods—tomatoes and artichokes—didn't hurt a bit. The combination may at first seem unusual, but once you taste the union, with the tomato's light acidity and the creamy richness of the puréed artichokes, I think you'll agree that they're a marriage made in heaven. This sauce can be spread on toasted homemade bread, used as a dip for vegetables, or tossed with hot pasta, such as farfalle.

½ cup (125 ml) Tomato Sauce (page 256)

4 small Marinated Baby Artichoke Hearts Preserved in Oil (page 18), drained and quartered

2 tablespoons extra-virgin olive oil

2 teaspoons fresh thyme leaves

Sea salt to taste

Combine all the ingredients in the bowl of a food processor and purée. Taste for seasoning. Transfer to a small bowl. The sauce can be refrigerated for up to 3 days. Bring to room temperature and stir before serving.

▪ Yield: ¾ cup (185 ml) sauce ▪

■ ■ ■

Tomato and Cream Sauce

Sugo di Pomodoro e Panna

*omato sauce all on its own is wonderful. Add a touch of cream and you've moved into another, more elegant world altogether. The garlic and peppers can be adjusted to personal tastes, though I enjoy a sauce with a good hit of both.

¼ cup (60 ml) extra-virgin olive oil

4 plump fresh garlic cloves, minced

Sea salt to taste

½ teaspoon crushed red peppers (hot red pepper flakes), or to taste

One 28-ounce (765-g) can peeled Italian plum tomatoes in juice or one 28-ounce (765-g) can crushed tomatoes in purée

1 cup (250 ml) heavy cream

In a large unheated skillet, combine the oil, garlic, salt, and crushed red peppers, stirring to coat with oil. Cook over moderate heat just until the garlic turns golden but does not brown, 2 to 3 minutes. If using whole canned tomatoes, place a food mill over the skillet and purée the tomatoes directly into it. Crushed tomatoes can be added directly from the can. Stir to blend and simmer, uncovered, until the sauce begins to thicken, about 15 minutes. Add the cream, stir, and heat for 1 minute. Taste for seasoning. Use over pasta, or with fresh lasagne (page 126).

■ Yield: 1 quart (1 l) sauce ■

Pungent Parsley Sauce

Salsa Prezzemolo

oss this with hot spaghetti, spread it on bread, use it as a dip for raw celery or strips of fresh fennel. Pungent and verdant parsley "pesto" can be found in specialty stores in Italy, but the sauce can be prepared at home in a minute.

3 to 5 plump fresh garlic cloves (to taste), degermed and minced

½ teaspoon fine sea salt, or to taste

6 flat anchovy fillets in olive oil, drained and minced

3 cups (750 ml) loosely packed fresh flat-leaf parsley leaves

3 tablespoons freshly squeezed lemon juice

½ cup (125 ml) extra-virgin olive oil

Place the minced garlic, salt, and anchovies in the bowl of a food processor. Add the parsley and pulse 2 or 3 times, or until the sauce is homogeneous. Scrape down the sides of the bowl. With the machine running, add the lemon juice and then the olive oil in a slow, steady stream. Taste for seasoning. Transfer to a small bowl. Serve immediately. Do not prepare more than 1 hour in advance. As the sauce sits, the anchovy flavor quickly overpowers the fresh parsley taste, so I prefer to prepare it at the last moment.

Yield: 1 cup (250 ml) sauce, or enough to sauce 1 pound (500 g) of pasta

■ ■ ■

Basil and Garlic Sauce

Pesto

Basil and garlic sauce, known as pesto, is so satisfying that one can never have too many versions. Here is the most traditional, including nothing more than basil, garlic, extra-virgin olive oil, and salt, enriched with Parmigiano-Reggiano cheese. Although most traditional recipes call for pine nuts, I choose not to use them here: They are expensive, and the few tablespoons used in most recipes don't play much of a role in enhancing flavor. I've included instructions for preparing the pesto by hand, using a mortar and pestle, or in the food processor.

4 plump fresh garlic cloves, degermed and minced

Fine sea salt to taste

2 cups (500 ml) loosely packed fresh basil leaves and flowers

½ cup (125 ml) extra-virgin olive oil

½ cup (2 ounces; 60 g) freshly grated Italian Parmigiano-Reggiano cheese

BY HAND: Place the garlic and salt in a mortar and mash with a pestle to form a paste. Add the basil, little by little, pounding and turning the pestle with a grinding motion to form a paste. Continue until all the basil has been used and the paste is homogeneous. Add the oil, little by little, working it in until you have a fairly fluid paste. Stir in the cheese. Taste for seasoning. Transfer to a bowl. Stir again before serving.

IN A FOOD PROCESSOR: Place the garlic, salt, and basil in the bowl of a food processor and process to a paste. Add the oil, and process again. Transfer to a bowl and stir in the cheese. Taste for seasoning. Stir again before serving.

Serve immediately, or cover and refrigerate. (The sauce can be stored in the refrigerator for up to 1 day. Bring to room temperature and stir before serving.)

■ Yield: ¾ cup (185 ml) sauce ■

Basil, Garlic, and Tomato Sauce

Pesto alla Santa Margherita

F ew flavors offer more pleasure than a fresh, vibrant tomato pesto sauce, a pungent combination of garlic, basil, oil, a touch of tomato, and a good hit of Parmigiano-Reggiano cheese. Lighter than the better-known sauce prepared without tomatoes, this version offers a welcome change of pace. I sampled it at a small restaurant off the harbor of Santa Margherita, in Liguria, the home of the traditional basil-rich sauce. I prefer to prepare the sauce by hand, using a mortar and pestle—it seems more genuine and earthy. But I'm aware not everyone wants to go that extra step, so I also offer instructions for preparing it in a food processor.

4 plump fresh garlic cloves, degermed and minced

Fine sea salt to taste

2 cups (500 ml) loosely packed fresh basil leaves and flowers

1 firm medium-size ripe tomato, peeled, cored, seeded, and chopped

½ cup (125 ml) extra-virgin olive oil

½ cup (2 ounces; 60 g) freshly grated Italian Parmigiano-Reggiano cheese

BY HAND: Place the garlic and salt in a mortar and mash with a pestle to form a paste. Add the basil, little by little, pounding and turning the pestle with a grinding motion to form a paste. Continue until all the basil has been used and the paste is homogeneous. Alternately add the tomato and oil in several additions, working until you have a fairly fluid paste. Stir in the cheese. Taste for seasoning. Transfer to a small bowl. Stir again before serving.

IN A FOOD PROCESSOR: Place the garlic, salt, and basil in the bowl of a food processor and process to a paste. Add the tomatoes and oil, and process again. Transfer to a small bowl and stir in the cheese. Taste for seasoning. Stir again before serving.

Serve immediately, or cover and refrigerate. (The sauce can be refrigerated for up to 1 day. Bring to room temperature and stir before serving.)

■ Yield: ¾ cup (185 ml) sauce ■

Red Pesto Sauce

Pesto Rosso

I first sampled this sauce one summer in the Lake Garda village of Torri del Benaco, where the local wine and specialty shop offered an abundant assortment of sauces, unusual jams, dried mushrooms, oils, vinegars, and, of course, great wines. Each day we walked to town to put together the makings of a grand lunch, and each day I would purchase a different item for sampling. This red pesto sauce is one of my favorites, for it symbolizes much of what is great about Italian cuisine: The combination of sun-dried tomatoes, black olives, a generous hit of fresh herbs, and a touch of garlic and hot pepper makes for a sauce that is complex in its simplicity. When you toss a tablespoon or two with hot spaghetti, or spread it very lightly on freshly toasted bread, you arrive at a symphony of flavors that is distinctly Italian, distinctly pleasurable. I prepare this with tomatoes I have dried at home. Of course the sauce can be made with purchased dried tomatoes or those in oil. The taste won't always be the same, so I will leave it up to you to taste carefully as you prepare the sauce. Whatever you use, the sauce should be pungent, surprising, and complex, filled with the flavors of fresh herbs, excellent oil, and olives. The tomatoes, in effect, serve as only a backdrop, but a vital one. I prefer this sauce with a good bite of crushed red peppers, but if you prefer a tamer sauce, leave them out.

10 Sun-Dried Tomatoes (page 284)

1 plump fresh garlic clove, degermed and minced

½ teaspoon crushed red peppers (hot red pepper flakes), or to taste

6 tablespoons extra-virgin olive oil

About 20 salt-cured black olives, such as Italian Gaeta or French Nyons olives (see page 280), pitted

2 teaspoons minced fresh thyme leaves

1 tablespoon minced fresh rosemary leaves

In the bowl of a food processor, combine all the ingredients and process until the sauce is lightly emulsified but still quite coarse and almost chunky. (You do not want a smooth sauce.) The sauce can be stored in a jar in the refrigerator for up to 1 month. If you do so, first cover the pesto with a film of olive oil.

■ Yield: ½ cup (125 ml) sauce ■

· · ·

Fresh Herb Sauce for Meats and Poultry

Salsa Verde

Vivid green and just slightly piquant, this is a fabulous all-purpose sauce for serving as one would mayonnaise, with boiled meats, poultry, or fish. I first sampled this sauce in Florence, at Sostanza, the quintessential old-fashioned trattoria. There it was served with boiled beef, but the sauce can also be served with poached chicken or fish. There are countless versions of salsa verde, which means you can customize the recipe to your tastes, mood, and what you have at hand. Since my garden is full of arugula, parsley, and sorrel, this is what I prefer. If you have only parsley, that's fine, too. (Just be sure to stem it thoroughly, using just the leaves for the sauce.) Red wine vinegar may be substituted for the lemon juice, capers may be added, and garlic may or may not be included in the repertoire, according to your whim. The only constants are top-quality extra-virgin olive oil and fresh greens. The sauce can be made ahead of time and refrigerated for up to one day. I like the old-fashioned quality of the mortar and pestle and the rather rough texture that results. Those interested in saving time can prepare the sauce in the food processor.

2 plump fresh garlic cloves, degermed

½ teaspoon fine sea salt, or to taste

4 flat anchovy fillets in olive oil, drained and minced

2 cups (500 ml) loosely packed fresh flat-leaf parsley leaves

1 cup (250 ml) loosely packed sorrel leaves, coarsely chopped

1 cup (250 ml) loosely packed arugula leaves, coarsely chopped

2 tablespoons freshly squeezed lemon juice

½ cup (125 ml) extra-virgin olive oil

BY HAND: Place the garlic and salt in a mortar and mash with a pestle to form a paste. Add the anchovies and pound to a paste. Add the greens, little by little, pounding into a thick paste. Continue until all the greens have been used and the paste is homogeneous. Slowly add the lemon juice, and then the oil, stirring until the sauce is well blended. Taste for seasoning.

IN A FOOD PROCESSOR: With the food processor running, add the garlic cloves and mince them. Add the salt and anchovies and pulse 2 or 3 times. Add the greens and pulse 2 or 3 times, or until the sauce is homogeneous. With the processor running, add the lemon juice and then the olive oil in a slow, steady stream. Taste for seasoning.

Transfer to a small bowl. Serve immediately. (The sauce can be stored, covered and refrigerated, for 1 day. Before serving, bring to room temperature. Stir, and taste for seasoning.)

■ Yield: 1 cup (250 ml) sauce ■

Meat Sauce

Ragù

All too often one thinks of ragù, or meat sauce, as a heavy, meaty sauce with just a tinge of red sauce. In most trattorias in Italy, what you find is quite the opposite: a very flavorful, light tomato sauce flecked with just a suggestion of meat. A sauce like that allows the pasta to star, not the meat or the sauce. Sometimes you'll find it flecked with bits of pungent hot peppers, sometimes the meat is so close to nonexistent it could almost fool a vegetarian, and other times the meat is noticeably chunky though never dominant. This all-purpose sauce is simply a suggestion: One can use a mix of meats, including nicely seasoned Italian sausage, or a mix of freshly ground pork, beef, and veal. Although I'm aware that many people try to stay away from any visible fat in their food, the best sauces do have a nice, overt veil of fat, so don't use meat that is too, too lean. For a vegetarian version, substitute half an ounce (15 g) of dried porcini mushrooms soaked in hot water and drained (see page 148). I generally make a large batch so I can have some for the freezer. Depending upon how I intend to use the sauce, I add more or less hot pepper.

3 tablespoons extra-virgin olive oil

1 small onion, minced

1 rib celery, minced

1 carrot, minced

¼ cup (60 ml) fresh flat-leaf parsley leaves, snipped with a scissors

Sea salt to taste

About 8 ounces (250 g) bulk sausage meat or a mix of chopped beef, pork, and veal

Two 28-ounce (765-g) cans peeled Italian plum tomatoes in juice, or two 28-ounce (765-g) cans crushed tomatoes in purée

1 teaspoon crushed red peppers (hot red pepper flakes), or to taste (optional)

In a large skillet, combine the oil, onion, celery, carrot, parsley, and salt, and toss to coat with oil. Cook over moderate heat until the vegetables are soft and fragrant, 3 to 4 minutes. Add the meat, making sure to break it up into small bits with a spatula, and toss to blend. Reduce the heat to low, and cook until the meat changes color, about 5 minutes more. If using whole canned tomatoes, place a food mill over the skillet and purée the tomatoes directly into it. Crushed tomatoes can be added directly from the can. Stir to blend, and, if using, add the crushed red peppers. Cover, and cook until the sauce begins to thicken, about 20 minutes. Taste for seasoning. The sauce can be refrigerated, covered, for up to 3 days or frozen for up to 1 month.

Yield: About 1 ½ quarts (1.5 l) sauce

White Sauce

Salsa Balsamella

A classic white sauce of milk, butter, and flour is used often in Italian cooking. It's a quick, easy, flavorful sauce to prepare at the last minute. The worst versions can taste like paste. The best serve as delicate binders that add fresh and refreshing herbal flavors and a pleasantly creamy texture to a dish. This recipe makes a medium-thick white sauce, ideal for baked pasta (page 154). Since milk so readily absorbs the flavors of fresh herbs, I like to infuse my white sauce with fresh bay leaves and rosemary.

2 cups (500 ml) whole milk

2 bay leaves, preferably fresh

1 tablespoon minced fresh rosemary leaves

4 tablespoons (2 ounces; 60 g) unsalted butter

3 tablespoons all-purpose flour

¼ teaspoon fine sea salt

1. In a medium-size saucepan, scald the milk over high heat, bringing it just to the boiling point. Add the bay leaves and rosemary, cover, and set aside to infuse for 10 minutes. Strain the milk through a fine-mesh sieve into a measuring cup with a pouring spout. Discard the herbs.

2. In a heavy medium-size saucepan, melt the butter over moderate heat. Whisk in the flour and cook, stirring constantly, for 1 minute. Do not let the flour brown. Remove the saucepan from the heat and whisk in the hot strained milk a few tablespoons at a time, stirring constantly until all the milk has been incorporated into the flour and butter.

3. Return the saucepan to the heat, add the salt, and whisk constantly until the sauce thickens, 2 to 3 minutes. Taste for seasoning. (White sauce should not be held for more than a few hours. If you prepare it an hour or two in advance, rub the surface with a lump of butter so that it melts and forms a thin coating that will prevent the sauce from drying out. At serving time, simply warm the sauce on the top of a double boiler, stirring the butter into the sauce.)

■ Yield: About 2 cups (500 ml) sauce ■

Tips For a Better White Sauce

■ Do not allow the flour to brown when cooking it with the butter, or the sauce will taste burnt.

■ Add the hot milk off the heat, and very gradually, to obtain a very smooth sauce without lumps.

■ Whisk, whisk, and whisk again, without distraction.

Chicken Stock

Brodo di Pollo

This is a light, freshly flavored chicken stock, similar to those found in Italian kitchens. I always have stock on hand in the freezer, a way to cut down on cooking time and to enrich my larder, enlarging my repertoire on days I don't have time to cook. And I adore the way my house smells when the stock is simmering away.

4 pounds (2 kg) chicken parts (necks and wings), rinsed

1 tablespoon sea salt, or to taste

1 large onion, halved, each half stuck with a whole clove

3 plump fresh garlic cloves

Several parsley stems, celery leaves, bay leaves, and sprigs of thyme, wrapped in the green part of a leek and tied in a bundle with cotton twine

4 large carrots, peeled

4 leeks, white and tender green part, trimmed and well rinsed

4 whole black peppercorns

1. In a large stockpot, combine the chicken parts, salt, and cold water to cover. Bring to a boil over high heat, skimming off any impurities that rise to the surface. With a slotted spoon, transfer the chicken parts to a large sieve. Rinse, drain, and set aside. Discard the blanching liquid.

2. Rinse out the stockpot, and add the blanched chicken parts and all the remaining ingredients. Add cold water to cover and bring just to a simmer over moderately high heat. Skim off the impurities that rise to the surface. Reduce the heat and simmer—as gently as possible—for 3 hours, skimming as necessary.

3. Line a fine-mesh sieve with dampened cheesecloth and set over a large bowl. Ladle—do not pour—the liquid into the bowl. Measure the liquid. If it exceeds 2 quarts (2 l), return to a saucepan and reduce over moderate heat. Cool to room temperature. Skim off and discard any fat that rises to the surface. The stock may be refrigerated for up to 2 days or frozen for up to 2 months.

■ Yield: About 2 quarts (2 l) light stock ■

Vegetable Broth

Brodo di Verdura

I once spent a very profitable and informative day in the kitchens with Chef Walter Tripodi at La Frateria di Padre Eligio in Tuscany. This is the quick vegetable stock he uses when preparing risotto. It can cook while you're doing other kitchen tasks, and should be ready just about the time you're ready to prepare your risotto. Because the broth is thin, delicate, and without the fat that would give it holding power, it should be used the same day it is prepared.

> *2 quarts (2 l) cold water*
>
> *3 onions, halved*
>
> *3 carrots, peeled*
>
> *2 ribs celery, rinsed*
>
> *Several parsley stems, celery leaves, bay leaves, and sprigs of fresh thyme, wrapped in the green part of a leek and tied in a bundle with cotton twine*
>
> *½ teaspoon sea salt*

In a large stockpot, combine all the ingredients and bring to a simmer over moderate heat. Simmer, uncovered, for about 1 hour. With a slotted spoon, remove and discard the vegetables and herb bundle. The broth can be used immediately.

■ Yield: About 1 ½ quarts (1.5 l) broth ■

Garlic Mayonnaise

Aïoli

One evening in the waterside town of Santa Margherita—not too far from the French border—I was served a side dish of sliced steamed potatoes and offered this garlic-pungent, French-inspired mayonnaise to toss with the potatoes. The combination has been a family favorite ever since. This is one sauce that simply cannot be made properly in the food processor: It turns to glue and is not worthy of its name. Serve garlic mayonnaise with any steamed or boiled vegetables, grilled fish, cold meats, and poultry.

6 plump fresh garlic cloves, degermed

½ teaspoon fine sea salt

2 large egg yolks, at room temperature

1 cup (250 ml) extra-virgin olive oil

1. Pour boiling water into a large mortar to warm it. Discard the water and dry the mortar. Place the garlic and salt in the mortar and mash together with a pestle to form as smooth a paste as possible. (The fresher the garlic, the easier it will be to crush.)

2. Add 1 of the egg yolks. Stir, pressing slowly and evenly with the pestle, always in the same direction, to thoroughly blend the garlic and yolk. Add the second yolk and repeat until well blended.

3. Very slowly work in the oil, drop by drop, until the mixture thickens. Then gradually whisk in the remaining oil in a slow, thin stream until the sauce is thickened to a mayonnaise consistency. (Garlic mayonnaise can be refrigerated, covered and well sealed, for up to 1 day. Bring to room temperature to serve.)

▪ Yield: About 1 cup (250 ml) mayonnaise ▪

Artichoke Cream

Crema di Carciofi

To anyone who loves artichokes as I do, this soothing, golden cream is like a taste of heaven on earth. Spread it on freshly grilled homemade bread, scoop it up with a wand of crisp celery, toss it with a bit of spaghetti for a very quick, nourishing meal. I first sampled this one summer along Lake Garda, where each day brought a new, specific flavor to my life, along with bold swaths of sunshine, friendship, and fun. Don't use just any marinated artichokes for this recipe: Make your own!

1 cup (250 ml) drained Marinated Baby Artichokes Preserved in Oil (page 18), marinade reserved

About ¼ cup (60 ml) reserved marinade liquid

Fine sea salt to taste (optional)

In the bowl of a food processor, combine the artichokes and about 2 tablespoons of the marinade liquid. Purée, adding additional liquid as necessary to create a light, fluffy cream. Taste for seasoning. This sauce will keep for several days, well covered, in the refrigerator. Bring to room temperature before serving.

▪ Yield: About 1 cup (250 ml) cream ▪

. . .

Black Olive Spread

Olivada

T his is one of my favorite Mediterranean flavors, a sunny blend of top-quality black olives, fresh herbs, oil, and a touch of capers and anchovies. Keep it on hand for those days you don't have time to cook and need a zesty pick-me-up.

2 plump fresh garlic cloves, degermed and minced

1 teaspoon fresh thyme leaves

2 tablespoons drained capers, rinsed

4 anchovy fillets, drained, rinsed, and coarsely chopped

2 tablespoons extra-virgin olive oil

1 tablespoon rum

2 cups (8 ounces; 250 g) salt-cured black olives, such as Italian Gaeta or French Nyons olives (see page 280), pitted

Combine all the ingredients except the olives in the bowl of a food processor and process just until blended. Add the olives and pulse about 10 times. The mixture should be fairly coarse. The spread can be used to dress pasta, or spread on toast. It can be stored in a jar in the refrigerator for up to 1 month. If you plan to do so, cover the olivada with a film of olive oil.

■ Yield: 2 cups (500 ml) spread ■

Green Olive Spread

Olivada Verde

While black olive spreads are well known in Italy and in France, the green olive version is, unfortunately, less common. I love this bright, brilliantly flavored spread, and think it's best when freshly made, when you have the slightly tangy mix of green olives, capers, anchovies, and a good hit of freshly ground black pepper, all flavors at their peak. I like to serve it as a condiment to spread on toast with a first course of Seasoned Raw Beef (page 12), or as a dip for wands of fresh celery.

2 tablespoons drained capers, rinsed

4 anchovy fillets, drained, rinsed, and coarsely chopped

¼ cup (60 ml) extra-virgin olive oil

Freshly ground black pepper to taste

2 cups (10 ounces; 300 g) drained pitted green olives

Combine all the ingredients except the olives in the bowl of a food processor and process just until blended. Add the olives and pulse about 10 times. The mixture should be just slightly chunky, but very spreadable, and should have a good flavor of freshly ground pepper. The spread can be used to dress pasta, or spread on toast. It can be stored in a jar in the refrigerator for up to 1 week, covered with a film of olive oil. (If stored longer than a week, the spread loses its bright, fresh flavor.)

■ Yield: 2 cups (500 ml) spread ■

• • •

Salt-Cured Anchovies

Acciughe sotto Sale

Pungent with the rich, salty flavors of the sea, salt-cured anchovies are essential to the Italian larder. Anchovies turn up in pasta sauces, are an essential ingredient in Lamb Braised in White Wine, Garlic, and Hot Peppers (page 242), and are delicious all on their own, on top of a slice of freshly grilled bread. When you find anchovies in your fish market, eat some fresh, marinated in lemon juice, herbs, and oil (see page 20). With the rest, prepare these simple cured anchovies for all-year eating.

2 pounds (1 kg) very fresh anchovies
2 pounds (1 kg) coarse sea salt
About 20 bay leaves, preferably fresh
About 20 sprigs fresh thyme

1. Lightly rinse (don't wash or soak) the anchovies. Individually head and gut the fish: Hold each anchovy firmly just beneath the head, and gently pull off the head and attached entrails. Discard the head and entrails. Place a thick layer of coarse salt on the bottom of a large sterilized canning jar. Place a layer of anchovies side by side on the salt, and sprinkle a thin layer of salt on top of the anchovies. Continue layering until all the anchovies and salt have been used, ending with a layer of salt. Every layer or so, add several bay leaves and sprigs of fresh thyme. Cover securely and store in a cool, dark place, or refrigerate. A brine will form as the anchovies absorb the salt and are cured. This should not be discarded. The anchovies are ready to eat in about 2 weeks and they can be stored for up to 1 year, in a cool, dark spot.

2. Properly cured anchovies are a deep mahogany color, much like ham. To eat, simply fillet the anchovies and use in any dish calling for cured anchovies.

▪ Yield: 2 quarts (2 l) anchovies ▪

Salt-Cured Black Olives

Olive Nere

Pure, salt-cured black olives are one of life's simple pleasures. Served as an appetizer with a glass of wine, tossed with pasta or with salads, stuffed into breads or rolls, or sprinkled on pizza, they are an integral part of Italian cooking.

As varieties of olives vary according to region, so do methods of curing them, and one finds Umbrian specialties flavored with orange zest, garlic, and bay leaves, as well as Sicilian salads of black olives crushed with oil, garlic, vinegar, and oregano, or with licorice-like fennel and orange and lemon zest. Note that different varieties are destined for different uses. However, as smooth green olives are those that were picked before they were ripe, smooth purple olives just as they ripened, and wrinkled black olives when they were overripe, in principle, all three could come from the same tree.

Although we don't all have olive trees in our backyards, fresh, uncured olives can be secured in parts of California, and on wintertime trips to Italy or France. Come harvesttime in December, markets in the south of Italy and France offer the bitter, wrinkled ripe olives for curing at home. Here is the simplest and most classic method: The olives are pricked all over with a small fork, then tossed in sea salt, using a traditional ratio of 2 pounds (1 kg) olives to 3½ ounces (100 g) coarse sea salt. Bay leaves, thyme, rosemary, and black peppercorns can also be added at this point. After being tossed daily, the olives are ready to be consumed in ten to fifteen days, and will stay fresh-tasting for about six months. If you're new to uncured olives, don't make the mistake so many people do, and pop one in your mouth. Uncured olives are unforgivably bitter and unpleasant.

2 pounds (1 kg) ripe uncured
black olives

3½ ounces (100 g) coarse sea salt

OPTIONAL FLAVORINGS

Sprigs of fresh thyme

Sprigs of fresh rosemary

Fresh bay leaves

Extra-virgin olive oil

Whole black peppercorns

Minced fresh garlic

Red wine vinegar

Grated lemon zest (yellow peel)

Grated orange zest (orange peel)

Dried red chile peppers

1. Do not wash the olives. If there are any leaves or stems still attached to the olives, remove and discard them. With a small seafood fork, prick each olive three or four times, all the way through to the center. (The pricking allows the olives to quickly absorb the salt.) Place the olives in a large, shallow bowl and add the salt. Toss with your hands to coat the olives with salt. Add, according to taste, sprigs of fresh thyme or rosemary, bay leaves, and/or a teaspoon of whole black peppercorns.

2. Leave the olives uncovered, at room temperature, tossing them once or twice a day. After 10 days, sample the olives. If they are still too bitter, let them cure for several more days. By this time much of the salt should be absorbed into the olives, but there may still be salt and some liquid at the bottom of the bowl. Do not discard this brine, for it will eventually be absorbed into the olives.

3. Once the olives are edible, pack them in pint (half-liter) glass jars, with any salt still attached, layering them with herbs as desired. Sprinkle with just enough olive oil to moisten. (Do not add citrus zest or garlic at this time, or the olives will lose their fresh, vibrant flavor.) Cover the jars and store, at room temperature, for up to 6 months.

4. At serving time, sample the olives. Should they be overly salty (though they shouldn't be), they can be rinsed in cold water. To serve, add, to taste, freshly minced garlic, a drop or two of red wine vinegar, citrus zest, black peppercorns, or hot red chile peppers.

■ Yield: 2 pounds (1 kg) olives ■

Brine-Cured Black Olives

Olive Nere

"If I could paint and had the necessary time, I should devote myself for a few years to making pictures only of olive trees."

ALDOUS HUXLEY

Brine-cured black olives are the "backbone" of cured olives, for they are basically indestructible. The ripe olives are simply placed in a 10 percent brine solution until they are edible, a process that takes several months. Unlike salt-cured olives, which are pricked with a fork to allow the salt to penetrate the meat of the olive, brine-cured olives are simply cured whole in the brine. The process can take three to four months, depending upon the size of the olives and the age of the brine. Once cured, they can be kept indefinitely, though I've never cured enough to last me more than a year.

2 pounds (1 kg) ripe uncured black olives

3½ ounces (100 g) fine sea salt

1 quart (1 l) water

OPTIONAL FLAVORINGS

Sprigs of fresh thyme

Sprigs of fresh rosemary

Fresh bay leaves

Extra-virgin olive oil

Whole black peppercorns

Red wine vinegar

Minced fresh garlic

Grated lemon zest (yellow peel)

Grated orange zest (orange peel)

Dried red chile peppers

1. Do not wash the olives. If there are any leaves or stems still attached to the olives, remove and discard them. In a large crock, combine the salt and water and stir to dissolve. Add the olives, cover, and set aside in a cool spot for several months, stirring from time to time. The olives should be covered with a small plate, to keep them all immersed in the brine. A scum will form on top, but it is harmless and should not be discarded, for it is the sign of a healthy, active brine. Do not add any seasonings other than salt and water to the brine. For specific flavorings, add those at serving time. When starting with a fresh brine, olives will take 3 to 4 months of curing before they are edible. Once cured, the olives can be kept indefinitely. Never discard a salt brine for olives, which will become black and inky. It can be used indefinitely, year after year.

2. To serve, remove the olives from the brine with a slotted spoon or wooden olive scoop with holes. Taste the olives. If they are excessively salty, they can be rinsed or soaked in cold water to remove some of the saltiness. Serve as they are, or season with any of the optional seasonings.

■ Yield: 2 pounds (1 kg) olives ■

Sun-Dried Tomatoes

Pomodori Secchi

T hese tomatoes are the essence of summer, serving to warm your soul in the depths of winter. Although sun-dried tomatoes are certainly more popular in America than in their native Italy (where they are sold at markets, but seldom show up in restaurant kitchens), they do have their place in the Italian kitchen. And the price of commercially sun-dried tomatoes makes it practical and economical to prepare them. I like to snip the dried tomatoes and toss them into a green salad for a cold-weather pick-me-up. They can also be tossed into a last-minute pasta dish, or served as is, with cheese.

It goes without saying that it's best to dry these on a dry day. I've had success with drying tomatoes in gas, electric, and convection ovens. The drying time will vary according to the size and moistness of the tomatoes, your oven, and the outdoor temperature. Since they are dried at the lowest possible oven temperature, there is little danger of burning the tomatoes. Be sure not to underdry: The tomatoes should be perfectly dry, with no interior moisture, and darkened to deep vermilion shades. Generally, there is no need to place a broiler pan beneath the tomatoes on the racks: They will dry better if there is good oven circulation. Look for small tomatoes of equal size so they will dry more quickly and in the same time. To ensure that the tomatoes do not fall through the racks as they dry and shrink, place them on cake racks set on the oven racks.

5 pounds (2.5 kg) Roma (oval) tomatoes
Fine sea salt

1. Preheat the oven to 200°F (100°C; gas mark 1), or the lowest setting possible. Remove the oven racks.

2. Trim and discard the stem ends of the tomatoes. Halve each tomato lengthwise. Arrange the tomatoes, cut side up, side by side and crosswise on cake racks set on the oven racks. Do not allow the tomatoes to touch one another. Sprinkle lightly with salt.

3. Place in the oven and bake until the tomatoes are shriveled and feel dry, anywhere from 6 to 12 hours. Check the tomatoes from time to time: They should remain rather flexible, not at all brittle. Once dried, remove the tomatoes from the oven and allow them to thoroughly cool on cake racks. (Smaller tomatoes will dry more quickly than larger ones. Remove each tomato from the oven as it is dried.)

4. Transfer the tomatoes to zipper-lock bags. The tomatoes will last indefinitely.

■ Yield: About 2 cups (500 ml) ■
dried tomatoes

THANK YOU, PIEMONTE

•

The Piedmont is certainly one of Italy's most appealing regions, with great wine, great food, and a solid, robust personality all of its own. This menu is a "thank-you note" to the cooks and restaurateurs who so kindly opened their doors to me on the trattoria tour. With the meal, I'd drink a young red Dolcetto d'Alba, while with dessert, I'd search out a good bottle of sweet, muscat-fragrant Moscato d'Asti.

SEASONED RAW BEEF
TAJARIN WITH ROSEMARY-INFUSED BUTTER
RABBIT WITH RED PEPPERS AND POLENTA
PANNA COTTA (ALMOND-VANILLA CREAMS)

·

DESSERTS, GRANITA, SORBET, AND ICE CREAMS

·

Summer Peaches and Raspberries

Insalata di Pesche e Lampone

ne sunny August afternoon we sat on the shaded terrace of La Stalla, a tranquil, country brick farmhouse-trattoria in the village of Gardone Riviera, on Lake Garda. We feasted on giant mixed salads of greens and vegetables, slices of grilled fontina cheese served with wild mushrooms, and this delightfully refreshing and simple dessert. The dish consists of a lightly sweetened peach purée that's spread out to fill the bottom of a flat serving plate, then edged with slices of fragrant ripe peaches. The center may be filled with raspberries or other small seasonal berries. Serve this with a bubbly white, such as the charming Italian Prosecco, and pass a basket of biscotti (page 314). Sort of makes you want to kick up your heels and dance!

5 ripe peaches (about 2 pounds; 1 kg)

¼ cup (50 g) Vanilla Sugar (page 324)

2 cups (8 ounces; 250 g) fresh raspberries

1. Peel the peaches: Bring a large pot of water to a rolling boil. Drop the peaches in, one by one, and scald just until the skins are softened, 1 to 2 minutes. Using a slotted spoon, remove the peaches and plunge directly into cold water, for easier handling. Once cool enough to handle, peel the peaches using the tip of a small sharp knife. Discard the skins.

2. Coarsely chop 3 of the peeled peaches and place in the bowl of a food processor. Add 2 tablespoons of the sugar and purée. Spoon the purée into a 10½-inch (27-cm) round porcelain baking dish and, using a spatula, evenly spread the purée over the bottom of the dish.

3. Cut the remaining 2 peeled peaches into 16 even slices. Place in a bowl and toss with 1 tablespoon of the sugar. Evenly arrange the peach slices, slightly overlapping, on top of the peach purée, forming a ring of peaches around the edge of the dish. Cover and refrigerate for up to 4 hours.

4. At serving time, toss the raspberries with the remaining 1 tablespoon sugar. Carefully spoon the berries on top of the peach purée, filling in the center of the dish. Serve immediately. Carefully spoon a few peach slices onto each dessert plate, and place a spoonful of purée, then a spoonful of berries, alongside.

■ Yield: 4 to 6 servings ■

WINE SUGGESTION: I love this with a fruity, fizzy Prosecco from the Veneto.

Almond Macaroons

Amaretti

I adore these fetching macaroons, rich with almond flavor. The cookies are prepared with simple pantry ingredients one is always likely to have on hand. They've become part of my repertoire, and make a great dessert, particularly when paired with biscotti. With this recipe, I find better results if one measures the egg whites (since volume varies), and prefer baking on parchment paper, for easier removal.

¾ cup (3½ ounces; 105 g) blanched almonds, ground to a fine powder

¾ cup (150 g) sugar

⅓ cup (80 ml) egg whites (about 2 large whites), at room temperature

½ teaspoon pure almond extract

1. Preheat the oven to 350°F (175°C; gas mark 4/5). Line 3 baking sheets with baking parchment. Set aside.

2. In a large bowl, combine the almonds and sugar, and stir to blend.

3. In another bowl, whisk together the egg whites and almond extract. Add the egg whites to the almond mixture, and stir to form a soft, sticky batter.

4. With a teaspoon, drop about ½ teaspoon of batter per cookie onto the baking sheets, spacing them slightly apart, for about 12 cookies per sheet.

5. Place the baking sheets in the center of the oven and bake until the macaroons are lightly browned around the edges and slightly firm to the touch, about 15 minutes. Remove the baking sheets from the oven and transfer the sheets of parchment to racks to cool until the cookies begin to firm up, just 3 to 4 minutes. With a sharp knife, gently lift the cookies from the parchment and transfer to racks to cool thoroughly. (The cookies can be stored in a tin box in a cool, dry spot for up to about 10 days.)

■ Yield: About 36 cookies ■

Tip

When buttering a pan, place about 1 tablespoon of softened butter in the pan, place your hand inside a small plastic sandwich bag, and carefully butter the pan. Discard the bag and come out with spotless hands. Likewise, keep a small shaker full of all-purpose flour at hand, using that to sprinkle the pan with flour.

• • •

Baked Peaches with Almond Macaroons

Pesche Ripiene alla Piemontese

Italian Dictum:

*"Peel a fig for a friend,
and a peach for an enemy."*

While this remarkably simple and delicious peach dessert is generally associated with the Piedmont, I've sampled these baked peaches stuffed with ground amaretti cookies all over Italy. Although a topping of whipped cream is not traditional here, remember, in your kitchen, you and your palate are boss.

Unsalted butter for preparing the baking dish

6 ripe peaches

10 full-size (5 pairs) amaretti cookies (Italian macaroons; see Mail Order Sources, page 325)

¼ cup (50 g) Vanilla Sugar (page 324)

1 large egg yolk

2 tablespoons (1 ounce; 30 g) unsalted butter

1. Preheat the oven to 350°F (175°C; gas mark 4/5).

2. Lightly butter a baking dish large enough to hold the peaches in a single layer. Rinse, halve, and stone the peaches, cutting along the natural line of the fruit. With a small spoon, scoop out about 1 teaspoon of the peach pulp from each half to enlarge the cavity. Reserve the scooped-out pulp. Place the peach halves, pitted side up, side by side in the buttered baking dish.

3. In the bowl of a food processor, process the amaretti to fine crumbs. (Do not process to a paste.) Transfer the mixture to a small mixing bowl. Stir in the reserved peach pulp, the sugar, and egg yolk, mixing thoroughly.

4. Spoon the filling into the cavity of each peach half, distributing it as evenly as possible. Dot each half with a bit of butter.

5. Place the dish in the center of the oven and bake until the peaches are soft and the filling firms up and begins to form a crust, about 40 minutes. Serve warm or at room temperature, transferring the peaches to an attractive serving platter or individual dessert bowls or plates.

■ Y i e l d : 6 s e r v i n g s ■

NOTE: If using miniature amaretti, use 20 cookies, about 2 ounces (30 g).

● ● ●

Coffee and Mascarpone Ladyfinger Cream

Tiramisù

Tiramisù—that hyper-rich layered modern Italian dessert—has become an international favorite, appealing particularly to sweet tooths that love soft, creamy, and cool. The name means "pick me up," and that's what happens when you offer your body a jolt of this brandy- and chocolate-flavored cream. It's easy as pie to make, especially when you begin with imported Italian ladyfingers, or sponge biscuits known as savoiardi. Although some versions call for sprinkling the top with cocoa powder, I always find this disagreeable: Inevitably a coughing fit follows the first bite. I prefer grated bitter chocolate. Perhaps the best version of this dish I ever sampled was in Venice, at the tiny, folksy trattoria Antica Besseta.

3 tablespoons very strong espresso coffee

1 tablespoon brandy or grappa

3 large eggs, at room temperature, separated

½ cup (100 g) Vanilla Sugar (page 324)

8 ounces (250 g) mascarpone, at room temperature

About 24 savoiardi or Italian lady fingers (see Mail Order Sources, page 325)

1 ounce (30 g) bittersweet chocolate, preferably Lindt Excellence

1. In a small bowl, combine the coffee and brandy. Set aside.

2. In the bowl of an electric mixer fitted with a whisk, whisk the egg whites until stiff and glossy but not dry. Set aside.

3. In a clean bowl of an electric mixer fitted with a whisk, combine the egg yolks and the vanilla sugar, and whisk until thick and lemon colored, about 2 minutes. Add the mascarpone and whisk to blend. With a large spatula, carefully fold the egg whites into the mascarpone mixture.

4. Place a single layer of 12 savoiardi (two rows of six each, end to end) in a 10-inch (25-cm) square baking dish or on a flat platter. Dip a pastry brush into the coffee mixture and soak the biscuits with the liquid. Spread about one-half of the mascarpone cream over the biscuits. Sprinkle with about one-half of the grated chocolate. Repeat with a second layer of biscuits, brush the biscuits with the remaining liquid, and cover with the remaining mascarpone cream. Reserve the final sprinkling of chocolate for serving time. Cover and refrigerate for at least 3 hours, allowing the cream to firm up slightly and the biscuits to absorb some of the liquid. (The tiramisù can also be prepared 1 day in advance). To serve, divide the tiramisù into rectangular slices and transfer to chilled dessert plates. Sprinkle with the remaining grated chocolate and serve immediately.

■ Y i e l d :   4   t o   8   s e r v i n g s ■

WINE SUGGESTION: Although tiramisù is almost too sweet for any wine, a velvety, amber Vin Santo would be right at home here.

A FROZEN TREAT: Haste in the kitchen usually spells disaster. But one day I prepared a last-minute tiramisù and slipped the prepared dessert in the freezer for about 30 minutes to help it stiffen up a bit before serving. The result was a pleasantly firm, chilled dessert, which I actually prefer to traditional tiramisù. The chilling somehow cuts through the richness of the mascarpone, making for a dessert that—to the palate at least—appears lighter than it really is.

Almond-Vanilla Creams

Panna Cotta

There's no question in my mind that panna cotta—an almond-and-vanilla-flavored cream—is up there among the top ten Italian desserts. It's so rich and creamy, this specialty of the Piedmont makes almost any other cream dessert taste like diet food! Panna cotta is a cinch to make, and can be even prepared a day or so in advance, a great boon to those looking for do-ahead desserts. And although the dessert is called "cooked cream," the cream is really only brought to a boil, to help dissolve the sugar and bring out the almond and vanilla flavors. For this dish, search out the freshest, most delicious cream you can find. One spring morning Chef Angelo Maionchi of Turin's Del Cambio kindly allowed me to work with him and his staff in their kitchen, and shared this recipe with me. Panna cotta can be prepared in a long loaf pan, set on a caramel base, or all on its own, in individual ramekins. I prefer the "special-ness" of having your very own dessert, and love the potential play of colors with the ivory-white panna cotta and brilliant and shiny fresh fruits, such as strawberries, raspberries, cherries, or raspberries.

Unsalted butter for preparing the ramekins

4 *teaspoons (about 2 packages) unflavored gelatin*

2 *cups (500 ml) whole milk*

1 *cup (120 g) confectioner's sugar*

2 *cups (500 ml) heavy cream*

1 *teaspoon pure vanilla extract*

½ *teaspoon pure almond extract*

Assorted soft fresh fruits, for garnish

1. Butter eight ½-cup (125-ml) ramekins. Place on a tray.

2. In a small bowl, sprinkle the gelatin over ¼ cup (60 ml) of the milk and stir to blend. Set aside until the gelatin completely absorbs the milk, 2 to 3 minutes.

3. In a large saucepan, combine the remaining 1¾ cups (440 ml) milk, the confectioner's sugar, and the cream, and bring just to a boil over moderate heat, whisking to dissolve the sugar. Remove from the heat, add the softened gelatin and milk and the vanilla and almond extracts, and whisk to completely dissolve the gelatin. Strain the mixture through a fine-mesh sieve into a large measuring cup or bowl with a pouring spout. Pour the mixture into the ramekins. Cover with plastic wrap and refrigerate until set, about 4 hours. (The panna cotta can be prepared up to 1 day in advance. Refrigerate until serving time.)

4. To serve, run a sharp knife along the inside of each ramekin, to help loosen the cream. Dip the bottom of each ramekin into a bowl of hot water, shaking to completely loosen the cream. Invert onto chilled dessert plates and serve with fresh fruit alongside, such as sliced strawberries, raspberries, or cherries.

■ Y i e l d : 8 s e r v i n g s ■

WINE SUGGESTION: This dreamy dessert deserves a fine, sweet wine, such as a Moscato d'Asti from the Piedmont.

VARIATION: While almond is the traditional flavoring for panna cotta, one also finds in Italy pure vanilla versions. For a more intense vanilla flavor, prepare the panna cotta with 2 teaspoons of pure vanilla extract, and omit the almond extract.

Individual Chocolate Flans

Budini di Cioccolato

Rich, creamy, and not overly sweet, these easy chocolate flans come from Cibrèo, a favorite Tuscan trattoria near the outdoor food market in Florence. I like to serve them with Hazelnut and Orange Biscotti (page 314), for I love the happy marriage of chocolate, coffee, and orange.

Unsalted butter for preparing the ramekins

8 ounces (250 g) bittersweet chocolate, preferably Lindt Excellence, finely chopped

⅔ cup (160 ml) whole milk

2 cups (500 ml) heavy cream

¼ cup (60 ml) espresso or very strong coffee (do not use instant)

1 tablespoon Vanilla Sugar (page 324)

2 large eggs, at room temperature, lightly beaten

2 large egg yolks, at room temperature, lightly beaten

1. Preheat the oven to 325°F (165°C; gas mark 4).

2. Cut 3 slits in a piece of waxed paper and use it to line a roasting pan. Butter six 1-cup (250-ml) ramekins and place them in the pan, on top of the paper. Set aside. (The paper will prevent the water added to the pan from boiling and splashing up on the custards.)

3. Prepare a large kettle of boiling water for the water bath; set aside.

4. In a large saucepan, combine the chocolate and milk. Melt the chocolate over low heat, stirring from time to time. Remove from the heat and set aside to cool for 5 minutes. Add the remaining ingredients, whisking to blend.

5. Divide the chocolate mixture evenly among the ramekins. Add enough boiling water to the roasting pan to reach about halfway up the sides of the ramekins. Place in the center of the oven and bake until the flans are just set at the edges but still trembling in the center, 45 to 50 minutes.

6. Remove from the oven and carefully remove the ramekins from the water. Serve in the ramekins warm or at room temperature, but not chilled.

■ Yield: 6 servings ■

· · ·

Ricotta Cheesecake with Pine Nuts and Raisins

Torta di Ricotta

T his is a delicate, tenderly sweet, and crustless ricotta cheesecake, studded lightly with pine nuts and raisins, and harboring a faint hint of lemon, orange, and spice. I frankly prefer it to the heavier, richer American-style cheesecake, and strongly recommend that cheesecake lovers add it to their repertoire. I sampled this dessert one sunny Saturday in December, at the excellent family-run trattoria Checchino dal 1887, in Rome.

Unsalted butter and all-purpose flour for preparing the cake pan

1 *cup (200 g) Vanilla Sugar (page 324)*

⅓ *cup (45 g) all-purpose flour, sifted*

½ *cup (2 ounces; 60 g) pine nuts*

½ *cup (70 g) golden raisins*

¼ *teaspoon fine sea salt*

2 *pounds (1 kg) whole-milk ricotta (or two 15-ounce containers)*

6 *large eggs, at room temperature, lightly beaten*

1 *teaspoon ground cinnamon*

1 *teaspoon freshly ground nutmeg*

2 *teaspoons pure vanilla extract*

Grated zest (yellow peel) of 1 lemon

Grated zest (orange peel) of 1 orange

Confectioner's sugar, for garnish

1. Preheat the oven to 300°F (150°C; gas mark 3/4).

2. Generously butter and flour a 9-inch (23-cm) springform pan, tapping out any excess flour. Set aside.

3. In a small bowl, stir together the vanilla sugar, flour, pine nuts, raisins, and salt. Set aside.

4. In the bowl of an electric mixer fitted with a paddle, gently beat the ricotta at low speed until smooth. Add the beaten eggs little by little, then add the vanilla sugar mixture and gently mix to blend. Add the spices, vanilla, and zests. Mix to blend thoroughly.

5. Pour the batter into the prepared cake pan. Place the pan in the center of the oven and bake until the cheesecake is a deep golden brown and fairly firm in the center, and a toothpick inserted in the center comes out clean, about 1 hour and 30 minutes. Transfer to a baking rack to cool. Once cooled, cover the cheesecake with plastic wrap and refrigerate until serving time. (The cake can be made up to 1 day in advance.)

6. To serve, release the sides of the springform pan, leaving the cheesecake on the pan base. Sprinkle the top generously with confectioner's sugar and serve, cutting into very thin wedges.

■ Yield: 16 to 20 servings ■

. . .

Toasted Hazelnut Cake

Torta di Nocciole

T he buttery, hazelnut-rich aroma that wafts from the oven as this cake bakes is enough of a reason to prepare it. The proof, as ever, is in the eating, and this is a moist, full-flavored, and satisfying cake. I first sampled torta di nocciole at the Panettiere Cravero, a bakery in the wine-making village of Barolo, where fresh rounds of the cake are stacked at the counter. Their version has the unusual addition of cocoa powder, which adds a lovely, rich touch to a cake that is already quite luxurious. Do take the time to toast the hazelnuts so they will better release their full, rich flavor and aroma. And don't be tempted to embellish this simple cake with frosting or even a dusting of confectioner's sugar. You'll see, it's perfectly fine all on its own.

Unsalted butter and all-purpose flour for preparing the cake pan

10 *tablespoons (5 ounces; 150 g) unsalted butter, at room temperature*

1¼ *cups (250 g) Vanilla Sugar (page 324)*

3 *large eggs, separated, at room temperature*

1 *teaspoon pure vanilla extract*

1 *cup (4 ounces; 125 g) hazelnuts (filberts), toasted and finely chopped*

2 *cups (265 g) all-purpose flour*

1 *tablespoon baking powder*

1 *tablespoon cocoa powder, preferably Dutch process*

¼ *teaspoon fine sea salt*

1. Preheat the oven to 350°F (175°C; gas mark 4/5).

2. Generously butter and flour a round 9-inch (23-cm) cake pan, preferably nonstick, tapping out any excess flour. Set aside.

3. In the bowl of an electric mixer fitted with a paddle, cream the butter and 1 cup (200 g) of the sugar until light and fluffy, 3 to 4 minutes. Add the egg yolks one by one, beating thoroughly after each addition. Beat in the vanilla and hazelnuts.

4. Sift the flour, baking powder, cocoa, and salt into a large bowl. Then sift the mixture over the hazelnut batter, folding gently until thoroughly blended. The batter will be very stiff, almost like a cookie dough.

5. In a clean bowl of an electric mixer fitted with a whisk, whisk the egg whites until fluffy. Add the remaining ¼ cup (50 g) of the sugar, a bit at a time, and whisk until the mixture is stiff and glossy but not dry.

6. With a large spatula, carefully fold the egg whites into the batter until there are no white patches in the batter.

7. Spoon the batter into the prepared cake pan, smoothing out the top with a spatula. Place the pan in the center of the oven. Bake until the cake is an even golden brown and a toothpick inserted in the center comes out clean, 40 to 50 minutes. Transfer to a wire rack to cool and firm up in the pan for 10 minutes. Then turn out of the pan and reinvert onto a serving plate. To serve, slice in wedges, for breakfast, as a snack, or for dessert.

■ Yield: 12 servings ■

WINE SUGGESTION: This cake is delicious with a slightly sweet muscatel, such as a Moscato d'Asti from the Piedmont.

Toasting for Flavor

Toasting nuts, such as hazelnuts, helps bring them to life, enhancing their flavor and reducing their moisture content. To toast: Spread the nuts out on a baking sheet. Toast in a preheated 350°F (175°C; gas mark 4/5) oven until lightly browned, about 10 minutes. Check every few minutes to avoid burning the nuts. Certain sophisticated recipes demand that the skins of hazelnuts be removed, by rubbing the nuts in a towel to loosen the skin. I don't find it necessary in this rustic cake. The nuts can easily be chopped in the food processor: Just be careful not to overprocess, or they turn to a paste. Hazelnuts are especially perishable and should be kept refrigerated or frozen, then thawed at room temperature before using.

Fragrant Orange and Lemon Cake

Torta di Arancio e Limone

One of the most romantic spots in Tuscany is the Locanda dell' Amorosa in Sinalunga. More than just an inn, this is a tiny U-shaped hamlet, set on a hill at the end of a long alley of cypresses. We stayed there one evening in late May, awakening to the sounds of thousands of tiny birds singing their little hearts out. Breakfast included cups of thick black coffee, unsalted Tuscan bread with homemade jams and honey, an assortment of sausages and cheeses, cereals, fruits, yogurt, and this magnificently golden cake studded with the flavorful zest of both lemon and orange. This version is based on the recipe that Chef Walter Ridaelli kindly shared with me that very day. This simple Italian delight, without the complication of a frosting, is always enjoyed with a beverage, making it the biscotti of the cake family. For special occasions, you may want to drizzle the cake with a simple icing, or serve it with sliced fruit macerated in rum or sweet wine.

(continued)

*Unsalted butter and all-purpose
flour for preparing the cake
pan*

3 cups (405 g) all-purpose flour

1½ teaspoons baking powder

½ teaspoon baking soda

¼ teaspoon fine sea salt

Grated zest and juice of 1 orange

Grated zest and juice of 1 lemon

¾ cup (185 ml) whole milk

*16 tablespoons (8 ounces; 225 g)
unsalted butter, softened*

*1½ cups (300 g) Vanilla Sugar
(page 324)*

5 large eggs

*Confectioner's sugar for dusting
(optional)*

1. Preheat the oven to 350°F (175°C; gas mark 4/5).

2. Evenly coat the interior of a 10-inch (12-cup; 2.5 l) Bundt pan with butter. Dust lightly with flour, shaking out the excess flour. Set aside.

3. Sift the flour, baking powder, baking soda, and salt into a large bowl. Stir in the orange and lemon zests.

4. Combine the orange and lemon juices and the milk, and set aside to "sour" the milk.

5. In a large bowl, using a hand-held electric mixer at high speed, beat the butter and vanilla sugar until light and fluffy, about 2 minutes. One at a time, beat in the eggs, mixing well after each addition. The mixture will looked curdled—don't worry. Alternating in thirds, add the flour and milk mixtures, beating well after each addition, and scraping down the sides of the bowl with a rubber spatula as needed.

6. Pour the batter into the prepared pan and place in the center of the oven. Bake until the cake is an even golden brown and a toothpick inserted in the center comes out clean, 45 to 55 minutes. (Don't worry if the cracks in the top of the cake don't look dry—use the toothpick test to test for doneness.) Transfer to a wire rack to cool in the pan for 10 minutes. Then turn out onto a serving plate. If desired, sift confectioner's sugar over the top of the cake. Slice into wedges and serve for breakfast, as a snack, or for dessert.

■ Yield: 10 to 14 servings ■

BEVERAGE RECOMMENDATION: I love this cake for breakfast, with a steaming cup of lemon-verbena herb tea. It could also be served for dessert, with a tiny glass of Tuscany's Vin Santo.

For Juicier Lemons

Place a room-temperature lemon on a flat work surface and, pressing down firmly with the palm of your hands, roll the lemon back and forth. This helps lemons give up the maximum amount of juice.

Lake Garda Apple Cake

Torta di Mele

. . .

Concentric circles of sweet, soft, golden-brown apples baked atop a vanilla-rich pound cake is one of my favorite Italian desserts. Late one summer on Lake Garda, a different version of torta di mele seemed to turn up every day, in trattorias, at open-air markets, at the local pastry shops along quiet side streets. This recipe is a montage, actually, a homage to all those apple cakes eaten in reality, or only with my eyes. I like its simple, old-fashioned quality, and enjoy it as much for breakfast or tea as for dessert after a meal.

Unsalted butter and all-purpose
flour for preparing the baking
pan

8 tablespoons (4 ounces; 125 g)
unsalted butter, at room
temperature

1 cup (200 g) Vanilla Sugar
(page 324)

1 teaspoon pure vanilla extract

3 tablespoons whole milk

Grated zest (yellow peel) of 1
lemon

3 large eggs, at room
temperature

1½ cups (200 g) all-purpose flour

¾ teaspoon baking powder

¼ teaspoon fine sea salt

½ teaspoon ground cinnamon

3 Golden Delicious apples
(about 1½ pounds; 750 g)

1. Preheat the oven to 350°F (175°C; gas mark 4/5).

2. Generously butter and flour a 9-inch (23-cm) springform pan, tapping out any excess flour. Set aside.

3. In the bowl of an electric mixer fitted with a paddle, cream the butter, ¾ cup (150 g) of the vanilla sugar, the vanilla, milk, and lemon zest until light and fluffy, 1 to 2 minutes. Add the eggs one by one, beating thoroughly after each addition.

4. Sift the flour, baking powder, and salt into a large bowl. Spoon the mixture into the batter and mix until thoroughly blended. Scrape down the sides of the bowl and mix once more. Set aside for 10 minutes to allow the flour to absorb the liquids.

5. In a large bowl, toss together 2 tablespoons of the vanilla sugar and ¼ teaspoon of the cinnamon. Peel and core the apples, and cut each lengthwise into 16 even wedges. Transfer the apples to the bowl, tossing with the cinnamon sugar. Set aside.

6. Spoon the batter into the prepared cake pan, smoothing out the top with a spatula. Starting just inside the edge of the pan, neatly overlap the wedges of apples—thicker curved outer side against the side of the pan—in 2 or 3 concentric circles, working toward the center. Fill in the center with the remaining apples. Toss together the remaining 2 tablespoons sugar and ¼ teaspoon cinnamon, and sprinkle over the apples.

7. Place the pan in the center of the oven. Bake until the apples are a deep golden brown and the cake feels quite firm when pressed with a fingertip, about 1 hour. Remove to a baking rack to cool. After 10 minutes, run a knife along the sides of the pan. Release and remove the side of the springform pan, leaving the cake on the pan base. Serve at room temperature, cutting into thin wedges.

■ Yield: 8 to 12 servings ■

■ ■ ■

Golden Lemon-Rice Cake

Torta di Riso

Golden and welcoming, with a happy, healthy glow, this lovely rice cake is one of my favorite desserts. I first sampled this spring-yellow cake in a Florentine café. I make it often, for it is inexpensive and usually can be prepared with ingredients I have on hand, and, what's more, it's a dessert that can easily be made a day in advance. This popular dessert gives proof to the fact that the Italians do much more with their marvelous Arborio rice than make risotto, for their repertoire of desserts is filled with a great variety of rice puddings and cakes. It is equally delicious prepared with orange zest and orange juice.

1 cup (180 g) Italian Arborio rice (see Mail Order Sources, page 325)

1 quart (1 l) whole milk

Pinch of fine sea salt

¾ cup (150 g) Vanilla Sugar (page 324)

Unsalted butter for preparing the pan

1 tablespoon semolina flour

3 large eggs, at room temperature

Grated zest (yellow peel) of 1 lemon

3 tablespoons freshly squeezed lemon juice

Confectioner's sugar, for garnish

1. In a 6-quart (6-l) saucepan, combine the rice, milk, salt, and ½ cup (100 g) of the sugar. Stir to blend, and bring to a simmer over moderate heat, stirring regularly to keep the rice from sticking to the bottom of the pan. (Watch the pan carefully so the milk does not boil over.) Reduce the heat to low and simmer until the rice is tender, most of the milk is absorbed, and the mixture is thick and porridge-like, 15 to 20 minutes. Continue stirring regularly to keep the rice from sticking to the bottom of the pan. Transfer the mixture to a bowl to cool for at least 1 hour.

2. Preheat the oven to 325°F (165°C; gas mark 4).

3. Thoroughly butter the bottom and sides of a 10-inch (25-cm) springform pan. Dust lightly with the semolina, tapping the sides to distribute it evenly. Shake out the excess, and set aside.

4. In the bowl of an electric mixer fitted with a whisk, combine the eggs and the remaining ¼ cup (50 g) sugar and whisk until thick and lemon-colored, about 2 minutes. Add the zest and lemon juice, and mix thoroughly. Stir in the rice mixture and blend thoroughly. Pour the mixture into the prepared cake pan, smoothing out the top with the back of a spoon.

5. Place the pan in the center of the oven and bake until the rice cake is a deep golden color and firm in the center, 25 to 30 minutes. Remove from the oven and transfer to a baking rack to cool. Once cooled, cover the rice cake with plastic wrap until ready to serve. (The cake can be made 1 day in advance.)

6. To serve, run a knife along the sides of the pan, and release and remove the side of the springform pan, leaving the rice cake on the pan base. Sprinkle the top generously with confectioner's sugar and serve, cutting into very thin wedges.

■ Yield: 8 to 12 servings ■

Lemon-Rice Tea Cakes

Budini di Riso

T he first time I sampled these sweet and golden little rice cakes—purchased at a bakery in Florence—they were a true revelation. Moist, golden, and not overly sweet, these soothing, gentle, flourless cakes (like elegant rice pudding in tea cake form) have become a favorite, perfect as a late morning or afternoon snack with a thick cup of espresso. They are most easily made in small muffin or cupcake tins. To ensure that the cakes do not stick to the pan, use paper liners (just be sure to remove the liners before serving). These tea cakes are best served at room temperature, sprinkled with a bit of confectioner's sugar. They look lovely arranged on a paper doily set on a footed cake stand.

3 cups (750 ml) whole milk

½ cup (90 g) Italian Arborio rice (see Mail Order Sources, page 325)

Pinch of fine sea salt

½ cup (100 g) Vanilla Sugar (page 324)

4 tablespoons (2 ounces; 60 g) unsalted butter

Grated zest (yellow peel) of 2 lemons

2 large eggs, separated, at room temperature

1 tablespoon freshly squeezed lemon juice

2 tablespoons dark rum

Confectioner's sugar, for garnish

1. Line fifteen ¼-cup (60-ml) muffin molds with cupcake liner papers. Set aside.

2. Rinse a 3-quart (3-l) saucepan with water, leaving a few drops of water clinging to the bottom of the pan. (This will help to keep the milk from sticking to the pan.) Add the milk and scald over high heat, bringing it just to the boiling point. Reduce the heat to medium, stir in the rice and salt, and bring to a simmer. Simmer for 10 minutes, stirring regularly. Add the sugar and butter, and simmer until the rice is cooked, about 7 minutes more, stirring regularly. At this point, the liquid should have the consistency of heavy cream. Transfer the mixture to a bowl to cool for at least 1 hour. During this time, the rice will absorb most of the liquid.

3. Preheat the oven to 375°F (190°C; gas mark 5).

4. When the rice mixture is cool, stir in the grated lemon zest, then the egg yolks, lemon juice, and rum, stirring to blend thoroughly.

5. In the bowl of an electric mixer fitted with a whisk, beat the egg whites until stiff but not dry. Gently fold the whites into the rice mixture. Spoon the mixture into the muffin molds, filling them to the top.

6. Place the muffin tins in the center of the oven and bake until the rice cakes are a deep golden brown and firm in the center, and a toothpick inserted in the center comes out clean, 25 to 30 minutes. Transfer the cakes to a wire rack to cool in the pan for 10 minutes. (Do not let sit longer, or the cakes are likely to stick to the paper.) Remove the cakes from the papers and place upright on a wire rack to cool completely. The cakes will sink slightly as they cool. At serving time, sprinkle generously with confectioner's sugar.

■ Yield: 15 tea cakes ■

Hazelnut and Orange Biscotti

Biscotti

Biscotti means "twice cooked," and that's just what you do to these fragrant, crunchy cookies studded with toasted whole nuts and scented with lemon zest, pure vanilla essence, and a warming touch of almond. Biscotti are made with no added fat—save for that in the eggs and nuts—and are intentionally dry, giving them an extra-long shelf life. During the day, they are ideal for dipping in a cup of espresso (softening them, and adding a zesty coffee flavor), while at dinnertime, they seem destined to be paired with a tiny glass of sherry, port, or the traditional Vin Santo.

About 2 cups (265 g) unbleached all-purpose flour

¼ *teaspoon baking powder*

¼ *teaspoon baking soda*

¼ *teaspoon fine sea salt*

3 *large eggs*

⅔ *cup (135 g) Vanilla Sugar (page 324)*

1 *teaspoon pure vanilla extract*

¾ *teaspoon pure almond extract*

Grated zest (yellow peel) of 1 lemon

Grated zest (orange peel) of 1 orange

1 *cup (4 ounces; 125 g) hazelnuts (filberts), toasted and cooled*

1 *egg mixed with ¼ teaspoon salt, for egg wash*

1. Preheat the oven to 350°F (175°C; gas mark 4/5). Line a baking sheet with baking parchment. Set aside.

2. In a sifter, combine 2 cups (265 g) flour, the baking powder, baking soda, and salt, and sift onto a clean work surface.

3. In a small bowl, combine the eggs, sugar, vanilla and almond extracts, and lemon and orange zest. Make a well in the center of the flour mixture, and slowly add the liquids to the well, drawing the flour mixture into the liquid and mixing gently with your hands. If necessary, add additional flour to form a firm and workable dough. Add the hazelnuts and work them evenly into the dough.

4. Divide the dough into 2 equal pieces. Flour your hands to keep the dough from sticking, and, with your palms, carefully roll each piece into an oval cylinder about 2 inches (5 cm) wide and 12 inches (31 cm) long. Carefully transfer each cylinder to the parchment-lined baking sheet. Evenly brush the dough with the egg wash.

5. Place the baking sheet in the center of the oven and bake until the dough is slightly risen and an even light golden brown, 25 to 30 minutes. Remove the baking sheet from the oven and transfer the cylinders to a cooling rack for 10 minutes.

6. Transfer each cylinder to a cutting board and slice the biscotti on a sharp diagonal (45-degree angle) at ½-inch (1-cm) intervals. Stand the biscotti upright on the baking sheet, about ½ inch (1 cm) apart. Return the baking sheet to the center of the oven and bake until the biscotti are a deep golden brown, about 15 minutes more. Remove from the oven, and transfer the biscotti to a rack to cool thoroughly. The cookies should be dry and crispy. (Once cooled, the biscotti can be stored in an airtight container for up to 1 month.)

■ Yield: About 50 biscotti ■

VARIATION: For Almond and Vanilla Biscotti, substitute 1 cup toasted unblanched whole almonds for the hazelnuts, and omit the orange zest.

WINE SUGGESTION: Vin Santo is the classic partner. If not available, try either port or sherry.

■ ■ ■

Light Orange Ice Cream

Gelato d'Arancia

ight fruit ice cream—which is what good fruity gelato should resemble—is a real
favorite. It offers the richness of ice cream without the heaviness, and the
fruitiness of a true sorbet with just a little boost from the cream. This orange gelato,
in fact, reminds me of the orange Creamsicles that were a favorite of my childhood.
Now I eat it out of a pretty little bowl, rather than lick it from a stick! Serve these with
Almond and Vanilla Biscotti (page 315) and maybe a few sips of Vin Santo.

2 cups (500 ml) water

Grated zest (orange peel) of 2 oranges

1 cup (200 g) Vanilla Sugar (page 324)

1 cup (250 ml) freshly squeezed orange juice

1 cup (250 ml) heavy cream

1. In a small saucepan, combine the water, orange zest, sugar, and orange juice, and
bring to a boil over moderate heat. Boil vigorously for 2 minutes. Place a sieve over
a bowl and strain the syrup through the sieve. Discard the solids. Let the syrup cool
to room temperature. (To speed cooling, place the bowl inside a larger bowl filled with
ice cubes and water. Stir occasionally until cold to the touch.)

2. When the syrup is thoroughly cooled, stir in the heavy cream. Transfer to an ice
cream maker and freeze according to the manufacturer's instructions.

■ Yield: About 1 quart (1 l) ice cream ■

Lemon Ice Cream

Gelato di Limone

"What one feels always in Italy is an extraordinary and direct min-gling of freshness and repose, as though all life were sunset and sun-rise, winter and spring."

C H A R L E S   M O R G A N, REFLECTIONS IN A MIRROR, 1944

L emon is one of my favorite flavors, and when I find myself at a gelato stand in Italy, it never takes me long to decide which flavor I'll select. The clerk behind the counter is always sad when I order a single flavor. I like my tastes pure! This is a simple, light, surefire recipe bound to thrill any lemon lover.

2¼ cups (560 ml) water

Grated zest (yellow peel) of 6 lemons

1½ cups Vanilla Sugar (page 324)

1 cup (250 ml) freshly squeezed lemon juice (about 8 to 10 lemons)

1 cup (250 ml) heavy cream

1. In a small saucepan, combine the water, lemon zest, sugar, and lemon juice, and bring to a boil over moderate heat. Boil vigorously for 2 minutes. Place a sieve over a bowl and strain the syrup through the sieve. Discard the solids. Let the syrup cool to room temperature. (To speed cooling, place the bowl inside a larger bowl filled with ice cubes and water. Stir occasionally until cool.)

2. When the syrup is thoroughly cooled, stir in the heavy cream. Transfer to an ice cream maker and freeze according to the manufacturer's instructions.

■   Y i e l d :   A b o u t   1   q u a r t   (1   l)   i c e   c r e a m   ■

Lemon Granita

Granita di Limone

I adore lemons. In the heat of summer, nothing is more refreshing than freshly squeezed lemon juice, a touch of sugar to chase away the pucker, and crushed ice. The Italians are masters at granita, a sort of half-ice, half-liquid drink made up of very fine-grained frozen crystals of fruit syrup. Whenever I see this "fruit slush" on the menu in Italian cafés, I order it. The best trattorias serve the granita from tall glasses with a straw and a long thin spoon, for sipping or for eating by the spoonful. At home, it's nice to serve out of shallow champagne coupes as an afternoon pick-me-up or a light dessert.

¼ cup (50 g) sugar

½ cup (125 ml) freshly squeezed lemon juice

1½ cups (375 ml) water

1. In a saucepan, combine the sugar, lemon juice, and water. Bring to a boil, stirring until the sugar is dissolved. Remove from the heat and allow the syrup to cool thoroughly.

2. Transfer the mixture to a shallow metal pan (or 2 metal ice cube trays with the grids removed). Carefully place in the freezer. After 15 minutes, remove from the freezer (be careful not to splash the sticky liquid!) and, with a fork, stir the contents to crush any lumps and break up the ice crystals, being sure to reach the crystals formed along the side and bottom of the pan. Return to the freezer and freeze for 15 minutes more. Stir the granita. Continue this every 15 minutes or so, for up to 3 hours. Spoon into chilled glasses and serve immediately: The granita will melt very quickly!

■ Yield: 4 to 6 servings ■

■ ■ ■

Pineapple Sorbet

Sorbetto di Ananas

Pineapple is among the most refreshing flavors I know, and this light, delicious, satisfying sorbet is as pure as you can get. Punctuated with just a hint of vanilla to accentuate the pineapple essence, it's a dessert I could easily enjoy on a regular basis. I sampled a superb version one sunny Sunday afternoon in the historic town of Sirmione, at the tip of Lake Garda. If you want to consume this as is, as a *frulatto*, or whip, simply eat it chilled as a snack or dessert, without freezing.

4 cups (1 l) cubed fresh pineapple (about 1 medium pineapple)

⅓ cup (65 g) Vanilla Sugar (page 324)

1 teaspoon pure vanilla extract

1. In the bowl of a food processor, combine the pineapple, sugar, and vanilla extract, and purée until light and fluffy.

2. Transfer to an ice cream maker and freeze according to the manufacturer's instructions.

■ Yield: About 1 quart (1 l) sorbet ■

Ricotta Gelato

Gelato di Ricotta

The tartness and tang of ricotta cheese blended with the richness of a traditional custard creates a sublime and elegant gelato. I love the purity of flavors here, unmarred by excess. Although the gelato appears to be extravagantly rich, the richness comes from the ricotta, not a heavy dose of cream.

CUSTARD BASE

1 plump, moist vanilla bean

2 cups (500 ml) whole milk

6 large egg yolks, at room temperature

¾ cup (150 g) Vanilla Sugar (page 324)

2 cups (500 ml) whole-milk ricotta

1 tablespoon dark rum

¼ cup (60 ml) heavy cream

1. Prepare the custard base: Flatten the vanilla bean and cut in half lengthwise. With a small spoon, scrape out the seeds and place them in the bowl of an electric mixer. Set aside. In a large saucepan, combine the milk and vanilla pods over moderate heat. Scald the milk (cook until tiny bubbles form around the edges), and remove from the heat. Cover and set aside to infuse for 15 minutes. Remove the vanilla pods.

2. In the bowl of an electric mixer, whisk the vanilla seeds, egg yolks, and sugar until thick, fluffy, and a pale-lemon color, 2 to 3 minutes. When you lift the whisk, the mixture should form a trail, or ribbon, on the surface. Set aside.

3. Return the simmered and infused milk to high heat and bring just to a boil. Remove from the heat and pour one-third of the boiling milk into the egg yolk mixture in the bowl, whisking constantly. Return the milk and egg yolk mixture to the saucepan, reduce the heat to low, and cool, stirring constantly with a wooden spoon, until the mixture thickens to a creamy consistency. To test, run your finger down the back of the wooden spoon: If the mixture is sufficiently cooked, the mark will hold. The entire process should take less than 5 minutes. (Alternatively, use a candy thermometer to test the custard. Cook until the thermometer registers 185°F; 85°C.)

4. Remove from the heat and immediately pass through a fine-mesh sieve into a bowl. Set the bowl in a larger bowl filled with ice cubes and water, and stir occasionally until the mixture is cold to the touch. The cooling process should take about 30 minutes.

5. In the bowl of an electric mixer fitted with a paddle, combine the ricotta, rum, and heavy cream, and mix until smooth. Fold the ricotta mixture into the cooled custard. Transfer to an ice cream maker and freeze according to the manufacturer's instructions.

■ Y i e l d :   A b o u t   1   q u a r t   (1   l)   i c e   c r e a m ■

Risotto Gelato

Gelato di Riso

Imagine cold, soothing rice pudding and you have it in this rich and memorable risotto ice cream. And if you come to love this delicious gelato as I do, almost anything short of a trip to Florence is worth the effort to sample it just one more time. Serve this with tiny almond macaroon cookies (page 290). The amount of rice seems infinitesimal, but the cooked rice swells up greatly, making for a rich vanilla ice cream flecked with sweet rice.

RICE	CUSTARD BASE
¼ cup (45 g) Italian Arborio rice (see Mail Order Sources, page 325)	2 plump, moist vanilla beans
1½ cups (375 ml) whole milk	2 cups (500 ml) whole milk
½ cup (100 g) Vanilla Sugar (page 324)	6 large egg yolks, at room temperature
¼ teaspoon fine sea salt	¾ cup (150 g) Vanilla Sugar (page 324)
	1 cup (250 ml) heavy cream

1. Prepare the rice: In a large saucepan, combine the rice, milk, sugar, and salt. Bring to a simmer over moderate heat, stirring often to keep the rice from sticking to the bottom of the pan. Reduce the heat and simmer until the rice is cooked, about 20 minutes, stirring often to keep the rice from sticking to the bottom of the pan. Transfer the mixture to a bowl to cool to room temperature. (To speed cooling, place the bowl inside a larger bowl filled with ice cubes and water. Stir occasionally until cool.) Place a sieve over a bowl and strain the cooled rice and liquid through the sieve. Discard the cooking liquid. Set the rice aside.

2. Prepare the custard base: Flatten the vanilla beans and cut in half lengthwise. With a small spoon, scrape out the seeds and place them in the bowl of an electric mixer. Set aside. In a large saucepan, combine the milk and vanilla pods over moderate heat. Scald the milk, and remove from the heat. Cover and set aside to infuse for 15 minutes. Remove the vanilla pods.

3. In the bowl of an electric mixer, whisk the vanilla seeds, egg yolks, and sugar until thick, fluffy, and a pale-lemon color, 2 to 3 minutes. When you lift the whisk, the mixture should form a trail, or ribbon, on the surface. Set aside.

4. Return the simmered and infused milk to high heat and bring just to a boil. Remove from the heat and pour one-third of the boiling milk into the egg yolk mixture in the bowl, whisking constantly. Return the milk and egg yolk mixture to the saucepan, reduce the heat to low, and cook, stirring constantly with a wooden spoon, until the mixture thickens to a creamy consistency. To test, run your finger down the back of the wooden spoon: If the mixture is sufficiently cooked, the mark will hold. The entire process should take less than 5 minutes. (Alternatively, use a candy thermometer to test the custard. Cook until the thermometer registers 185°F; 85°C.)

5. Remove from the heat and immediately stir in the heavy cream to stop the cooking. Pass through a fine-mesh sieve into a bowl, and let cool completely. (To speed cooling, place the bowl inside a larger bowl filled with ice cubes and water. Stir occasionally until cool.)

6. When thoroughly cooled, stir in the cooled rice. Transfer to an ice cream maker and freeze according to the manufacturer's instructions.

■ Yield: About 1 quart (1 l) ice cream ■

Vanilla Sugar

Zucchero di Vaniglia

Vanilla plays a lovely supporting role in many Italian desserts. Little packages of vanilla sugar can be purchased in the supermarket for scenting traditional desserts, including the famed sponge cake *pan di spagna*, as well as milk-and-egg-based desserts such as *budini*. Whenever I bake, I use vanilla sugar, rather than the "unscented" variety. You'll be well rewarded for the few seconds it takes to prepare a batch at home.

4 plump moist vanilla beans

4 cups (800 g) sugar

Flatten the vanilla beans and cut them in half lengthwise. With a small spoon, scrape out the seeds and place them in a small bowl; reserve the seeds for another use. Combine the pods and sugar in a jar. Cover securely and set aside at room temperature for several days to scent and flavor the sugar. Use in place of regular sugar when preparing desserts. Vanilla sugar can be stored indefinitely. As the vanilla sugar is used, replace with new sugar. (When baking, I return rinsed and thoroughly dried pods to the sugar mixture as an added boost.)

■ Yield: 4 cups (800 g) vanilla sugar ■

Mail Order Sources

The following companies offer mail-order catalogs and/or newsletters, for purchasing specialty and hard-to-find ingredients and equipment. There is a charge for most catalogs.

APPLE PIE FARM, INCORPORATED (THE HERB PATCH), Union Hill Road #5, Malvern, PA 19355. Tel: (215) 933–4215.

THE CHEF'S CATALOG, 3215 Commercial Avenue, Northbrook, IL 60062–1900. Tel: (800) 338–3232; Fax: (708) 480–8929.

A COOK'S WARES, 211 37th Street, Beaver Falls, PA 15010–2103. Tel: (412) 846–9490.

CORTI BROTHERS, 5810 Folsom Boulevard, P.O. Box 191358, Sacramento, CA 95819. Tel: (916) 736–3800; Fax: (916) 736–3807.

LA CUISINE, 323 Cameron Street, Alexandria, VA 22314. Tel: (800) 521–1176.

DEAN & DELUCA, 560 Broadway, New York, NY 10012. Tel: (800) 221–7714 or (212) 431–1691.

FERRARA, 195 Grand Street, New York, NY 10013. Tel: (212) 226–6150.

G. B. RATTO & COMPANY, 821 Washington Street, Oakland, CA 94607. Tel: (800) 325–3483; Fax: (510) 836–2250.

GIANT ARTICHOKE, 11241 Merritt Street, Castroville, CA 95012. Tel: (408) 633–2778.

THE HERBFARM, 32804 Issaquah–Fall City Road, Fall City, WA 98024. Tel: (800) 866–HERB.

HERB GATHERING INC., 5742 Kenwood Avenue, Kansas City, MO 64110. Tel: (816) 523–2653.

Ideal Cheese, 1205 Second Avenue, New York, NY 10021. Tel: (212) 688–7579.

Island Farmcrafters, Waldron Island, WA 98297. Tel: (206) 739–2286.

Kermit Lynch Wine Merchant, 1605 San Pablo Avenue, Berkeley, CA 94702–1317. Tel: (510) 524–1524; Fax: (510) 528–7026.

King Arthur Flour Baker's Catalogue, P.O. Box 876, Norwich, VT 05055. Tel: (800) 827–6836.

Mozzarella Company, 2944 Elm Street, Dallas, TX 75226. Tel: (800) 798–2954 or (214) 741–4072; Fax: (214) 741–4076.

Nichols Garden Nursery, 1190 North Pacific Highway, Albany, OR 97321. Tel: (503) 928–9280.

Northwest Select, 14724 184th Street NE, Arlington, WA 98223. Tel: (800) 852–7132 or (206) 435–8577.

Penzey's Spice House, 1921 S. West Avenue, Waukesha, WI 53186. Tel: (414) 574-0277; Fax: (414) 574-0278.

Shepherd's Garden Seeds, 6116 Highway 9, Felton, CA 95018. Tel: (408) 335–6910.

Todaro Brothers, 555 Second Avenue, New York, NY 10016. Tel: (212) 679–7766.

Walnut Acres Organic Farms, Walnut Acres, Penns Creek, PA 17862. Tel: (800) 433–3998.

Well-Sweep Herb Farm, 317 Mount Bethal Road, Port Murray, NJ 07865. Tel: (908) 852–5390.

Williams-Sonoma, Mail Order Department, P.O. Box 7456, San Francisco, CA 94120–7456. Tel: (415) 421–4242; Fax: (415) 421–5153.

HARD-TO-FIND PANTRY ITEMS

SALTED ANCHOVIES

Todaro Brothers

AMARETTI COOKIES

Ferrara

G. B. Ratto & Company

BEANS, DRIED ASSORTED

(borlotti, cannellini, cranberry)

Corti Brothers

Dean & Deluca

G. B. Ratto & Company

SALTED CAPERS, ANCHOVIES IN OIL

Dean & Deluca

Todaro Brothers

OLIVES, OILS, VINEGARS

Corti Brothers

Dean & Deluca

G. B. Ratto & Company

Kermit Lynch Wine Merchant

IMPORTED PASTA

G. B. Ratto & Company

POLENTA, ARBORIO RICE

Dean & Deluca

G. B. Ratto & Company

Williams-Sonoma

DRIED PORCINI MUSHROOMS,

DRIED TOMATOES

Dean & Deluca

G. B. Ratto & Company

RED PEPPER FLAKES, PURE

SPANISH SAFFRON

Penzey's Spice House

SAVOIARDI BISCUITS

Ferrara

SEMOLINA FLOUR

G. B. Ratto & Company

King Arthur Flour Baker's Catalogue

IMPORTED TUNA IN OIL

G. B. Ratto & Company

PURE VANILLA EXTRACT, VANILLA BEANS

Penzey's Spice House

Williams-Sonoma

WHEAT BERRIES

King Arthur Flour Baker's Catalogue

Walnut Acres Organic Farms

■

CHEESE, CURED MEATS, AND PRODUCE

FRESH BABY ARTICHOKES

Giant Artichoke

Northwest Select

PLUMP ORGANIC GARLIC BRAIDS

Island Farmcrafters

DOMESTIC GOAT'S CHEESE, MASCARPONE, MOZZARELLA, PECORINO, RICOTTA

Mozzarella Company

FRESH HERB AND BAY LEAF PLANTS

The Herbfarm

Nichols Garden Nursery

Well-Sweep Herb Farm

FRESH-CUT HERBS

Apple Pie Farm, Inc.

Herb Gathering Inc.

IMPORTED ITALIAN CHEESES

Ideal Cheese

PANCETTA

Dean & Deluca

PARMIGIANO-REGGIANO

Dean & Deluca

G. B. Ratto & Company

Ideal Cheese

■

GARDEN SEEDS FOR GROWING IT YOURSELF

FLAT-LEAF PARSLEY, SAGE, AND OTHER HERBS

Herb Gathering Inc.

Shepherd's Garden Seeds

Well-Sweep Herb Farm

ARUGULA, CHILES, RADICCHIO, BORLOTTI BEANS

Shepherd's Garden Seeds

■

KITCHEN AND BAKING EQUIPMENT

The Chef's Catalog

Dean & Deluca

King Arthur Flour Baker's Catalogue

La Cuisine

Williams-Sonoma

Index

Frittata fredda alla rustica,
     26–27
Fritto di zucca e fiori di zucca,
     56–57
Frittura di pesce, 212–213
Frying, tips for, 58, 214
Fusilli:
     with eggplant, tomatoes, and
          mozzarella, 100–101
     with walnut and garlic sauce,
          110–111
Fusilli salsa di noci,
     110–111

Garbanzo bean(s):
     and pasta soup, 82–83
     spicy, cubed pork with garlic,
          spinach, and, 234–235
Garlic:
     and arugula sauce, tagliatelle
          with, 146–147
     basil, and tomato sauce,
          262–263
     basil, and tomato sauce,
          lasagne with, 133
     and basil sauce, 261
     braised artichokes with parsley
          and, 66–67
     cubed pork with spinach,
          spicy chick peas and,
          234–235
     germ of, 3
     and goat cheese spread, 2–3
     lamb braised in white wine, hot
          peppers and, 242–243
     mayonnaise, 275
     sautéed spinach with lemon, oil
          and, 62–63
     shrimp with oil, hot peppers
          and, 204–205
     spaghetti with oil, hot peppers
          and, 96–97
     spaghetti with shrimp, clams,
          and mussels in tomato
          sauce, 117–119
     and walnut sauce, fusilli with,
          110–111
Gelato:
     d'arancia, 316
     di limone, 317
     di ricotta, 320–321
     di riso, 322–323
Gelato
     ricotta, 320–321
     risotto, 322–323
Gemelli:
     with eggplant, tomatoes, and
          mozzarella, 100–101
     tossing of, 107
Gemelli alla Siciliana, 100–101

Goat's cheese:
     and fresh fava bean salad,
          38–39
     and garlic spread, 2–3
     and thyme spread, 3
     and walnut salad, 48
Gorgonzola soufflés, individual,
     28–29
Gran farro, 78–79
Granita, lemon, 318
Granita di limone, 318
Grilling, tips for, 17, 86

Ham, *see* Prosciutto
Hand blenders, 77
Hazelnut(s), 304
     and orange biscotti, 314–315
     toasted, cake, 302–303
     toasting of, 304
Herb(s):
     fresh, sauce, poached chicken
          with, 226–227
     fresh, sauce for meats and
          poultry, 266–267
     -infused savory custards,
          30–31
     lemon risotto, 158–159

Ice cream:
     lemon, 317
     light orange, 316
     ricotta, 320–321
     risotta, 322–323
Immersion mixers, 77
Insalata:
     di borlotti, 40–41
     di calamari, 200–201
     di carne cruda, 12
     di noci e pecorino, 48
     di olive, 36
     *di olive verde, tonno, sedano, e
          peperoni,* 37
     di pesche e lampone, 288–289
     di puntarelle, 34–35
     di rughetta, pignoli, e Parmi,
          46–47

Ladyfinger cream, coffee and
     mascarpone, 294–295
Lamb:
     braised in white wine, garlic,
          and hot peppers, 242–243
     chops, grilled marinated, with
          lemon and oil, 240–241
     chops, Parmesan-breaded baby,
          238–239
     cubed, with garlic, spinach,
          and spicy chick peas,
          234–235
     to test for doneness, 241

Lasagne:
     with basil, garlic, and tomato
          sauce, 133
     speedy, 122–123
     with tomato-cream sauce and
          mozzarella, 150–151
Lasagne al pesto, 133
Lasagne rapide, 122–123
Lemon(s), 132
     -and-oregano-seasoned tuna
          mousse, 8
     granita, 318
     grilled chicken with oil, black
          pepper and, 224–225
     grilled marinated lamb chops
          with oil and, 240–241
     ice cream, 317
     -infused baked pasta or rice,
          technique for, 156
     juice, anchovies marinated in
          olive oil, thyme and,
          20–21
     juicing of, 307
     and orange cake, fragrant,
          305–307
     and parsley garnish, braised
          veal shanks with, 244–245
     rice cake, golden, 310–311
     rice tea cakes, 312–313
     risotto, 158–159
     sauce, tagliarini with, 130–131
     sautéed chicken breasts with
          fresh sage, 216–217
     sautéed spinach with garlic, oil
          and, 62–63
     zest, 132, 156

Macaroons, almond, 290–291
     baked peaches with, 292–293
Main courses:
     baked risotto with asparagus,
          spinach, and Parmesan,
          166–167
     baked risotto with tomato sauce
          and pecorino, 168–169
     baked sea bass with artichokes,
          210–211
     baked swordfish with tomatoes
          and green olives, 206–207
     beef braised in Barolo wine,
          247–249
     braised oxtail with tomatoes,
          onions, and celery,
          251–253
     braised veal shanks with lemon
          and parsley garnish,
          244–245
     chicken cacciatora, 228–229
     chicken cooked under bricks,
          218–219